# The Quran With Tafsir Ibn Kathir
## Part 12 of 30: Hud 006 To Yusuf 052

# The Quran With Tafsir Ibn Kathir
# Part 12 of 30:
# Hud 006 To
# Yusuf 052

With
Arabic Script, Transliteration of Arabic, Meaning in English
and Ibn Kathir's Abridged Tafsir (Explanation)

Muhammad Saed Abdul-Rahman

BSc, DipHE

MSA Publication Limited

© Muhammad Saed Abdul-Rahman, 2012
ISBN 978-1-86179-861-9

All Rights reserved

British Library Cataloguing in Publication Data. A Catalogue record for this book is available from the British Library

Designed, Typeset and produced by:
MSA Publication Limited, 4 Bello Close, Herne Hill,
London SE24 9BW
United Kingdom

Cover design: Houriyah Abdul-Rahman

# TABLE OF CONTENTS

TABLE OF CONTENTS .................................................................................................. V

PRELUDE ................................................................................................................... XI

OPENING SERMAN ........................................................................................................... XI
OUR MISSION .................................................................................................................. XII
BIOGRAPHY OF HAFIZ IBN KATHIR (701 H - 774 H) ............................................................. XII
    Ibn Kathir's Teachers ................................................................................................. xii
    Ibn Kathir's Students ................................................................................................. xiii
    Ibn Kathir's Books ..................................................................................................... xiii
    Ibn Kathir's Death ..................................................................................................... xiv

PREFACE .................................................................................................................. XV

ABOUT THIS BOOK ........................................................................................................... XV
PERFORMING PROSTRATION WHILE READING THE QUR'AN ................................................. XV

PART 12 FULL ARABIC TEXT ........................................................................................ 1

INTRODUCTION TO CHAPTER (SURAH) 11: HUD ........................................................ 12

IBN KATHIR'S INTRODUCTION .......................................................................................... 12
    Surah Hud made the Prophet's Hair turn Gray ........................................................ 12

CHAPTER (SURAH) 11: HUD, VERSES 006-123 .......................................................... 12

*Surah: 11 Ayah: 6* .......................................................................................................... 12
    Tafsir Ibn Kathir ........................................................................................................ 13
        Allah is Responsible for the Provisions of All Creatures ..................................... 13
*Surah: 11 Ayah: 7 & Ayah: 8* ......................................................................................... 13
    Tafsir Ibn Kathir ........................................................................................................ 14
        Allah created the Heavens and the Earth in Six Days ....................................... 14
        The Polytheists hasten their Torment by arguing against Resurrection after Death ......... 16
        The Meanings of the Word Ummah ................................................................... 17
*Surah: 11 Ayah: 9, Ayah: 10 & Ayah: 11* ....................................................................... 18
    Tafsir Ibn Kathir ........................................................................................................ 18
        The changing of Man's Attitude in Happiness and Hardship ............................ 18
*Surah: 11 Ayah: 12, Ayah: 13 & Ayah: 14* ..................................................................... 20
    Tafsir Ibn Kathir ........................................................................................................ 20
        The Messenger grieving by the Statements of the Polytheists, and His Gratification ........ 20
        An Explanation concerning the Miracle of the Qur'an ....................................... 21
*Surah: 11 Ayah: 15 & Ayah: 16* ..................................................................................... 21
    Tafsir Ibn Kathir ........................................................................................................ 22
        Whoever wants the Worldly Life, then He will have no Share of the Hereafter ............... 22
*Surah: 11 Ayah: 17* ....................................................................................................... 23
    Tafsir Ibn Kathir ........................................................................................................ 23
        The One Who believes in the Qur'an is upon Clear Proof from His Lord ........... 23

| | |
|---|---|
| Every Hadith is confirmed by the Qur'an | 25 |
| *Surah: 11 Ayah: 18, Ayah: 19, Ayah: 20, Ayah: 21 & Ayah: 22* | *26* |
| Tafsir Ibn Kathir | 27 |
| Those Who invent Lies against Allah and hinder Others from His Path are the Greatest Losers | 27 |
| *Surah: 11 Ayah: 23 & Ayah: 24* | *29* |
| Tafsir Ibn Kathir | 30 |
| Rewarding the People of Faith | 30 |
| The Parable of the Believers and the Disbelievers | 30 |
| *Surah: 11 Ayah: 25, Ayah: 26 & Ayah: 27* | *31* |
| Tafsir Ibn Kathir | 31 |
| The Story of Nuh and His Conversation with His People | 31 |
| *Surah: 11 Ayah: 28* | *33* |
| Tafsir Ibn Kathir | 33 |
| The Response of Nuh | 33 |
| *Surah: 11 Ayah: 29 & Ayah: 30* | *33* |
| Tafsir Ibn Kathir | 34 |
| *Surah: 11 Ayah: 31* | *34* |
| Tafsir Ibn Kathir | 35 |
| *Surah: 11 Ayah: 32, Ayah: 33 & Ayah: 34* | *35* |
| Tafsir Ibn Kathir | 36 |
| The People's Request of Nuh to bring the Torment and His Response to Them | 36 |
| *Surah: 11 Ayah: 35* | *36* |
| Tafsir Ibn Kathir | 37 |
| An Interruption to verify the Truthfulness of the Prophet | 37 |
| *Surah: 11 Ayah: 36, Ayah: 37, Ayah: 38 & Ayah: 39* | *37* |
| Tafsir Ibn Kathir | 38 |
| The Revelation to Nuh concerning what would happen to the People and the Command to prepare for It | 38 |
| *Surah: 11 Ayah: 40* | *39* |
| Tafsir Ibn Kathir | 39 |
| The beginning of the Flood and Nuh loads Every Creature in Pairs upon the Ship | 39 |
| *Surah: 11 Ayah: 41, Ayah: 42 & Ayah: 43* | *40* |
| Tafsir Ibn Kathir | 40 |
| The riding upon the Ship and Its sailing through the huge Waves | 40 |
| The Story of the drowning of Nuh's Disbelieving Son | 41 |
| *Surah: 11 Ayah: 44* | *42* |
| Tafsir Ibn Kathir | 42 |
| The End of the Flood | 42 |
| *Surah: 11 Ayah: 45, Ayah: 46 & Ayah: 47* | *43* |
| Tafsir Ibn Kathir | 44 |
| A Return to the Story of the Son of Nuh and mentioning what transpired between Nuh and Allah concerning Him | 44 |
| *Surah: 11 Ayah: 48* | *44* |

# Table of Contents

Tafsir Ibn Kathir .................................................................................................................. 45
    The Command to descend from the Ship with Peace and Blessings ................... 45
*Surah: 11 Ayah: 49* ............................................................................................................ 45
    Tafsir Ibn Kathir .............................................................................................................. 46
        The Explanation of These Stories is a Proof of the Revelation of Allah to His Messenger. 46
*Surah: 11 Ayah: 50, Ayah: 51 & Ayah: 52* ......................................................................... 46
    Tafsir Ibn Kathir .............................................................................................................. 47
        The Story of Prophet Hud and the People of `Ad ........................................................ 47
*Surah: 11 Ayah: 53, Ayah: 54, Ayah: 55 & Ayah: 56* ......................................................... 48
    Tafsir Ibn Kathir .............................................................................................................. 48
        The Conversation between (the People of) `Ad and Hud ........................................... 48
*Surah: 11 Ayah: 57, Ayah: 58, Ayah: 59 & Ayah: 60* ......................................................... 49
    Tafsir Ibn Kathir .............................................................................................................. 50
        The Destruction of the People of `Ad and the Salvation of Those among Them Who believed ........................................................................................................................ 51
*Surah: 11 Ayah: 61* ............................................................................................................ 51
    Tafsir Ibn Kathir .............................................................................................................. 51
        The Story of Salih and the People of Thamud ............................................................ 51
*Surah: 11 Ayah: 62 & Ayah: 63* ......................................................................................... 52
    Tafsir Ibn Kathir .............................................................................................................. 53
        The Conversation between Salih and the People of Thamud .................................... 53
*Surah: 11 Ayah: 64, Ayah: 65, Ayah: 66, Ayah: 67 & Ayah: 68* ......................................... 53
    Tafsir Ibn Kathir .............................................................................................................. 54
*Surah: 11 Ayah: 69, Ayah: 70, Ayah: 71, Ayah: 72 & Ayah: 73* ......................................... 54
    Tafsir Ibn Kathir .............................................................................................................. 55
        The Coming of the Angels to Ibrahim and Their Glad Tidings to Him of Ishaq and Ya`qub 55
*Surah: 11 Ayah: 74, Ayah: 75 & Ayah: 76* ......................................................................... 58
    Tafsir Ibn Kathir .............................................................................................................. 58
        The Dispute of Ibrahim over the People of Lut ........................................................... 58
*Surah: 11 Ayah: 77, Ayah: 78 & Ayah: 79* ......................................................................... 59
    Tafsir Ibn Kathir .............................................................................................................. 60
        The Coming of the Angels to Lut, His Grief, and His Discussion with His People ....... 60
*Surah: 11 Ayah: 80 & Ayah: 81* ......................................................................................... 61
    Tafsir Ibn Kathir .............................................................................................................. 62
        Lut's Inability, His Desire for Strength and the Angels' Informing Him of the Reality ....... 62
*Surah: 11 Ayah: 82 & Ayah: 83* ......................................................................................... 63
    Tafsir Ibn Kathir .............................................................................................................. 63
        The Town of Lut's People is overturned and Their Destruction .................................. 63
*Surah: 11 Ayah: 84* ............................................................................................................ 64
    Tafsir Ibn Kathir .............................................................................................................. 65
        The Story of the People of Madyan and the Call of Shu`ayb ..................................... 65
*Surah: 11 Ayah: 85 & Ayah: 86* ......................................................................................... 65
    Tafsir Ibn Kathir .............................................................................................................. 65
*Surah: 11 Ayah: 87* ............................................................................................................ 66

- Tafsir Ibn Kathir ... 66
  - The Response of Shu`ayb's People ... 66
- *Surah: 11 Ayah: 88* ... 67
  - Tafsir Ibn Kathir ... 67
    - Shu`ayb's Refutation of His People ... 67
- *Surah: 11 Ayah: 89 & Ayah: 90* ... 68
  - Tafsir Ibn Kathir ... 68
- *Surah: 11 Ayah: 91 & Ayah: 92* ... 69
  - Tafsir Ibn Kathir ... 69
    - The Response of Shu`ayb's People ... 69
    - Shu`ayb's Refutation of His People ... 70
- *Surah: 11 Ayah: 93, Ayah: 94 & Ayah: 95* ... 70
  - Tafsir Ibn Kathir ... 71
    - Shu`ayb's threatening of His People When the Prophet of Allah, Shu`ayb, despaired of their response to him, he said, "O my people, ... 71
- *Surah: 11 Ayah: 96, Ayah: 97, Ayah: 98 & Ayah: 99* ... 71
  - Tafsir Ibn Kathir ... 72
    - The Story of Musa and Fir`awn ... 72
- *Surah: 11 Ayah: 100 & Ayah: 101* ... 73
  - Tafsir Ibn Kathir ... 74
    - The Lesson taken from the Destroyed Towns ... 74
- *Surah: 11 Ayah: 102* ... 74
  - Tafsir Ibn Kathir ... 75
- *Surah: 11 Ayah: 103, Ayah: 104 & Ayah: 105* ... 75
  - Tafsir Ibn Kathir ... 76
    - The Destruction of the Towns is a Proof of the Establishment of the Hour (Judgement) . 76
- *Surah: 11 Ayah: 106 & Ayah: 107* ... 77
  - Tafsir Ibn Kathir ... 77
    - The Condition of the Wretched People and their Destination ... 77
- *Surah: 11 Ayah: 108* ... 79
  - Tafsir Ibn Kathir ... 79
    - The Condition of the Happy People and their Destination ... 79
- *Surah: 11 Ayah: 109, Ayah: 110 & Ayah: 111* ... 80
  - Tafsir Ibn Kathir ... 81
    - Associating Partners with Allah is no doubt Misguidance ... 81
- *Surah: 11 Ayah: 112 & Ayah: 113* ... 82
  - Tafsir Ibn Kathir ... 82
    - The Command to Stand Firm and Straight ... 82
- *Surah: 11 Ayah: 114 & Ayah: 115* ... 83
  - Tafsir Ibn Kathir ... 83
    - The Command to establish the Prayer ... 83
    - The Good Deeds wipe away the Evil Deeds ... 84
- *Surah: 11 Ayah: 116 & Ayah: 117* ... 86
  - Tafsir Ibn Kathir ... 86

# Table of Contents

There must be a Group of People Who forbid Lewdness .................................................. 86

*Surah: 11 Ayah: 118 & Ayah: 119* ................................................................................. 88
    Tafsir Ibn Kathir .......................................................................................................... 88
        Allah has not made Faith universally accepted .................................................. 88

*Surah: 11 Ayah: 120* ...................................................................................................... 90
    Tafsir Ibn Kathir .......................................................................................................... 90
        The Conclusion ..................................................................................................... 90

*Surah: 11 Ayah: 121 & Ayah: 122* ................................................................................. 90
    Tafsir Ibn Kathir .......................................................................................................... 91
        Allah, the Exalted, commands His Messenger to say to those who disbelieve in what he has come with from his Lord, by way of warning, ......................................................... 91

*Surah: 11 Ayah: 123* ...................................................................................................... 91
    Tafsir Ibn Kathir .......................................................................................................... 91
        Allah, the Exalted, informs that He is the All-Knower of the unseen of the heavens and the earth and that unto Him is the final return. .......................................................... 91

## CHAPTER (SURAH) 12: YUSUF (JOSEPH), VERSES 001-052 ..................................... 92

*Surah: 12 Ayah: 1, Ayah: 2 & Ayah: 3* ........................................................................... 92
    Tafsir Ibn Kathir .......................................................................................................... 93
        Qualities of the Qur'an ......................................................................................... 93
        Reason behind revealing Ayah (12:3) .................................................................. 93

*Surah: 12 Ayah: 4* .......................................................................................................... 94
    Tafsir Ibn Kathir .......................................................................................................... 94
        Yusuf's Dream ....................................................................................................... 94

*Surah: 12 Ayah: 5* .......................................................................................................... 95
    Tafsir Ibn Kathir .......................................................................................................... 95
        Ya`qub orders Yusuf to hide His Vision to avoid Shaytan's Plots ...................... 95

*Surah: 12 Ayah: 6* .......................................................................................................... 96
    Tafsir Ibn Kathir .......................................................................................................... 96
        Interpretation of Yusuf's Vision ........................................................................... 96

*Surah: 12 Ayah: 7, Ayah: 8, Ayah: 9 & Ayah: 10* .......................................................... 97
    Tafsir Ibn Kathir .......................................................................................................... 97
        There are Lessons to draw from the Story of Yusuf ........................................... 97

*Surah: 12 Ayah: 11 & Ayah: 12* ..................................................................................... 99
    Tafsir Ibn Kathir .......................................................................................................... 99
        Yusuf's Brothers ask for Their Father's Permission to take Yusuf with Them ... 99

*Surah: 12 Ayah: 13 & Ayah: 14* ..................................................................................... 99
    Tafsir Ibn Kathir ........................................................................................................ 100
        Ya`qub's Answer to Their Request ..................................................................... 100

*Surah: 12 Ayah: 15* ...................................................................................................... 100
    Tafsir Ibn Kathir ........................................................................................................ 100
        Yusuf is thrown in a Well ................................................................................... 100

*Surah: 12 Ayah: 16, Ayah: 17 & Ayah: 18* ................................................................... 101
    Tafsir Ibn Kathir ........................................................................................................ 102

- Yusuf's Brothers try to deceive Their Father .................................................................. 102
- **Surah: 12 Ayah: 19 & Ayah: 20** .................................................................................. 103
  - Tafsir Ibn Kathir ........................................................................................................... 103
  - Yusuf is Rescued from the Well and sold as a Slave ................................................... 103
- **Surah: 12 Ayah: 21 & Ayah: 22** .................................................................................. 104
  - Tafsir Ibn Kathir ........................................................................................................... 105
  - Yusuf in Egypt .............................................................................................................. 105
- **Surah: 12 Ayah: 23** ...................................................................................................... 106
  - Tafsir Ibn Kathir ........................................................................................................... 106
  - Wife of the `Aziz loves Yusuf and plots against Him ................................................... 106
- **Surah: 12 Ayah: 24** ...................................................................................................... 107
  - Tafsir Ibn Kathir ........................................................................................................... 107
- **Surah: 12 Ayah: 25, Ayah: 26, Ayah: 27, Ayah: 28 & Ayah: 29** ................................. 108
  - Tafsir Ibn Kathir ........................................................................................................... 109
- **Surah: 12 Ayah: 30, Ayah: 31, Ayah: 32, Ayah: 33 & Ayah: 34** ................................. 110
  - Tafsir Ibn Kathir ........................................................................................................... 111
  - The News reaches Women in the City, Who also plot against Yusuf .......................... 111
- **Surah: 12 Ayah: 35** ...................................................................................................... 114
  - Tafsir Ibn Kathir ........................................................................................................... 114
  - Yusuf is imprisoned without Justification ................................................................... 114
- **Surah: 12 Ayah: 36** ...................................................................................................... 114
  - Tafsir Ibn Kathir ........................................................................................................... 115
  - Two Jail Mates ask Yusuf to interpret their Dreams .................................................... 115
- **Surah: 12 Ayah: 37 & Ayah: 38** .................................................................................. 115
  - Tafsir Ibn Kathir ........................................................................................................... 116
  - Yusuf calls His Jail Mates to Tawhid even before He interprets Their Dreams ........... 116
- **Surah: 12 Ayah: 39 & Ayah: 40** .................................................................................. 116
  - Tafsir Ibn Kathir ........................................................................................................... 117
- **Surah: 12 Ayah: 41** ...................................................................................................... 118
  - Tafsir Ibn Kathir ........................................................................................................... 118
  - The Interpretation of the Dreams ................................................................................ 118
- **Surah: 12 Ayah: 42** ...................................................................................................... 119
  - Tafsir Ibn Kathir ........................................................................................................... 119
  - Yusuf asks the King's Distiller to mention Him to the King ........................................ 119
- **Surah: 12 Ayah: 43, Ayah: 44, Ayah: 45, Ayah: 46, Ayah: 47, Ayah: 48 & Ayah: 49** ...... 119
  - Tafsir Ibn Kathir ........................................................................................................... 121
  - The Dream of the King of Egypt .................................................................................. 121
  - Yusuf's Interpretation of the King's Dream ................................................................. 121
- **Surah: 12 Ayah: 50, Ayah: 51 & Ayah: 52** .................................................................. 122
  - Tafsir Ibn Kathir ........................................................................................................... 123
  - The King investigates what happened between the Wife of the `Aziz, the Women in the City, and Yusuf ......................................................................................................... 123

# PRELUDE

# Opening Serman

Indeed, all praise is due to Allah. We praise Him and seek His help and forgiveness. We seek refuge with Allah from our soul's evil and our wrong doings. He whom Allah guides, no one can misguide; and he whom He misguides, no one can guide

I bear witness that there is no (true) god except Allah – alone without a partner, and I bear witness that Muhammad (peace and blessings of Allah be upon him) is His 'abd (servant) and messenger.

يَٰٓأَيُّهَا ٱلَّذِينَ ءَامَنُواْ ٱتَّقُواْ ٱللَّهَ حَقَّ تُقَاتِهِۦ وَلَا تَمُوتُنَّ إِلَّا وَأَنتُم مُّسْلِمُونَ

O you who believe! Fear Allâh (by doing all that He has ordered and by abstaining from all that He has forbidden) as He should be feared. (Obey Him, be thankful to Him, and remember Him always), and die not except in a state of Islâm (as Muslims (with complete submission to Allâh)).

يَٰٓأَيُّهَا ٱلنَّاسُ ٱتَّقُواْ رَبَّكُمُ ٱلَّذِى خَلَقَكُم مِّن نَّفْسٍ وَٰحِدَةٍ وَخَلَقَ مِنْهَا زَوْجَهَا وَبَثَّ مِنْهُمَا رِجَالاً كَثِيرًا وَنِسَآءً وَٱتَّقُواْ ٱللَّهَ ٱلَّذِى تَسَآءَلُونَ بِهِۦ وَٱلْأَرْحَامَ إِنَّ ٱللَّهَ كَانَ عَلَيْكُمْ رَقِيبًا

O mankind! Be dutiful to your Lord, Who created you from a single person (Adam), and from him (Adam) He created his wife (Hawwâ (Eve)) and from them both He created many men and women; and fear Allâh through Whom you demand (your mutual rights), and (do not cut the relations of) the wombs (kinship). Surely, Allâh is Ever an All-Watcher over you.

يُصْلِحْ لَكُمْ أَعْمَٰلَكُمْ وَيَغْفِرْ لَكُمْ ذُنُوبَكُمْ وَمَن يُطِعِ ٱللَّهَ وَرَسُولَهُۥ فَقَدْ فَازَ فَوْزًا عَظِيمًا

He will direct you to do righteous good deeds and will forgive you your sins. And whosoever obeys Allâh and His Messenger (peace be upon him), he has indeed achieved a great achievement (i.e. he will be saved from the Hell-fire and will be admitted to Paradise).

Indeed, the best speech is Allah's Book and the best guidance is Muhammad's () guidance. The worst affairs (of religion) are those innovated (by people), for every such innovation is an act of misguidance leading to the Fire

## Our Mission

Our mission is to gather in one place, for the English-speaking public, all relevant information needed to make the Qur'an more understandable and easier to study. This book tries to do this by providing the following:

1. The Arabic Text for those who are able to read Arabic
2. Transliteration of the Arabic text for those who are unable to read the Arabic script. This will give them a sample of the sound of the Qur'an, which they could not otherwise comprehend from reading the English meaning.
3. The meaning of the qur'an (translated by Dr. Muhammad Taqi-ud-Din Al-Hilali, Ph.D. and Dr. Muhammad Muhsin Khan)
4. Explanation (abridged Tafsir) by Ibn Kathir (translated by Safi-ur-Rahman al-Mubarakpuri)

We hope that by doing this an ordinary English-speaker will be able to pick up a copy of this book and study and comprehend The Glorious Qur'an in a way that is acceptable to the understanding of the Rightly-guided Muslim Ummah (Community).

## Biography of Hafiz Ibn Kathir (701 H - 774 H)

By the Honored Shaykh `Abdul-Qadir Al-Arna'ut, may Allah protect him.

He is the respected Imam, Abu Al-Fida', `Imad Ad-Din Isma il bin 'Umar bin Kathir Al-Qurashi Al-Busrawi - Busraian in origin; Dimashqi in training, learning and residence.

Ibn Kathir was born in the city of Busra in 701 H. His father was the Friday speaker of the village, but he died while Ibn Kathir was only four years old. Ibn Kathir's brother, Shaykh Abdul-Wahhab, reared him and taught him until he moved to Damascus in 706 H., when he was five years old.

### Ibn Kathir's Teachers

Ibn Kathir studied Fiqh - Islamic jurisprudence - with Burhan Ad-Din, Ibrahim bin `Abdur-Rahman Al-Fizari, known as Ibn Al-Firkah (who died in 729 H). Ibn Kathir heard Hadiths from `Isa bin Al-Mutim, Ahmad bin Abi Talib, (Ibn Ash-Shahnah) (who died in 730 H), Ibn Al-Hajjar, (who died in 730 H), and the Hadith narrator of Ash-Sham (modern day Syria and surrounding areas); Baha Ad-Din Al-Qasim bin Muzaffar bin `Asakir (who died in 723 H), and Ibn Ash-Shirdzi, Ishaq bin Yahya Al-Ammuddi, also known as `Afif Ad-Din, the Zahiriyyah Shaykh who died in 725 H, and Muhammad bin Zarrad. He remained with Jamal Ad-Din, Yusuf bin Az-Zaki AlMizzi who died in 724 H, he benefited from his knowledge and also married his daughter. He also read with Shaykh Al-Islam, Taqi Ad-Din Ahmad bin `Abdul-Halim bin `Abdus-Salam bin Taymiyyah who died in 728 H. He also read with the Imam Hafiz and historian Shams Ad-Din, Muhammad bin Ahmad bin Uthman bin Qaymaz Adh-Dhahabi, who died in 748 H. Also, Abu Musa Al-Qarafai, Abu Al-Fath Ad-Dabbusi and

'Ali bin `Umar As-Suwani and others who gave him permission to transmit the knowledge he learned with them in Egypt.

In his book, Al-Mu jam Al-Mukhtas, Al-Hafiz Adh-Dhaliabi wrote that Ibn Kathir was, "The Imam, scholar of jurisprudence, skillful scholar of Hadith, renowned Fagih and scholar of Tafsir who wrote several beneficial books."

Further, in Ad-Durar Al-Kdminah, Al-Hafiz Ibn Hajar AlAsqalani said, "Ibn Kathir worked on the subject of the Hadith in the areas of texts and chains of narrators. He had a good memory, his books became popular during his lifetime, and people benefited from them after his death."

Also, the renowned historian Abu Al-Mahasin, Jamal Ad-Din Yusuf bin Sayf Ad-Din (Ibn Taghri Bardi), said in his book, AlManhal As-Safi, "He is the Shaykh, the Imam, the great scholar `Imad Ad-Din Abu Al-Fida'. He learned extensively and was very active in collecting knowledge and writing. He was excellent in the areas of Fiqh, Tafsfr and Hadith. He collected knowledge, authored (books), taught, narrated Hadith and wrote. He had immense knowledge in the fields of Hadith, Tafsir, Fiqh, the Arabic language, and so forth. He gave Fatawa (religious verdicts) and taught until he died, may Allah grant him mercy. He was known for his precision and vast knowledge, and as a scholar of history, Hadith and Tafsir."

## Ibn Kathir's Students

Ibn Hajji was one of Ibn Kathir's students, and he described Ibn Kathir: "He had the best memory of the Hadith texts. He also had the most knowledge concerning the narrators and authenticity, his contemporaries and teachers admitted to these qualities. Every time I met him I gained some benefit from him."

Also, Ibn Al-`Imad Al-Hanbali said in his book, Shadhardt Adh-Dhahab, "He is the renowned Hafiz `Imad Ad-Din, whose memory was excellent, whose forgetfulness was miniscule, whose understanding was adequate, and who had good knowledge in the Arabic language." Also, Ibn Habib said about Ibn Kathir, "He heard knowledge and collected it and wrote various books. He brought comfort to the ears with his Fatwas and narrated Hadith and brought benefit to other people. The papers that contained his Fatwas were transmitted to the various (Islamic) provinces. Further, he was known for his precision and encompassing knowledge."

## Ibn Kathir's Books

1 - One of the greatest books that Ibn Kathir wrote was his Tafsir of the Noble Qur'an, which is one of the best Tafsir that rely on narrations [of Ahadith, the Tafsir of the Companions, etc.]. The Tafsir by Ibn Kathir was printed many times and several scholars have summarized it.

2- The History Collection known as Al-Biddyah, which was printed in 14 volumes under the name Al-Bidayah wanNihdyah, and contained the stories of the Prophets and previous nations, the Prophet's Seerah (life story) and Islamic history until his time. He also added a book Al-Fitan, about the Signs of the Last Hour.

3- At-Takmil ft Ma`rifat Ath-Thiqat wa Ad-Du'afa wal Majdhil which Ibn Kathir collected from the books of his two Shaykhs Al-Mizzi and Adh-Dhahabi; Al-Kdmal and Mizan Al-Ftiddl. He added several benefits regarding the subject of Al-Jarh and AtT'adil.

4- Al-Hadi was-Sunan ft Ahadith Al-Masdnfd was-Sunan which is also known by, Jami` Al-Masdnfd. In this book, Ibn Kathir collected the narrations of Imams Ahmad bin Hanbal, Al-Bazzar, Abu Ya`la Al-Mawsili, Ibn Abi Shaybah and from the six collections of Hadith: the Two Sahihs [Al-Bukhari and Muslim] and the Four Sunan [Abu Dawud, At-Tirmidhi, AnNasa and Ibn Majah]. Ibn Kathir divided this book according to areas of Fiqh.

5-Tabaqat Ash-Shaf iyah which also contains the virtues of Imam Ash-Shafi.

6- Ibn Kathir wrote references for the Ahadith of Adillat AtTanbfh, from the Shafi school of Fiqh.

7- Ibn Kathir began an explanation of Sahih Al-Bukhari, but he did not finish it.

8- He started writing a large volume on the Ahkam (Laws), but finished only up to the Hajj rituals.

9- He summarized Al-Bayhaqi's 'Al-Madkhal. Many of these books were not printed.

10- He summarized `Ulum Al-Hadith, by Abu `Amr bin AsSalah and called it Mukhtasar `Ulum Al-Hadith. Shaykh Ahmad Shakir, the Egyptian Muhaddith, printed this book along with his commentary on it and called it Al-Ba'th Al-Hathfth fi Sharh Mukhtasar `Ulum Al-Hadith.

11- As-Sfrah An-Nabawiyyah, which is contained in his book Al-Biddyah, and both of these books are in print.

12- A research on Jihad called Al-Ijtihad ft Talabi Al-Jihad, which was printed several times.

## Ibn Kathir's Death

Al-Hafiz Ibn Hajar Al-Asgalani said, "Ibn Kathir lost his sight just before his life ended. He died in Damascus in 774 H." May Allah grant mercy upon Ibn Kathir and make him among the residents of His Paradise.

# PREFACE

In the name of Allah, Most Gracious, Most Merciful.

## About this book

The previous publication of this book included some background information to the chapters of the Qur'an by an Islamic scholar known as Abul Ala Maududi. This information was used to shed more light on the chapters by giving a summery of why each chapter was given its name, It's period of revelation and the circumstances surrounding its revelatiom. However, some Muslims objected to the inclusion of the contributions of Maududi.

In this new publication of Tafsir Ibn Kathir, we have removed all traces of the contribution of Abul Ala Maududi. Personally, I do not know the reasons for the objections to Maududi, but this work concerns only the tafsir of Ibn Kathir, so we have not included anything from Maududi in it. We have also corrected all the typing and formatting errors found in the previous publication. We have not alter the structure of the book. The reader is still able to read the full Arabic Text of the thirty Parts of the Qur'an and follow its meanings in the English language. The transliteration of the Arabic text should also give the reader a taste of the sound of the original Arabic.

May Almighty Allah accept this effort from us, and make it a source of blessings for us in this world and in the next. I bear witness that there is none worthy of worship but Allah and I bear witness that Muhammad ( may the peace and blessings of Allah be upon him) is the slave and messenger of Allah.

## Performing Prostration While Reading the Qur'an

Question:

Could you please give a list of the Qur'anic verses when a prostration is recommended? What happens if we read these verses and not perform a prostration?

A. Jalil

Answer:

There are 15 verses in the Qur'an that mention prostration before God Almighty as a good action by God-fearing believers. Therefore, it is strongly recommended to perform such a prostration when we read or listen to any of these verses, whether during prayer or in any situation.

Some scholars are of the view that even if one has not performed ablution, one should prostrate oneself. These verses are given here, starting with the Arabic title of the surah which is followed by two numbers, the first indicating the surah, and the second indicating the verse,: Al-Araf 7: 206; Al-Raad 13: 15; Al-Nahl 16: 50; Al-Isra 17: 109; Maryam 19: 58; Al-Hajj 22: 18 & 22: 77; Al-Furqan 25: 60; Al-Naml 27: 26;

Al-Sajdah 32: 15; Saad 38: 25; Fussilat 41: 38; Al-Najm 53: 62; Al-Inshiqaq 84: 21 and Al-Alaq 96: 19.

If you do not perform a prostration when you read or listen to any of these verses, you have done badly because you miss out on the reward of performing a prostration for God. You incur no sin and violate no divine order.

Reference:
http://archive.arabnews.com/?page=5&section=0&article=97811&d=1&m=7&y=2007

# The Glorious Qur'an Juz' 12 (Part 12): Chapter (Surah) 11: Hud (Hud)) 006 To Chapter (Surah) 12: Yusuf (Joseph) 052

**PART 12 FULL ARABIC TEXT**

## Chapter (Surah) 11: Hud 006-123

﴿ إِلَّا ٱلَّذِينَ صَبَرُواْ وَعَمِلُواْ ٱلصَّٰلِحَٰتِ أُوْلَٰٓئِكَ لَهُم مَّغْفِرَةٌ وَأَجْرٌ كَبِيرٌ ۝ فَلَعَلَّكَ تَارِكٌۢ بَعْضَ مَا يُوحَىٰٓ إِلَيْكَ وَضَآئِقٌۢ بِهِۦ صَدْرُكَ أَن يَقُولُواْ لَوْلَآ أُنزِلَ عَلَيْهِ كَنزٌ أَوْ جَآءَ مَعَهُۥ مَلَكٌ ۚ إِنَّمَآ أَنتَ نَذِيرٌ ۚ وَٱللَّهُ عَلَىٰ كُلِّ شَىْءٍ وَكِيلٌ ۝ أَمْ يَقُولُونَ ٱفْتَرَىٰهُ ۖ قُلْ فَأْتُواْ بِعَشْرِ سُوَرٍ مِّثْلِهِۦ مُفْتَرَيَٰتٍ وَٱدْعُواْ مَنِ ٱسْتَطَعْتُم مِّن دُونِ ٱللَّهِ إِن كُنتُمْ صَٰدِقِينَ ۝ فَإِلَّمْ يَسْتَجِيبُواْ لَكُمْ فَٱعْلَمُوٓاْ أَنَّمَآ أُنزِلَ بِعِلْمِ ٱللَّهِ وَأَن لَّآ إِلَٰهَ إِلَّا هُوَ ۖ فَهَلْ أَنتُم مُّسْلِمُونَ ۝ مَن كَانَ يُرِيدُ ٱلْحَيَوٰةَ ٱلدُّنْيَا وَزِينَتَهَا نُوَفِّ إِلَيْهِمْ أَعْمَٰلَهُمْ فِيهَا وَهُمْ فِيهَا لَا يُبْخَسُونَ ۝ أُوْلَٰٓئِكَ ٱلَّذِينَ لَيْسَ لَهُمْ فِى ٱلْءَاخِرَةِ إِلَّا ٱلنَّارُ ۖ وَحَبِطَ مَا صَنَعُواْ فِيهَا وَبَٰطِلٌ مَّا كَانُواْ يَعْمَلُونَ ۝ أَفَمَن كَانَ عَلَىٰ بَيِّنَةٍ مِّن رَّبِّهِۦ وَيَتْلُوهُ شَاهِدٌ مِّنْهُ وَمِن قَبْلِهِۦ كِتَٰبُ مُوسَىٰٓ إِمَامًا وَرَحْمَةً ۚ أُوْلَٰٓئِكَ يُؤْمِنُونَ بِهِۦ ۚ وَمَن يَكْفُرْ بِهِۦ مِنَ ٱلْأَحْزَابِ فَٱلنَّارُ مَوْعِدُهُۥ ۚ فَلَا تَكُ فِى مِرْيَةٍ مِّنْهُ ۚ إِنَّهُ ٱلْحَقُّ مِن رَّبِّكَ وَلَٰكِنَّ أَكْثَرَ ٱلنَّاسِ لَا يُؤْمِنُونَ ۝ وَمَنْ أَظْلَمُ مِمَّنِ ٱفْتَرَىٰ عَلَى ٱللَّهِ كَذِبًا ۚ أُوْلَٰٓئِكَ يُعْرَضُونَ عَلَىٰ رَبِّهِمْ وَيَقُولُ ٱلْأَشْهَٰدُ هَٰٓؤُلَآءِ ٱلَّذِينَ كَذَبُواْ عَلَىٰ رَبِّهِمْ ۚ أَلَا لَعْنَةُ ٱللَّهِ عَلَى ٱلظَّٰلِمِينَ ۝ ٱلَّذِينَ يَصُدُّونَ عَن سَبِيلِ ٱللَّهِ وَيَبْغُونَهَا عِوَجًا وَهُم بِٱلْءَاخِرَةِ هُمْ كَٰفِرُونَ ۝ أُوْلَٰٓئِكَ لَمْ يَكُونُواْ مُعْجِزِينَ فِى ٱلْأَرْضِ وَمَا كَانَ لَهُم مِّن دُونِ ٱللَّهِ مِنْ أَوْلِيَآءَ

يُضَعَفُ لَهُمُ ٱلْعَذَابُ ۚ مَا كَانُوا۟ يَسْتَطِيعُونَ ٱلسَّمْعَ وَمَا كَانُوا۟ يُبْصِرُونَ ۞ أُو۟لَـٰٓئِكَ ٱلَّذِينَ خَسِرُوٓا۟ أَنفُسَهُمْ وَضَلَّ عَنْهُم مَّا كَانُوا۟ يَفْتَرُونَ ۞ لَا جَرَمَ أَنَّهُمْ فِى ٱلْـَٔاخِرَةِ هُمُ ٱلْأَخْسَرُونَ ۞ إِنَّ ٱلَّذِينَ ءَامَنُوا۟ وَعَمِلُوا۟ ٱلصَّـٰلِحَـٰتِ وَأَخْبَتُوٓا۟ إِلَىٰ رَبِّهِمْ أُو۟لَـٰٓئِكَ أَصْحَـٰبُ ٱلْجَنَّةِ ۖ هُمْ فِيهَا خَـٰلِدُونَ ۞ ۞ مَثَلُ ٱلْفَرِيقَيْنِ كَٱلْأَعْمَىٰ وَٱلْأَصَمِّ وَٱلْبَصِيرِ وَٱلسَّمِيعِ ۚ هَلْ يَسْتَوِيَانِ مَثَلًا ۚ أَفَلَا تَذَكَّرُونَ ۞ وَلَقَدْ أَرْسَلْنَا نُوحًا إِلَىٰ قَوْمِهِۦٓ إِنِّى لَكُمْ نَذِيرٌ مُّبِينٌ ۞ أَن لَّا تَعْبُدُوٓا۟ إِلَّا ٱللَّهَ ۖ إِنِّىٓ أَخَافُ عَلَيْكُمْ عَذَابَ يَوْمٍ أَلِيمٍ ۞ فَقَالَ ٱلْمَلَأُ ٱلَّذِينَ كَفَرُوا۟ مِن قَوْمِهِۦ مَا نَرَىٰكَ إِلَّا بَشَرًا مِّثْلَنَا وَمَا نَرَىٰكَ ٱتَّبَعَكَ إِلَّا ٱلَّذِينَ هُمْ أَرَاذِلُنَا بَادِىَ ٱلرَّأْىِ وَمَا نَرَىٰ لَكُمْ عَلَيْنَا مِن فَضْلٍ بَلْ نَظُنُّكُمْ كَـٰذِبِينَ ۞ قَالَ يَـٰقَوْمِ أَرَءَيْتُمْ إِن كُنتُ عَلَىٰ بَيِّنَةٍ مِّن رَّبِّى وَءَاتَىٰنِى رَحْمَةً مِّنْ عِندِهِۦ فَعُمِّيَتْ عَلَيْكُمْ أَنُلْزِمُكُمُوهَا وَأَنتُمْ لَهَا كَـٰرِهُونَ ۞ وَيَـٰقَوْمِ لَآ أَسْـَٔلُكُمْ عَلَيْهِ مَالًا ۖ إِنْ أَجْرِىَ إِلَّا عَلَى ٱللَّهِ ۚ وَمَآ أَنَا۠ بِطَارِدِ ٱلَّذِينَ ءَامَنُوٓا۟ ۚ إِنَّهُم مُّلَـٰقُوا۟ رَبِّهِمْ وَلَـٰكِنِّىٓ أَرَىٰكُمْ قَوْمًا تَجْهَلُونَ ۞ وَيَـٰقَوْمِ مَن يَنصُرُنِى مِنَ ٱللَّهِ إِن طَرَدتُّهُمْ ۚ أَفَلَا تَذَكَّرُونَ ۞ وَلَآ أَقُولُ لَكُمْ عِندِى خَزَآئِنُ ٱللَّهِ وَلَآ أَعْلَمُ ٱلْغَيْبَ وَلَآ أَقُولُ إِنِّى مَلَكٌ وَلَآ أَقُولُ لِلَّذِينَ تَزْدَرِىٓ أَعْيُنُكُمْ لَن يُؤْتِيَهُمُ ٱللَّهُ خَيْرًا ۖ ٱللَّهُ أَعْلَمُ بِمَا فِىٓ أَنفُسِهِمْ ۖ إِنِّىٓ إِذًا لَّمِنَ ٱلظَّـٰلِمِينَ ۞ قَالُوا۟ يَـٰنُوحُ قَدْ جَـٰدَلْتَنَا فَأَكْثَرْتَ جِدَٰلَنَا فَأْتِنَا بِمَا تَعِدُنَآ إِن كُنتَ مِنَ ٱلصَّـٰدِقِينَ ۞ قَالَ إِنَّمَا يَأْتِيكُم بِهِ ٱللَّهُ إِن شَآءَ وَمَآ أَنتُم بِمُعْجِزِينَ ۞ وَلَا يَنفَعُكُمْ نُصْحِىٓ إِنْ أَرَدتُّ أَنْ أَنصَحَ لَكُمْ إِن كَانَ ٱللَّهُ يُرِيدُ أَن يُغْوِيَكُمْ ۚ هُوَ رَبُّكُمْ وَإِلَيْهِ تُرْجَعُونَ ۞ أَمْ يَقُولُونَ ٱفْتَرَىٰهُ ۖ قُلْ إِنِ ٱفْتَرَيْتُهُۥ فَعَلَىَّ إِجْرَامِى وَأَنَا۠ بَرِىٓءٌ مِّمَّا تُجْرِمُونَ ۞ وَأُوحِىَ إِلَىٰ نُوحٍ

Juz' 12 (Part 12): Hud (Hud) 6 - Yusuf (Joseph) 52

أَنَّهُۥ لَن يُؤْمِنَ مِن قَوْمِكَ إِلَّا مَن قَدْ ءَامَنَ فَلَا تَبْتَئِسْ بِمَا كَانُوا۟ يَفْعَلُونَ ۝ وَٱصْنَعِ ٱلْفُلْكَ بِأَعْيُنِنَا وَوَحْيِنَا وَلَا تُخَٰطِبْنِى فِى ٱلَّذِينَ ظَلَمُوٓا۟ إِنَّهُم مُّغْرَقُونَ ۝ وَيَصْنَعُ ٱلْفُلْكَ وَكُلَّمَا مَرَّ عَلَيْهِ مَلَأٌ مِّن قَوْمِهِۦ سَخِرُوا۟ مِنْهُ ۚ قَالَ إِن تَسْخَرُوا۟ مِنَّا فَإِنَّا نَسْخَرُ مِنكُمْ كَمَا تَسْخَرُونَ ۝ فَسَوْفَ تَعْلَمُونَ مَن يَأْتِيهِ عَذَابٌ يُخْزِيهِ وَيَحِلُّ عَلَيْهِ عَذَابٌ مُّقِيمٌ ۝ حَتَّىٰٓ إِذَا جَآءَ أَمْرُنَا وَفَارَ ٱلتَّنُّورُ قُلْنَا ٱحْمِلْ فِيهَا مِن كُلٍّ زَوْجَيْنِ ٱثْنَيْنِ وَأَهْلَكَ إِلَّا مَن سَبَقَ عَلَيْهِ ٱلْقَوْلُ وَمَنْ ءَامَنَ ۚ وَمَآ ءَامَنَ مَعَهُۥٓ إِلَّا قَلِيلٌ ۝ ۞ وَقَالَ ٱرْكَبُوا۟ فِيهَا بِسْمِ ٱللَّهِ مَجْر۪ىٰهَا وَمُرْسَىٰهَآ ۚ إِنَّ رَبِّى لَغَفُورٌ رَّحِيمٌ ۝ وَهِىَ تَجْرِى بِهِمْ فِى مَوْجٍ كَٱلْجِبَالِ وَنَادَىٰ نُوحٌ ٱبْنَهُۥ وَكَانَ فِى مَعْزِلٍ يَٰبُنَىَّ ٱرْكَب مَّعَنَا وَلَا تَكُن مَّعَ ٱلْكَٰفِرِينَ ۝ قَالَ سَـَٔاوِىٓ إِلَىٰ جَبَلٍ يَعْصِمُنِى مِنَ ٱلْمَآءِ ۚ قَالَ لَا عَاصِمَ ٱلْيَوْمَ مِنْ أَمْرِ ٱللَّهِ إِلَّا مَن رَّحِمَ ۚ وَحَالَ بَيْنَهُمَا ٱلْمَوْجُ فَكَانَ مِنَ ٱلْمُغْرَقِينَ ۝ وَقِيلَ يَٰٓأَرْضُ ٱبْلَعِى مَآءَكِ وَيَٰسَمَآءُ أَقْلِعِى وَغِيضَ ٱلْمَآءُ وَقُضِىَ ٱلْأَمْرُ وَٱسْتَوَتْ عَلَى ٱلْجُودِىِّ ۖ وَقِيلَ بُعْدًا لِّلْقَوْمِ ٱلظَّٰلِمِينَ ۝ وَنَادَىٰ نُوحٌ رَّبَّهُۥ فَقَالَ رَبِّ إِنَّ ٱبْنِى مِنْ أَهْلِى وَإِنَّ وَعْدَكَ ٱلْحَقُّ وَأَنتَ أَحْكَمُ ٱلْحَٰكِمِينَ ۝ قَالَ يَٰنُوحُ إِنَّهُۥ لَيْسَ مِنْ أَهْلِكَ ۖ إِنَّهُۥ عَمَلٌ غَيْرُ صَٰلِحٍ ۖ فَلَا تَسْـَٔلْنِ مَا لَيْسَ لَكَ بِهِۦ عِلْمٌ ۖ إِنِّىٓ أَعِظُكَ أَن تَكُونَ مِنَ ٱلْجَٰهِلِينَ ۝ قَالَ رَبِّ إِنِّىٓ أَعُوذُ بِكَ أَنْ أَسْـَٔلَكَ مَا لَيْسَ لِى بِهِۦ عِلْمٌ ۖ وَإِلَّا تَغْفِرْ لِى وَتَرْحَمْنِىٓ أَكُن مِّنَ ٱلْخَٰسِرِينَ ۝ قِيلَ يَٰنُوحُ ٱهْبِطْ بِسَلَٰمٍ مِّنَّا وَبَرَكَٰتٍ عَلَيْكَ وَعَلَىٰٓ أُمَمٍ مِّمَّن مَّعَكَ ۚ وَأُمَمٌ سَنُمَتِّعُهُمْ ثُمَّ يَمَسُّهُم مِّنَّا عَذَابٌ أَلِيمٌ ۝ تِلْكَ مِنْ أَنۢبَآءِ ٱلْغَيْبِ نُوحِيهَآ إِلَيْكَ ۖ مَا كُنتَ تَعْلَمُهَآ أَنتَ وَلَا قَوْمُكَ مِن قَبْلِ هَٰذَا ۖ فَٱصْبِرْ ۖ إِنَّ ٱلْعَٰقِبَةَ لِلْمُتَّقِينَ ۝ وَإِلَىٰ عَادٍ

أَخَاهُمْ هُودًا ۗ قَالَ يَـٰقَوْمِ ٱعْبُدُوا۟ ٱللَّهَ مَا لَكُم مِّنْ إِلَـٰهٍ غَيْرُهُۥٓ ۖ إِنْ أَنتُمْ إِلَّا مُفْتَرُونَ ۝ يَـٰقَوْمِ لَآ أَسْـَٔلُكُمْ عَلَيْهِ أَجْرًا ۖ إِنْ أَجْرِىَ إِلَّا عَلَى ٱلَّذِى فَطَرَنِىٓ ۚ أَفَلَا تَعْقِلُونَ ۝ وَيَـٰقَوْمِ ٱسْتَغْفِرُوا۟ رَبَّكُمْ ثُمَّ تُوبُوٓا۟ إِلَيْهِ يُرْسِلِ ٱلسَّمَآءَ عَلَيْكُم مِّدْرَارًا وَيَزِدْكُمْ قُوَّةً إِلَىٰ قُوَّتِكُمْ وَلَا تَتَوَلَّوْا۟ مُجْرِمِينَ ۝ قَالُوا۟ يَـٰهُودُ مَا جِئْتَنَا بِبَيِّنَةٍ وَمَا نَحْنُ بِتَارِكِىٓ ءَالِهَتِنَا عَن قَوْلِكَ وَمَا نَحْنُ لَكَ بِمُؤْمِنِينَ ۝ إِن نَّقُولُ إِلَّا ٱعْتَرَىٰكَ بَعْضُ ءَالِهَتِنَا بِسُوٓءٍ ۗ قَالَ إِنِّىٓ أُشْهِدُ ٱللَّهَ وَٱشْهَدُوٓا۟ أَنِّى بَرِىٓءٌ مِّمَّا تُشْرِكُونَ ۝ مِن دُونِهِۦ ۖ فَكِيدُونِى جَمِيعًا ثُمَّ لَا تُنظِرُونِ ۝ إِنِّى تَوَكَّلْتُ عَلَى ٱللَّهِ رَبِّى وَرَبِّكُم ۚ مَّا مِن دَآبَّةٍ إِلَّا هُوَ ءَاخِذٌۢ بِنَاصِيَتِهَآ ۚ إِنَّ رَبِّى عَلَىٰ صِرَٰطٍ مُّسْتَقِيمٍ ۝ فَإِن تَوَلَّوْا۟ فَقَدْ أَبْلَغْتُكُم مَّآ أُرْسِلْتُ بِهِۦٓ إِلَيْكُمْ ۚ وَيَسْتَخْلِفُ رَبِّى قَوْمًا غَيْرَكُمْ وَلَا تَضُرُّونَهُۥ شَيْـًٔا ۚ إِنَّ رَبِّى عَلَىٰ كُلِّ شَىْءٍ حَفِيظٌ ۝ وَلَمَّا جَآءَ أَمْرُنَا نَجَّيْنَا هُودًا وَٱلَّذِينَ ءَامَنُوا۟ مَعَهُۥ بِرَحْمَةٍ مِّنَّا وَنَجَّيْنَـٰهُم مِّنْ عَذَابٍ غَلِيظٍ ۝ وَتِلْكَ عَادٌ ۖ جَحَدُوا۟ بِـَٔايَـٰتِ رَبِّهِمْ وَعَصَوْا۟ رُسُلَهُۥ وَٱتَّبَعُوٓا۟ أَمْرَ كُلِّ جَبَّارٍ عَنِيدٍ ۝ وَأُتْبِعُوا۟ فِى هَـٰذِهِ ٱلدُّنْيَا لَعْنَةً وَيَوْمَ ٱلْقِيَـٰمَةِ ۗ أَلَآ إِنَّ عَادًا كَفَرُوا۟ رَبَّهُمْ ۗ أَلَا بُعْدًا لِّعَادٍ قَوْمِ هُودٍ ۝ وَإِلَىٰ ثَمُودَ أَخَاهُمْ صَـٰلِحًا ۚ قَالَ يَـٰقَوْمِ ٱعْبُدُوا۟ ٱللَّهَ مَا لَكُم مِّنْ إِلَـٰهٍ غَيْرُهُۥ ۖ هُوَ أَنشَأَكُم مِّنَ ٱلْأَرْضِ وَٱسْتَعْمَرَكُمْ فِيهَا فَٱسْتَغْفِرُوهُ ثُمَّ تُوبُوٓا۟ إِلَيْهِ ۚ إِنَّ رَبِّى قَرِيبٌ مُّجِيبٌ ۝ قَالُوا۟ يَـٰصَـٰلِحُ قَدْ كُنتَ فِينَا مَرْجُوًّا قَبْلَ هَـٰذَآ ۖ أَتَنْهَىٰنَآ أَن نَّعْبُدَ مَا يَعْبُدُ ءَابَآؤُنَا وَإِنَّنَا لَفِى شَكٍّ مِّمَّا تَدْعُونَآ إِلَيْهِ مُرِيبٍ ۝ قَالَ يَـٰقَوْمِ أَرَءَيْتُمْ إِن كُنتُ عَلَىٰ بَيِّنَةٍ مِّن رَّبِّى وَءَاتَىٰنِى مِنْهُ رَحْمَةً فَمَن يَنصُرُنِى مِنَ ٱللَّهِ إِنْ عَصَيْتُهُۥ ۖ فَمَا تَزِيدُونَنِى غَيْرَ تَخْسِيرٍ ۝ وَيَـٰقَوْمِ هَـٰذِهِۦ نَاقَةُ ٱللَّهِ لَكُمْ ءَايَةً فَذَرُوهَا تَأْكُلْ فِىٓ أَرْضِ ٱللَّهِ وَلَا تَمَسُّوهَا بِسُوٓءٍ فَيَأْخُذَكُمْ

عَذَابٌ قَرِيبٌ ۝ فَعَقَرُوهَا فَقَالَ تَمَتَّعُوا۟ فِى دَارِكُمْ ثَلَٰثَةَ أَيَّامٍ ۖ ذَٰلِكَ وَعْدٌ غَيْرُ مَكْذُوبٍ ۝ فَلَمَّا جَآءَ أَمْرُنَا نَجَّيْنَا صَٰلِحًا وَٱلَّذِينَ ءَامَنُوا۟ مَعَهُۥ بِرَحْمَةٍ مِّنَّا وَمِنْ خِزْىِ يَوْمِئِذٍ ۗ إِنَّ رَبَّكَ هُوَ ٱلْقَوِىُّ ٱلْعَزِيزُ ۝ وَأَخَذَ ٱلَّذِينَ ظَلَمُوا۟ ٱلصَّيْحَةُ فَأَصْبَحُوا۟ فِى دِيَٰرِهِمْ جَٰثِمِينَ ۝ كَأَن لَّمْ يَغْنَوْا۟ فِيهَآ ۗ أَلَآ إِنَّ ثَمُودَا۟ كَفَرُوا۟ رَبَّهُمْ ۗ أَلَا بُعْدًا لِّثَمُودَ ۝ وَلَقَدْ جَآءَتْ رُسُلُنَآ إِبْرَٰهِيمَ بِٱلْبُشْرَىٰ قَالُوا۟ سَلَٰمًا ۖ قَالَ سَلَٰمٌ ۖ فَمَا لَبِثَ أَن جَآءَ بِعِجْلٍ حَنِيذٍ ۝ فَلَمَّا رَءَآ أَيْدِيَهُمْ لَا تَصِلُ إِلَيْهِ نَكِرَهُمْ وَأَوْجَسَ مِنْهُمْ خِيفَةً ۚ قَالُوا۟ لَا تَخَفْ إِنَّآ أُرْسِلْنَآ إِلَىٰ قَوْمِ لُوطٍ ۝ وَٱمْرَأَتُهُۥ قَآئِمَةٌ فَضَحِكَتْ فَبَشَّرْنَٰهَا بِإِسْحَٰقَ وَمِن وَرَآءِ إِسْحَٰقَ يَعْقُوبَ ۝ قَالَتْ يَٰوَيْلَتَىٰٓ ءَأَلِدُ وَأَنَا۠ عَجُوزٌ وَهَٰذَا بَعْلِى شَيْخًا ۖ إِنَّ هَٰذَا لَشَىْءٌ عَجِيبٌ ۝ قَالُوٓا۟ أَتَعْجَبِينَ مِنْ أَمْرِ ٱللَّهِ ۖ رَحْمَتُ ٱللَّهِ وَبَرَكَٰتُهُۥ عَلَيْكُمْ أَهْلَ ٱلْبَيْتِ ۚ إِنَّهُۥ حَمِيدٌ مَّجِيدٌ ۝ فَلَمَّا ذَهَبَ عَنْ إِبْرَٰهِيمَ ٱلرَّوْعُ وَجَآءَتْهُ ٱلْبُشْرَىٰ يُجَٰدِلُنَا فِى قَوْمِ لُوطٍ ۝ إِنَّ إِبْرَٰهِيمَ لَحَلِيمٌ أَوَّٰهٌ مُّنِيبٌ ۝ يَٰٓإِبْرَٰهِيمُ أَعْرِضْ عَنْ هَٰذَآ ۖ إِنَّهُۥ قَدْ جَآءَ أَمْرُ رَبِّكَ ۖ وَإِنَّهُمْ ءَاتِيهِمْ عَذَابٌ غَيْرُ مَرْدُودٍ ۝ وَلَمَّا جَآءَتْ رُسُلُنَا لُوطًا سِىٓءَ بِهِمْ وَضَاقَ بِهِمْ ذَرْعًا وَقَالَ هَٰذَا يَوْمٌ عَصِيبٌ ۝ وَجَآءَهُۥ قَوْمُهُۥ يُهْرَعُونَ إِلَيْهِ وَمِن قَبْلُ كَانُوا۟ يَعْمَلُونَ ٱلسَّيِّـَٔاتِ ۚ قَالَ يَٰقَوْمِ هَٰٓؤُلَآءِ بَنَاتِى هُنَّ أَطْهَرُ لَكُمْ ۖ فَٱتَّقُوا۟ ٱللَّهَ وَلَا تُخْزُونِ فِى ضَيْفِىٓ ۖ أَلَيْسَ مِنكُمْ رَجُلٌ رَّشِيدٌ ۝ قَالُوا۟ لَقَدْ عَلِمْتَ مَا لَنَا فِى بَنَاتِكَ مِنْ حَقٍّ وَإِنَّكَ لَتَعْلَمُ مَا نُرِيدُ ۝ قَالَ لَوْ أَنَّ لِى بِكُمْ قُوَّةً أَوْ ءَاوِىٓ إِلَىٰ رُكْنٍ شَدِيدٍ ۝ قَالُوا۟ يَٰلُوطُ إِنَّا رُسُلُ رَبِّكَ لَن يَصِلُوٓا۟ إِلَيْكَ ۖ فَأَسْرِ بِأَهْلِكَ بِقِطْعٍ مِّنَ ٱلَّيْلِ وَلَا يَلْتَفِتْ مِنكُمْ أَحَدٌ إِلَّا ٱمْرَأَتَكَ ۖ إِنَّهُۥ مُصِيبُهَا مَآ أَصَابَهُمْ ۚ إِنَّ مَوْعِدَهُمُ ٱلصُّبْحُ ۚ أَلَيْسَ ٱلصُّبْحُ بِقَرِيبٍ ۝

فَلَمَّا جَآءَ أَمْرُنَا جَعَلْنَا عَٰلِيَهَا سَافِلَهَا وَأَمْطَرْنَا عَلَيْهَا حِجَارَةً مِّن سِجِّيلٍ مَّنضُودٍ ۝ مُّسَوَّمَةً عِندَ رَبِّكَ ۖ وَمَا هِىَ مِنَ ٱلظَّٰلِمِينَ بِبَعِيدٍ ۝ ۞ وَإِلَىٰ مَدْيَنَ أَخَاهُمْ شُعَيْبًا ۚ قَالَ يَٰقَوْمِ ٱعْبُدُوا۟ ٱللَّهَ مَا لَكُم مِّنْ إِلَٰهٍ غَيْرُهُۥ ۖ وَلَا تَنقُصُوا۟ ٱلْمِكْيَالَ وَٱلْمِيزَانَ ۚ إِنِّىٓ أَرَىٰكُم بِخَيْرٍ وَإِنِّىٓ أَخَافُ عَلَيْكُمْ عَذَابَ يَوْمٍ مُّحِيطٍ ۝ وَيَٰقَوْمِ أَوْفُوا۟ ٱلْمِكْيَالَ وَٱلْمِيزَانَ بِٱلْقِسْطِ ۖ وَلَا تَبْخَسُوا۟ ٱلنَّاسَ أَشْيَآءَهُمْ وَلَا تَعْثَوْا۟ فِى ٱلْأَرْضِ مُفْسِدِينَ ۝ بَقِيَّتُ ٱللَّهِ خَيْرٌ لَّكُمْ إِن كُنتُم مُّؤْمِنِينَ ۚ وَمَآ أَنَا۠ عَلَيْكُم بِحَفِيظٍ ۝ قَالُوا۟ يَٰشُعَيْبُ أَصَلَوٰتُكَ تَأْمُرُكَ أَن نَّتْرُكَ مَا يَعْبُدُ ءَابَآؤُنَآ أَوْ أَن نَّفْعَلَ فِىٓ أَمْوَٰلِنَا مَا نَشَٰٓؤُا۟ ۖ إِنَّكَ لَأَنتَ ٱلْحَلِيمُ ٱلرَّشِيدُ ۝ قَالَ يَٰقَوْمِ أَرَءَيْتُمْ إِن كُنتُ عَلَىٰ بَيِّنَةٍ مِّن رَّبِّى وَرَزَقَنِى مِنْهُ رِزْقًا حَسَنًا ۚ وَمَآ أُرِيدُ أَنْ أُخَالِفَكُمْ إِلَىٰ مَآ أَنْهَىٰكُمْ عَنْهُ ۚ إِنْ أُرِيدُ إِلَّا ٱلْإِصْلَٰحَ مَا ٱسْتَطَعْتُ ۚ وَمَا تَوْفِيقِىٓ إِلَّا بِٱللَّهِ ۚ عَلَيْهِ تَوَكَّلْتُ وَإِلَيْهِ أُنِيبُ ۝ وَيَٰقَوْمِ لَا يَجْرِمَنَّكُمْ شِقَاقِىٓ أَن يُصِيبَكُم مِّثْلُ مَآ أَصَابَ قَوْمَ نُوحٍ أَوْ قَوْمَ هُودٍ أَوْ قَوْمَ صَٰلِحٍ ۚ وَمَا قَوْمُ لُوطٍ مِّنكُم بِبَعِيدٍ ۝ وَٱسْتَغْفِرُوا۟ رَبَّكُمْ ثُمَّ تُوبُوٓا۟ إِلَيْهِ ۚ إِنَّ رَبِّى رَحِيمٌ وَدُودٌ ۝ قَالُوا۟ يَٰشُعَيْبُ مَا نَفْقَهُ كَثِيرًا مِّمَّا تَقُولُ وَإِنَّا لَنَرَىٰكَ فِينَا ضَعِيفًا ۖ وَلَوْلَا رَهْطُكَ لَرَجَمْنَٰكَ ۖ وَمَآ أَنتَ عَلَيْنَا بِعَزِيزٍ ۝ قَالَ يَٰقَوْمِ أَرَهْطِىٓ أَعَزُّ عَلَيْكُم مِّنَ ٱللَّهِ وَٱتَّخَذْتُمُوهُ وَرَآءَكُمْ ظِهْرِيًّا ۖ إِنَّ رَبِّى بِمَا تَعْمَلُونَ مُحِيطٌ ۝ وَيَٰقَوْمِ ٱعْمَلُوا۟ عَلَىٰ مَكَانَتِكُمْ إِنِّى عَٰمِلٌ ۖ سَوْفَ تَعْلَمُونَ مَن يَأْتِيهِ عَذَابٌ يُخْزِيهِ وَمَنْ هُوَ كَٰذِبٌ ۖ وَٱرْتَقِبُوٓا۟ إِنِّى مَعَكُمْ رَقِيبٌ ۝ وَلَمَّا جَآءَ أَمْرُنَا نَجَّيْنَا شُعَيْبًا وَٱلَّذِينَ ءَامَنُوا۟ مَعَهُۥ بِرَحْمَةٍ مِّنَّا وَأَخَذَتِ ٱلَّذِينَ ظَلَمُوا۟ ٱلصَّيْحَةُ فَأَصْبَحُوا۟ فِى دِيَٰرِهِمْ جَٰثِمِينَ ۝ كَأَن لَّمْ يَغْنَوْا۟ فِيهَآ ۗ أَلَا بُعْدًا لِّمَدْيَنَ

كَمَا بَعِدَتْ ثَمُودُ ۝ وَلَقَدْ أَرْسَلْنَا مُوسَىٰ بِـَٔايَـٰتِنَا وَسُلْطَـٰنٍ مُّبِينٍ ۝ إِلَىٰ فِرْعَوْنَ وَمَلَإِيْهِۦ فَٱتَّبَعُوٓا۟ أَمْرَ فِرْعَوْنَ ۖ وَمَآ أَمْرُ فِرْعَوْنَ بِرَشِيدٍ ۝ يَقْدُمُ قَوْمَهُۥ يَوْمَ ٱلْقِيَـٰمَةِ فَأَوْرَدَهُمُ ٱلنَّارَ ۖ وَبِئْسَ ٱلْوِرْدُ ٱلْمَوْرُودُ ۝ وَأُتْبِعُوا۟ فِى هَـٰذِهِۦ لَعْنَةً وَيَوْمَ ٱلْقِيَـٰمَةِ ۚ بِئْسَ ٱلرِّفْدُ ٱلْمَرْفُودُ ۝ ذَٰلِكَ مِنْ أَنۢبَآءِ ٱلْقُرَىٰ نَقُصُّهُۥ عَلَيْكَ ۖ مِنْهَا قَآئِمٌ وَحَصِيدٌ ۝ وَمَا ظَلَمْنَـٰهُمْ وَلَـٰكِن ظَلَمُوٓا۟ أَنفُسَهُمْ ۖ فَمَآ أَغْنَتْ عَنْهُمْ ءَالِهَتُهُمُ ٱلَّتِى يَدْعُونَ مِن دُونِ ٱللَّهِ مِن شَىْءٍ لَّمَّا جَآءَ أَمْرُ رَبِّكَ ۖ وَمَا زَادُوهُمْ غَيْرَ تَتْبِيبٍ ۝ وَكَذَٰلِكَ أَخْذُ رَبِّكَ إِذَآ أَخَذَ ٱلْقُرَىٰ وَهِىَ ظَـٰلِمَةٌ ۚ إِنَّ أَخْذَهُۥٓ أَلِيمٌ شَدِيدٌ ۝ إِنَّ فِى ذَٰلِكَ لَـَٔايَةً لِّمَنْ خَافَ عَذَابَ ٱلْـَٔاخِرَةِ ۚ ذَٰلِكَ يَوْمٌ مَّجْمُوعٌ لَّهُ ٱلنَّاسُ وَذَٰلِكَ يَوْمٌ مَّشْهُودٌ ۝ وَمَا نُؤَخِّرُهُۥٓ إِلَّا لِأَجَلٍ مَّعْدُودٍ ۝ يَوْمَ يَأْتِ لَا تَكَلَّمُ نَفْسٌ إِلَّا بِإِذْنِهِۦ ۚ فَمِنْهُمْ شَقِىٌّ وَسَعِيدٌ ۝ فَأَمَّا ٱلَّذِينَ شَقُوا۟ فَفِى ٱلنَّارِ لَهُمْ فِيهَا زَفِيرٌ وَشَهِيقٌ ۝ خَـٰلِدِينَ فِيهَا مَا دَامَتِ ٱلسَّمَـٰوَٰتُ وَٱلْأَرْضُ إِلَّا مَا شَآءَ رَبُّكَ ۚ إِنَّ رَبَّكَ فَعَّالٌ لِّمَا يُرِيدُ ۝ ۞ وَأَمَّا ٱلَّذِينَ سُعِدُوا۟ فَفِى ٱلْجَنَّةِ خَـٰلِدِينَ فِيهَا مَا دَامَتِ ٱلسَّمَـٰوَٰتُ وَٱلْأَرْضُ إِلَّا مَا شَآءَ رَبُّكَ ۖ عَطَآءً غَيْرَ مَجْذُوذٍ ۝ فَلَا تَكُ فِى مِرْيَةٍ مِّمَّا يَعْبُدُ هَـٰٓؤُلَآءِ ۚ مَا يَعْبُدُونَ إِلَّا كَمَا يَعْبُدُ ءَابَآؤُهُم مِّن قَبْلُ ۚ وَإِنَّا لَمُوَفُّوهُمْ نَصِيبَهُمْ غَيْرَ مَنقُوصٍ ۝ وَلَقَدْ ءَاتَيْنَا مُوسَى ٱلْكِتَـٰبَ فَٱخْتُلِفَ فِيهِ ۚ وَلَوْلَا كَلِمَةٌ سَبَقَتْ مِن رَّبِّكَ لَقُضِىَ بَيْنَهُمْ ۚ وَإِنَّهُمْ لَفِى شَكٍّ مِّنْهُ مُرِيبٍ ۝ وَإِنَّ كُلًّا لَّمَّا لَيُوَفِّيَنَّهُمْ رَبُّكَ أَعْمَـٰلَهُمْ ۚ إِنَّهُۥ بِمَا يَعْمَلُونَ خَبِيرٌ ۝ فَٱسْتَقِمْ كَمَآ أُمِرْتَ وَمَن تَابَ مَعَكَ وَلَا تَطْغَوْا۟ ۚ إِنَّهُۥ بِمَا تَعْمَلُونَ بَصِيرٌ ۝ وَلَا تَرْكَنُوٓا۟ إِلَى ٱلَّذِينَ ظَلَمُوا۟ فَتَمَسَّكُمُ ٱلنَّارُ وَمَا لَكُم مِّن دُونِ ٱللَّهِ مِنْ أَوْلِيَآءَ ثُمَّ لَا تُنصَرُونَ ۝ وَأَقِمِ ٱلصَّلَوٰةَ طَرَفَىِ ٱلنَّهَارِ وَزُلَفًا مِّنَ

ٱلَّيْلِ ۚ إِنَّ ٱلْحَسَنَـٰتِ يُذْهِبْنَ ٱلسَّيِّـَٔاتِ ۚ ذَٰلِكَ ذِكْرَىٰ لِلذَّٰكِرِينَ ۞ وَٱصْبِرْ فَإِنَّ ٱللَّهَ لَا يُضِيعُ أَجْرَ ٱلْمُحْسِنِينَ ۞ فَلَوْلَا كَانَ مِنَ ٱلْقُرُونِ مِن قَبْلِكُمْ أُوْلُواْ بَقِيَّةٍ يَنْهَوْنَ عَنِ ٱلْفَسَادِ فِى ٱلْأَرْضِ إِلَّا قَلِيلًا مِّمَّنْ أَنجَيْنَا مِنْهُمْ ۗ وَٱتَّبَعَ ٱلَّذِينَ ظَلَمُواْ مَآ أُتْرِفُواْ فِيهِ وَكَانُواْ مُجْرِمِينَ ۞ وَمَا كَانَ رَبُّكَ لِيُهْلِكَ ٱلْقُرَىٰ بِظُلْمٍ وَأَهْلُهَا مُصْلِحُونَ ۞ وَلَوْ شَآءَ رَبُّكَ لَجَعَلَ ٱلنَّاسَ أُمَّةً وَٰحِدَةً ۖ وَلَا يَزَالُونَ مُخْتَلِفِينَ ۞ إِلَّا مَن رَّحِمَ رَبُّكَ ۚ وَلِذَٰلِكَ خَلَقَهُمْ ۗ وَتَمَّتْ كَلِمَةُ رَبِّكَ لَأَمْلَأَنَّ جَهَنَّمَ مِنَ ٱلْجِنَّةِ وَٱلنَّاسِ أَجْمَعِينَ ۞ وَكُلًّا نَّقُصُّ عَلَيْكَ مِنْ أَنْبَآءِ ٱلرُّسُلِ مَا نُثَبِّتُ بِهِ فُؤَادَكَ ۚ وَجَآءَكَ فِى هَـٰذِهِ ٱلْحَقُّ وَمَوْعِظَةٌ وَذِكْرَىٰ لِلْمُؤْمِنِينَ ۞ وَقُل لِّلَّذِينَ لَا يُؤْمِنُونَ ٱعْمَلُواْ عَلَىٰ مَكَانَتِكُمْ إِنَّا عَـٰمِلُونَ ۞ وَٱنتَظِرُوٓاْ إِنَّا مُنتَظِرُونَ ۞ وَلِلَّهِ غَيْبُ ٱلسَّمَـٰوَٰتِ وَٱلْأَرْضِ وَإِلَيْهِ يُرْجَعُ ٱلْأَمْرُ كُلُّهُ فَٱعْبُدْهُ وَتَوَكَّلْ عَلَيْهِ ۚ وَمَا رَبُّكَ بِغَـٰفِلٍ عَمَّا تَعْمَلُونَ ۞

(Hud 011-123)

# Chapter (Surah) 12: Yusuf 001-052

بِسْمِ ٱللَّهِ ٱلرَّحْمَـٰنِ ٱلرَّحِيمِ

﴿ الٓر ۚ تِلْكَ ءَايَـٰتُ ٱلْكِتَـٰبِ ٱلْمُبِينِ ۞ إِنَّآ أَنزَلْنَـٰهُ قُرْءَٰنًا عَرَبِيًّا لَّعَلَّكُمْ تَعْقِلُونَ ۞ نَحْنُ نَقُصُّ عَلَيْكَ أَحْسَنَ ٱلْقَصَصِ بِمَآ أَوْحَيْنَآ إِلَيْكَ هَـٰذَا ٱلْقُرْءَانَ وَإِن كُنتَ مِن قَبْلِهِ لَمِنَ ٱلْغَـٰفِلِينَ ۞ إِذْ قَالَ يُوسُفُ لِأَبِيهِ يَـٰٓأَبَتِ إِنِّى رَأَيْتُ أَحَدَ عَشَرَ كَوْكَبًا وَٱلشَّمْسَ وَٱلْقَمَرَ رَأَيْتُهُمْ لِى سَـٰجِدِينَ ۞ قَالَ يَـٰبُنَىَّ لَا تَقْصُصْ رُءْيَاكَ عَلَىٰٓ إِخْوَتِكَ فَيَكِيدُواْ لَكَ كَيْدًا ۖ إِنَّ ٱلشَّيْطَـٰنَ لِلْإِنسَـٰنِ عَدُوٌّ مُّبِينٌ ۞ وَكَذَٰلِكَ يَجْتَبِيكَ رَبُّكَ وَيُعَلِّمُكَ مِن تَأْوِيلِ ٱلْأَحَادِيثِ وَيُتِمُّ نِعْمَتَهُ عَلَيْكَ وَعَلَىٰٓ ءَالِ يَعْقُوبَ كَمَآ أَتَمَّهَا عَلَىٰٓ أَبَوَيْكَ مِن

قَبۡلُ إِبۡرَٰهِيمَ وَإِسۡحَٰقَ ۚ إِنَّ رَبَّكَ عَلِيمٌ حَكِيمٌ ۝ ۞ لَّقَدۡ كَانَ فِي يُوسُفَ وَإِخۡوَتِهِۦٓ ءَايَٰتٌ لِّلسَّآئِلِينَ ۝ إِذۡ قَالُواْ لَيُوسُفُ وَأَخُوهُ أَحَبُّ إِلَىٰٓ أَبِينَا مِنَّا وَنَحۡنُ عُصۡبَةٌ إِنَّ أَبَانَا لَفِي ضَلَٰلٍ مُّبِينٍ ۝ ٱقۡتُلُواْ يُوسُفَ أَوِ ٱطۡرَحُوهُ أَرۡضًا يَخۡلُ لَكُمۡ وَجۡهُ أَبِيكُمۡ وَتَكُونُواْ مِنۢ بَعۡدِهِۦ قَوۡمًا صَٰلِحِينَ ۝ قَالَ قَآئِلٌ مِّنۡهُمۡ لَا تَقۡتُلُواْ يُوسُفَ وَأَلۡقُوهُ فِي غَيَٰبَتِ ٱلۡجُبِّ يَلۡتَقِطۡهُ بَعۡضُ ٱلسَّيَّارَةِ إِن كُنتُمۡ فَٰعِلِينَ ۝ قَالُواْ يَٰٓأَبَانَا مَا لَكَ لَا تَأۡمَ۫نَّا عَلَىٰ يُوسُفَ وَإِنَّا لَهُۥ لَنَٰصِحُونَ ۝ أَرۡسِلۡهُ مَعَنَا غَدًا يَرۡتَعۡ وَيَلۡعَبۡ وَإِنَّا لَهُۥ لَحَٰفِظُونَ ۝ قَالَ إِنِّي لَيَحۡزُنُنِيٓ أَن تَذۡهَبُواْ بِهِۦ وَأَخَافُ أَن يَأۡكُلَهُ ٱلذِّئۡبُ وَأَنتُمۡ عَنۡهُ غَٰفِلُونَ ۝ قَالُواْ لَئِنۡ أَكَلَهُ ٱلذِّئۡبُ وَنَحۡنُ عُصۡبَةٌ إِنَّآ إِذًا لَّخَٰسِرُونَ ۝ فَلَمَّا ذَهَبُواْ بِهِۦ وَأَجۡمَعُوٓاْ أَن يَجۡعَلُوهُ فِي غَيَٰبَتِ ٱلۡجُبِّ ۚ وَأَوۡحَيۡنَآ إِلَيۡهِ لَتُنَبِّئَنَّهُم بِأَمۡرِهِمۡ هَٰذَا وَهُمۡ لَا يَشۡعُرُونَ ۝ وَجَآءُوٓ أَبَاهُمۡ عِشَآءٗ يَبۡكُونَ ۝ قَالُواْ يَٰٓأَبَانَآ إِنَّا ذَهَبۡنَا نَسۡتَبِقُ وَتَرَكۡنَا يُوسُفَ عِندَ مَتَٰعِنَا فَأَكَلَهُ ٱلذِّئۡبُ ۖ وَمَآ أَنتَ بِمُؤۡمِنٍ لَّنَا وَلَوۡ كُنَّا صَٰدِقِينَ ۝ وَجَآءُو عَلَىٰ قَمِيصِهِۦ بِدَمٍ كَذِبٖ ۚ قَالَ بَلۡ سَوَّلَتۡ لَكُمۡ أَنفُسُكُمۡ أَمۡرٗا ۖ فَصَبۡرٞ جَمِيلٞ ۖ وَٱللَّهُ ٱلۡمُسۡتَعَانُ عَلَىٰ مَا تَصِفُونَ ۝ وَجَآءَتۡ سَيَّارَةٞ فَأَرۡسَلُواْ وَارِدَهُمۡ فَأَدۡلَىٰ دَلۡوَهُۥ ۖ قَالَ يَٰبُشۡرَىٰ هَٰذَا غُلَٰمٞ ۚ وَأَسَرُّوهُ بِضَٰعَةٗ ۚ وَٱللَّهُ عَلِيمُۢ بِمَا يَعۡمَلُونَ ۝ وَشَرَوۡهُ بِثَمَنٍۭ بَخۡسٖ دَرَٰهِمَ مَعۡدُودَةٖ وَكَانُواْ فِيهِ مِنَ ٱلزَّٰهِدِينَ ۝ وَقَالَ ٱلَّذِي ٱشۡتَرَىٰهُ مِن مِّصۡرَ لِٱمۡرَأَتِهِۦٓ أَكۡرِمِي مَثۡوَىٰهُ عَسَىٰٓ أَن يَنفَعَنَآ أَوۡ نَتَّخِذَهُۥ وَلَدٗا ۚ وَكَذَٰلِكَ مَكَّنَّا لِيُوسُفَ فِي ٱلۡأَرۡضِ وَلِنُعَلِّمَهُۥ مِن تَأۡوِيلِ ٱلۡأَحَادِيثِ ۚ وَٱللَّهُ غَالِبٌ عَلَىٰٓ أَمۡرِهِۦ وَلَٰكِنَّ أَكۡثَرَ ٱلنَّاسِ لَا يَعۡلَمُونَ ۝ وَلَمَّا بَلَغَ أَشُدَّهُۥٓ ءَاتَيۡنَٰهُ حُكۡمٗا وَعِلۡمٗا ۚ وَكَذَٰلِكَ نَجۡزِي ٱلۡمُحۡسِنِينَ ۝ وَرَٰوَدَتۡهُ ٱلَّتِي هُوَ فِي بَيۡتِهَا عَن نَّفۡسِهِۦ وَغَلَّقَتِ ٱلۡأَبۡوَٰبَ وَقَالَتۡ هَيۡتَ لَكَ ۚ

قَالَ مَعَاذَ ٱللَّهِ إِنَّهُ رَبِّى أَحْسَنَ مَثْوَاىَ إِنَّهُ لَا يُفْلِحُ ٱلظَّـٰلِمُونَ ۝ وَلَقَدْ هَمَّتْ بِهِۦ وَهَمَّ بِهَا لَوْلَآ أَن رَّءَا بُرْهَـٰنَ رَبِّهِۦ كَذَٰلِكَ لِنَصْرِفَ عَنْهُ ٱلسُّوٓءَ وَٱلْفَحْشَآءَ إِنَّهُۥ مِنْ عِبَادِنَا ٱلْمُخْلَصِينَ ۝ وَٱسْتَبَقَا ٱلْبَابَ وَقَدَّتْ قَمِيصَهُۥ مِن دُبُرٍ وَأَلْفَيَا سَيِّدَهَا لَدَا ٱلْبَابِ قَالَتْ مَا جَزَآءُ مَنْ أَرَادَ بِأَهْلِكَ سُوٓءًا إِلَّآ أَن يُسْجَنَ أَوْ عَذَابٌ أَلِيمٌ ۝ قَالَ هِىَ رَٰوَدَتْنِى عَن نَّفْسِى وَشَهِدَ شَاهِدٌ مِّنْ أَهْلِهَآ إِن كَانَ قَمِيصُهُۥ قُدَّ مِن قُبُلٍ فَصَدَقَتْ وَهُوَ مِنَ ٱلْكَـٰذِبِينَ ۝ وَإِن كَانَ قَمِيصُهُۥ قُدَّ مِن دُبُرٍ فَكَذَبَتْ وَهُوَ مِنَ ٱلصَّـٰدِقِينَ ۝ فَلَمَّا رَءَا قَمِيصَهُۥ قُدَّ مِن دُبُرٍ قَالَ إِنَّهُۥ مِن كَيْدِكُنَّ إِنَّ كَيْدَكُنَّ عَظِيمٌ ۝ يُوسُفُ أَعْرِضْ عَنْ هَـٰذَا وَٱسْتَغْفِرِى لِذَنۢبِكِ إِنَّكِ كُنتِ مِنَ ٱلْخَاطِـِٔينَ ۝ ۞ وَقَالَ نِسْوَةٌ فِى ٱلْمَدِينَةِ ٱمْرَأَتُ ٱلْعَزِيزِ تُرَٰوِدُ فَتَىٰهَا عَن نَّفْسِهِۦ قَدْ شَغَفَهَا حُبًّا إِنَّا لَنَرَىٰهَا فِى ضَلَـٰلٍ مُّبِينٍ ۝ فَلَمَّا سَمِعَتْ بِمَكْرِهِنَّ أَرْسَلَتْ إِلَيْهِنَّ وَأَعْتَدَتْ لَهُنَّ مُتَّكَـًٔا وَءَاتَتْ كُلَّ وَٰحِدَةٍ مِّنْهُنَّ سِكِّينًا وَقَالَتِ ٱخْرُجْ عَلَيْهِنَّ فَلَمَّا رَأَيْنَهُۥٓ أَكْبَرْنَهُۥ وَقَطَّعْنَ أَيْدِيَهُنَّ وَقُلْنَ حَـٰشَ لِلَّهِ مَا هَـٰذَا بَشَرًا إِنْ هَـٰذَآ إِلَّا مَلَكٌ كَرِيمٌ ۝ قَالَتْ فَذَٰلِكُنَّ ٱلَّذِى لُمْتُنَّنِى فِيهِ وَلَقَدْ رَٰوَدتُّهُۥ عَن نَّفْسِهِۦ فَٱسْتَعْصَمَ وَلَئِن لَّمْ يَفْعَلْ مَآ ءَامُرُهُۥ لَيُسْجَنَنَّ وَلَيَكُونًا مِّنَ ٱلصَّـٰغِرِينَ ۝ قَالَ رَبِّ ٱلسِّجْنُ أَحَبُّ إِلَىَّ مِمَّا يَدْعُونَنِى إِلَيْهِ وَإِلَّا تَصْرِفْ عَنِّى كَيْدَهُنَّ أَصْبُ إِلَيْهِنَّ وَأَكُن مِّنَ ٱلْجَـٰهِلِينَ ۝ فَٱسْتَجَابَ لَهُۥ رَبُّهُۥ فَصَرَفَ عَنْهُ كَيْدَهُنَّ إِنَّهُۥ هُوَ ٱلسَّمِيعُ ٱلْعَلِيمُ ۝ ثُمَّ بَدَا لَهُم مِّنۢ بَعْدِ مَا رَأَوُا۟ ٱلْـَٔايَـٰتِ لَيَسْجُنُنَّهُۥ حَتَّىٰ حِينٍ ۝ وَدَخَلَ مَعَهُ ٱلسِّجْنَ فَتَيَانِ قَالَ أَحَدُهُمَآ إِنِّىٓ أَرَىٰنِىٓ أَعْصِرُ خَمْرًا وَقَالَ ٱلْـَٔاخَرُ إِنِّىٓ أَرَىٰنِىٓ أَحْمِلُ فَوْقَ رَأْسِى خُبْزًا تَأْكُلُ ٱلطَّيْرُ مِنْهُ نَبِّئْنَا بِتَأْوِيلِهِۦٓ إِنَّا نَرَىٰكَ مِنَ ٱلْمُحْسِنِينَ ۝ قَالَ لَا يَأْتِيكُمَا طَعَامٌ تُرْزَقَانِهِۦٓ إِلَّا نَبَّأْتُكُمَا بِتَأْوِيلِهِۦ قَبْلَ

أَن يَأْتِيَكُمَا ۚ ذَٰلِكُمَا مِمَّا عَلَّمَنِى رَبِّى ۚ إِنِّى تَرَكْتُ مِلَّةَ قَوْمٍ لَّا يُؤْمِنُونَ بِٱللَّهِ وَهُم بِٱلْءَاخِرَةِ هُمْ كَٰفِرُونَ ۝ وَٱتَّبَعْتُ مِلَّةَ ءَابَآءِىٓ إِبْرَٰهِيمَ وَإِسْحَٰقَ وَيَعْقُوبَ ۚ مَا كَانَ لَنَآ أَن نُّشْرِكَ بِٱللَّهِ مِن شَىْءٍ ۚ ذَٰلِكَ مِن فَضْلِ ٱللَّهِ عَلَيْنَا وَعَلَى ٱلنَّاسِ وَلَٰكِنَّ أَكْثَرَ ٱلنَّاسِ لَا يَشْكُرُونَ ۝ يَٰصَٰحِبَىِ ٱلسِّجْنِ ءَأَرْبَابٌ مُّتَفَرِّقُونَ خَيْرٌ أَمِ ٱللَّهُ ٱلْوَٰحِدُ ٱلْقَهَّارُ ۝ مَا تَعْبُدُونَ مِن دُونِهِۦٓ إِلَّآ أَسْمَآءً سَمَّيْتُمُوهَآ أَنتُمْ وَءَابَآؤُكُم مَّآ أَنزَلَ ٱللَّهُ بِهَا مِن سُلْطَٰنٍ ۚ إِنِ ٱلْحُكْمُ إِلَّا لِلَّهِ ۚ أَمَرَ أَلَّا تَعْبُدُوٓا۟ إِلَّآ إِيَّاهُ ۚ ذَٰلِكَ ٱلدِّينُ ٱلْقَيِّمُ وَلَٰكِنَّ أَكْثَرَ ٱلنَّاسِ لَا يَعْلَمُونَ ۝ يَٰصَٰحِبَىِ ٱلسِّجْنِ أَمَّآ أَحَدُكُمَا فَيَسْقِى رَبَّهُۥ خَمْرًا ۖ وَأَمَّا ٱلْءَاخَرُ فَيُصْلَبُ فَتَأْكُلُ ٱلطَّيْرُ مِن رَّأْسِهِۦ ۚ قُضِىَ ٱلْأَمْرُ ٱلَّذِى فِيهِ تَسْتَفْتِيَانِ ۝ وَقَالَ لِلَّذِى ظَنَّ أَنَّهُۥ نَاجٍ مِّنْهُمَا ٱذْكُرْنِى عِندَ رَبِّكَ فَأَنسَىٰهُ ٱلشَّيْطَٰنُ ذِكْرَ رَبِّهِۦ فَلَبِثَ فِى ٱلسِّجْنِ بِضْعَ سِنِينَ ۝ وَقَالَ ٱلْمَلِكُ إِنِّىٓ أَرَىٰ سَبْعَ بَقَرَٰتٍ سِمَانٍ يَأْكُلُهُنَّ سَبْعٌ عِجَافٌ وَسَبْعَ سُنۢبُلَٰتٍ خُضْرٍ وَأُخَرَ يَابِسَٰتٍ ۖ يَٰٓأَيُّهَا ٱلْمَلَأُ أَفْتُونِى فِى رُءْيَٰىَ إِن كُنتُمْ لِلرُّءْيَا تَعْبُرُونَ ۝ قَالُوٓا۟ أَضْغَٰثُ أَحْلَٰمٍ ۖ وَمَا نَحْنُ بِتَأْوِيلِ ٱلْأَحْلَٰمِ بِعَٰلِمِينَ ۝ وَقَالَ ٱلَّذِى نَجَا مِنْهُمَا وَٱدَّكَرَ بَعْدَ أُمَّةٍ أَنَا۠ أُنَبِّئُكُم بِتَأْوِيلِهِۦ فَأَرْسِلُونِ ۝ يُوسُفُ أَيُّهَا ٱلصِّدِّيقُ أَفْتِنَا فِى سَبْعِ بَقَرَٰتٍ سِمَانٍ يَأْكُلُهُنَّ سَبْعٌ عِجَافٌ وَسَبْعِ سُنۢبُلَٰتٍ خُضْرٍ وَأُخَرَ يَابِسَٰتٍ لَّعَلِّىٓ أَرْجِعُ إِلَى ٱلنَّاسِ لَعَلَّهُمْ يَعْلَمُونَ ۝ قَالَ تَزْرَعُونَ سَبْعَ سِنِينَ دَأَبًا فَمَا حَصَدتُّمْ فَذَرُوهُ فِى سُنۢبُلِهِۦٓ إِلَّا قَلِيلًا مِّمَّا تَأْكُلُونَ ۝ ثُمَّ يَأْتِى مِنۢ بَعْدِ ذَٰلِكَ سَبْعٌ شِدَادٌ يَأْكُلْنَ مَا قَدَّمْتُمْ لَهُنَّ إِلَّا قَلِيلًا مِّمَّا تُحْصِنُونَ ۝ ثُمَّ يَأْتِى مِنۢ بَعْدِ ذَٰلِكَ عَامٌ فِيهِ يُغَاثُ ٱلنَّاسُ وَفِيهِ يَعْصِرُونَ ۝ وَقَالَ ٱلْمَلِكُ ٱئْتُونِى بِهِۦ ۖ فَلَمَّا جَآءَهُ ٱلرَّسُولُ قَالَ ٱرْجِعْ إِلَىٰ رَبِّكَ فَسْـَٔلْهُ مَا بَالُ ٱلنِّسْوَةِ ٱلَّٰتِى قَطَّعْنَ أَيْدِيَهُنَّ ۚ إِنَّ رَبِّى بِكَيْدِهِنَّ عَلِيمٌ ۝

$$\text{قَالَ مَا خَطْبُكُنَّ إِذْ رَاوَدتُّنَّ يُوسُفَ عَن نَّفْسِهِ قُلْنَ حَاشَ لِلَّهِ مَا عَلِمْنَا عَلَيْهِ مِن سُوءٍ قَالَتِ امْرَأَتُ الْعَزِيزِ الْـَٔنَ حَصْحَصَ الْحَقُّ أَنَا۠ رَاوَدتُّهُۥ عَن نَّفْسِهِۦ وَإِنَّهُۥ لَمِنَ الصَّـٰدِقِينَ ۝ ذَٰلِكَ لِيَعْلَمَ أَنِّى لَمْ أَخُنْهُ بِالْغَيْبِ وَأَنَّ اللَّهَ لَا يَهْدِى كَيْدَ الْخَآئِنِينَ ۝}$$

(Yusuf 001-052)

## INTRODUCTION TO CHAPTER (SURAH) 11: HUD

## Ibn Kathir's Introduction

### Surah Hud made the Prophet's Hair turn Gray

Abu `Isa At-Tirmidhi recorded from Ibn `Abbas that Abu Bakr said, "O Messenger of Allah, verily your hair has turned gray." The Prophet replied,

$$\text{«شَيَّبَتْنِي هُودٌ وَالْوَاقِعَةُ وَالْمُرْسَلَاتُ وَعَمَّ يَتَسَاءَلُونَ وَإِذَا الشَّمْسُ كُوِّرَتْ»}$$

(Surahs Hud, Al-Waqi`ah, Al-Mursalat, `Amma Yatasa'lun (An-Naba') and Idhash-Shamsu Kuwwirat (At-Takwir) have turned my hair gray.) In another narration he said,

$$\text{«هُودٌ وَأَخَوَاتُهَا»}$$

(Surah Hud and its sisters...)

## CHAPTER (SURAH) 11: HUD, VERSES 006-123

### Surah: 11 Ayah: 6

$$\text{﴿ وَمَا مِن دَآبَّةٍ فِى الْأَرْضِ إِلَّا عَلَى اللَّهِ رِزْقُهَا وَيَعْلَمُ مُسْتَقَرَّهَا وَمُسْتَوْدَعَهَا كُلٌّ فِى كِتَـٰبٍ مُّبِينٍ ۝ ﴾}$$

41. And no moving (living) creature is there on earth but its provision is due from Allâh. And He knows its dwelling place and its deposit (in the uterus, grave). All is in a Clear Book (Al-Lauh Al-Mahfûz - the Book of Decrees with Allâh).

### Transliteration

6. Wama min dabbatin fee al-ardi illa AAala Allahi rizquha wayaAAlamu mustaqarraha wamustawdaAAaha kullun fee kitabin mubeenin

## Tafsir Ibn Kathir

### Allah is Responsible for the Provisions of All Creatures

Allah, the Exalted, informs that He is responsible for the provisions of all the creatures that dwell in the earth, whether they are small, large, sea-dwelling or land-dwelling. He knows their place of dwelling and their place of deposit. This means that He knows where their journeying will end in the earth and where they will seek shelter when they wish to nest. This place of nesting is also considered their place of deposit. `Ali bin Abi Talhah and others reported from Ibn `Abbas that he said concerning the statement,

(And He knows its dwelling place) that it means where it resides. In reference to the statement,

(and its deposit.) he (Ibn `Abbas) said it means where it will die. Allah informs us that all of this is written in a Book with Allah that explains it in detail. This is similar to Allah's statement,

(There is not a moving creature on earth, nor a bird that flies with its two wings, but are communities like you. We have neglected nothing in the Book, then unto their Lord they (all) shall be gathered.) (6:38), and

(And with Him are the keys of the Ghayb (all that is hidden and unseen), none knows them but He. And He knows whatever there is in the land and in the sea; not a leaf falls, but he knows it. There is not a grain in the darkness of the earth nor anything fresh or dry, but is written in a Clear Record.) (6:59)

### Surah: 11 Ayah: 7 & Ayah: 8

﴿ وَهُوَ ٱلَّذِى خَلَقَ ٱلسَّمَـٰوَٰتِ وَٱلْأَرْضَ فِى سِتَّةِ أَيَّامٍ وَكَانَ عَرْشُهُ عَلَى ٱلْمَآءِ لِيَبْلُوَكُمْ أَيُّكُمْ أَحْسَنُ عَمَلًا ۗ وَلَئِن قُلْتَ إِنَّكُم مَّبْعُوثُونَ مِنۢ بَعْدِ ٱلْمَوْتِ لَيَقُولَنَّ ٱلَّذِينَ كَفَرُوٓا۟ إِنْ هَـٰذَآ إِلَّا سِحْرٌ مُّبِينٌ ﴿٧﴾

42. And He it is Who has created the heavens and the earth in six Days and His Throne was on the water, that He might try you, which of you is the best in deeds. But if you were to say to them: "You shall indeed be raised up after death," those who disbelieve would be sure to say, "This is nothing but obvious magic."

﴿ وَلَئِنْ أَخَّرْنَا عَنْهُمُ ٱلْعَذَابَ إِلَىٰٓ أُمَّةٍ مَّعْدُودَةٍ لَّيَقُولُنَّ مَا يَحْبِسُهُۥٓ ۗ أَلَا يَوْمَ يَأْتِيهِمْ لَيْسَ مَصْرُوفًا عَنْهُمْ وَحَاقَ بِهِم مَّا كَانُوا۟ بِهِۦ يَسْتَهْزِءُونَ ﴿٨﴾

43. And if We delay the torment for them till a determined term, they are sure to say, "What keeps it back?" Verily, on the day it reaches them, nothing will turn it

away from them, and they will be surrounded by (or fall in) that at which they used to mock!

### Transliteration

7. Wahuwa allathee khalaqa alssamawati waal-arda fee sittati ayyamin wakana AAarshuhu AAala alma-i liyabluwakum ayyukum ahsanu AAamalan wala-in qulta innakum mabAAoothoona min baAAdi almawti layaqoolanna allatheena kafaroo in hatha illa sihrun mubeenun 8. Wala-in akhkharna AAanhumu alAAathaba ila ommatin maAAdoodatin layaqoolunna ma yahbisuhu ala yawma ya/teehim laysa masroofan AAanhum wahaqa bihim ma kanoo bihi yastahzi-oona

### Tafsir Ibn Kathir

## Allah created the Heavens and the Earth in Six Days

Allah, the Exalted, informs of His power over all things, and that He created the heavens and the earth in six days. He mentions that His Throne was over the water before that, just as Imam Ahmad recorded that `Imran bin Husayn said, "The Messenger of Allah said,

«اقْبَلُوا الْبُشْرَى يَا بَنِي تَمِيم»

(Accept the glad tidings, O tribe of Tamim!) They said, `Verily you have brought us glad tidings and you have given us.' Then he said,

«اقْبَلُوا الْبُشْرَى يَا أَهْلَ الْيَمَن»

(Accept the glad tidings, O people of Yemen!) They said, `We accept. Therefore, inform us about the beginning of this matter and how it was.' He said,

«كَانَ اللهُ قَبْلَ كُلِّ شَيْءٍ، وَكَانَ عَرْشُهُ عَلَى الْمَاءِ، وَكَتَبَ فِي اللَّوْحِ الْمَحْفُوظِ ذِكْرَ كُلِّ شَيْءٍ»

(Allah was before everything and His Throne was over the water. He then wrote in the Preserved Tablet mentioning everything.) Then a man came to me and said, "O `Imran, your she camel has escaped from her fetter." I then went out after her and I do not know what was said after I left." This Hadith has been recorded in the Two Sahihs of Al-Bukhari and Muslim with a variety of wordings. In Sahih Muslim, it is recorded that `Abdullah bin `Amr bin Al-`As said that the Messenger of Allah said,

# Chapter 11: Hud (Hud), Verses 006-123

«إِنَّ اللهَ قَدَّرَ مَقَادِيرَ الْخَلَائِقِ قَبْلَ أَنْ يَخْلُقَ السَّمٰوَاتِ وَالْأَرْضَ بِخَمْسِينَ أَلْفَ سَنَةٍ وَكَانَ عَرْشُهُ عَلَى الْمَاءِ»

(Verily Allah measured the amount of sustenance of the creatures fifty thousand years before He created the heavens and the earth, and His Throne was over the water.) Under the explanation of this verse, Al-Bukhari recorded from Abu Hurayrah that the Messenger of Allah said,

«قَالَ اللهُ عَزَّ وَجَلَّ: أَنْفِقْ أُنْفِقْ عَلَيْكَ»

(Allah, the Mighty and Sublime, said, `Spend and I will spend on you.') And he said,

«يَدُ اللهِ مَلْأَى لَا يَغِيضُهَا نَفَقَةٌ، سَحَّاءُ اللَّيْلَ وَالنَّهَارَ»

(Allah's Hand is full, and it is not diminished by spending throughout the night and the day.) He also said,

«أَفَرَأَيْتُمْ مَا أَنْفَقَ مُنْذُ خَلَقَ السَّمٰوَاتِ وَالْأَرْضَ فَإِنَّهُ لَمْ يَغِضْ مَا فِي يَمِينِهِ، وَكَانَ عَرْشُهُ عَلَى الْمَاءِ، وَبِيَدِهِ الْمِيزَانُ يَخْفِضُ وَيَرْفَعُ»

(Have you seen what has been spent since the creation of the heavens and the earth Verily it does not diminish what is in His Right Hand (in the slightest) and His Throne was over the water. In His Hand is the Scale and he lowers and raises it.) Concerning Allah's statement,

(that He might try you, which of you is the best in deeds.) This means that He created the heavens and the earth for the benefit of His servants, whom He created so that they may worship Him and not associate anything with Him as a partner. Allah did not create this creation (of the heavens and the earth) out of mere frivolity. This is similar to His statement,

(And We created not the heaven and the earth and all that is between them without purpose! That is the consideration of those who disbelieve! Then woe to those who disbelieve from the Fire!) (38: 27) Allah the Exalted, said,

(Did you think that We created you in play (without any purpose), and that you would not be brought back to Us So Exalted is Allah, the True King: there is no God but He, the Lord of the Supreme Throne!) (23:115-116) Allah, the Exalted, said,

(And I (Allah) created not the Jinn and mankind except that they should worship Me (Alone).) (51:56) Concerning the statement of Allah, (that He might try you,) It means so that He (Allah) may test you. Concerning the statement,

(which of you is the best in deeds.) It is important to note here that Allah did not say, "Which of you has done the most deeds." Rather, He said, "Best in deeds." A deed cannot be considered a good deed until it is done sincerely for Allah, the Mighty and Sublime, and it must be in accordance with the legislation of the Messenger of Allah. Whenever a deed lacks one of these conditions, then it is null and void.

## The Polytheists hasten their Torment by arguing against Resurrection after Death

Concerning Allah's statement,

(But if you were to say to them: "You shall indeed be raised up after death.") Allah, the Exalted, is saying, "O Muhammad, if you were to inform these polytheists that Allah is going to resurrect them after their death, just as He created them originally (they would still reject)." Even though they know that Allah, the Exalted, is the One Who created the heavens and the earth, just as He said,

(And if you ask them who created them, they will surely say: "Allah.")(43:87) Allah says,

(And if you were to ask them: "Who has created the heavens and the earth and subjected the sun and the moon" They will surely reply: "Allah.") (29:61) Even after their awareness of this (Allah's creating), they still reject the resurrection and the promised return on the Day of Judgement. Yet, in reference to ability, the resurrection is easier (for Allah to perform) than the original creation. As Allah said,

(And He it is Who originates the creation, then He will repeat it (after it has perished); and this is easier for Him.) (30:27) Allah also said,

(The creation of you all and the resurrection of you all are only as (the creation and resurrection of) a single person.) (31:28) Concerning the statement,

(This is nothing but obvious magic.) The polytheists say this due to their disbelief and obstinacy. They say, "We do not believe your claim that resurrection will occur." They also say, "He (Muhammad) only says this (resurrection of the dead) because he is bewitched, and he wants you to follow him in what his bewitchment tells him. Concerning Allah's statement,

(And if We delay the torment for them till a determined term,) Allah, the Exalted, is saying "If We delay the torment and the destruction of these polytheists until an appointed time and a period determined, and We promise them a specific time period (of life), they would still say, in rejection and haste;

(What keeps it back) They mean by this, "What delays this torment from overtaking us" Both rejection and doubt are their very nature. Therefore, they have no escape or refuge from the torment.

## The Meanings of the Word Ummah

The word Ummah is used in the Qur'an and Sunnah with a number of different meanings. Sometimes when it is used it means a specified period of time. An example is the statement of Allah, the Exalted, in this verse,

(till a determined Ummah (term),) This is also the meaning in the statement of Allah in Surah Yusuf,

(Then the man who was released, now after Ummah (some time) remembered.) (12:45) The word Ummah is also used to refer to the Imam (leader) who is followed. An example of this is in the statement of Allah,

(Verily, Ibrahim was an Ummah, obedient to Allah, Hanif, and he was not of those who were polytheists.) (16:120) The word Ummah is also used to mean religion and religious creed. This is as Allah mentions concerning the polytheists, that they said,

(Verily, we found our fathers following a certain way and religion, and we will indeed follow their footsteps. ) (43:23) The word Ummah is also used to mean a group (of people). This is as Allah says,

(And when he arrived at the water (well) of Madyan, he found there a group of men watering (their flocks).) (28:23) Allah also said,

(And verily, We have sent among every Ummah a Messenger (proclaiming): "Worship Allah (Alone), and avoid Taghut.") (16:36) Allah also said,

(And for every Ummah there is a Messenger; when their Messenger comes, the matter will be judged between them with justice, and they will not be wronged.) (10:47) The meaning of Ummah here is those people who have had a Messenger sent among them. The meaning of Ummah in this context includes the believers and the disbelievers among them. This is like what has been recorded in Sahih Muslim,

«وَالَّذِي نَفْسِي بِيَدِهِ لَا يَسْمَعُ بِي أَحَدٌ مِنْ هَذِهِ الْأُمَّةِ يَهُودِيٌّ وَلَا نَصْرَانِيٌّ ثُمَّ لَا يُؤْمِنُ بِي إِلَّا دَخَلَ النَّارِ»

(By He in Whose Hand is my soul! there is no one of this Ummah, whether he be a Jew or Christian, who hears of me and does not believe in me, except that he will enter the Hell- fire.) In reference to the Ummah of followers, then they are those who believe in the Messengers, as Allah said,

(You (the followers of Prophet Muhammad) are the best Ummah ever raised up for mankind.) (3:110) In the Sahih the Prophet said,

«فَأَقُولُ: أُمَّتِي أُمَّتِي»

(Then I will say, "My Ummah (followers), my Ummah!") The word Ummah is also used to mean a sect or party. An example of this usage is in the statement of Allah,

(And of the people of Musa there is an Ummah who lead (the men) with truth and established justice therewith.) (7:159) Likewise is His statement,

(A party of the People of the Scripture stand for the right.) (3:113)

### Surah: 11 Ayah: 9, Ayah: 10 & Ayah: 11

﴿ وَلَئِنْ أَذَقْنَا ٱلْإِنسَـٰنَ مِنَّا رَحْمَةً ثُمَّ نَزَعْنَـٰهَا مِنْهُ إِنَّهُۥ لَيَـُٔوسٌ كَفُورٌ ۝ ﴾

44. And if We give man a taste of Mercy from Us, and then withdraw it from him, verily! he is despairing, ungrateful.

﴿ وَلَئِنْ أَذَقْنَـٰهُ نَعْمَآءَ بَعْدَ ضَرَّآءَ مَسَّتْهُ لَيَقُولَنَّ ذَهَبَ ٱلسَّيِّئَاتُ عَنِّىٓ إِنَّهُۥ لَفَرِحٌ فَخُورٌ ۝ ﴾

45. But if We let him taste good (favor) after evil (poverty and harm) has touched him, he is sure to say: "Ills have departed from me." Surely, he is exultant, and boastful (ungrateful to Allâh).

﴿ إِلَّا ٱلَّذِينَ صَبَرُواْ وَعَمِلُواْ ٱلصَّـٰلِحَـٰتِ أُوْلَـٰٓئِكَ لَهُم مَّغْفِرَةٌ وَأَجْرٌ كَبِيرٌ ۝ ﴾

46. Except those who show patience and do righteous good deeds: those, theirs will be forgiveness and a great reward (Paradise).

### Transliteration

9. Wala-in athaqna al-insana minna rahmatan thumma nazaAAnaha minhu innahu layaoosun kafoorun   10. Wala-in athaqnahu naAAmaa baAAda darraa massat-hu layaqoolanna thahaba alssayyi-atu AAannee innahu lafarihun fakhoorun   11. Illa allatheena sabaroo waAAamiloo alssalihati ola-ika lahum maghfiratun waajrun kabeerun

### Tafsir Ibn Kathir

### The changing of Man's Attitude in Happiness and Hardship

Allah, the Exalted, informs about mankind and the blameworthy characteristics that he possesses, except for those believing servants upon whom Allah has bestowed His mercy. Allah explains that when any hardship befalls man, after he has experienced blessings, he is disheartened and he despairs of any good in the future. He denies and rejects (the bounties of) his previous condition. Thus, he behaves as if he has never seen any good and he loses all hope for relief (from his situation). Likewise, if any blessing befalls him after displeasure,

(he is sure to say, "Ills have departed from me.") This means that he will claim that no harm or calamity will afflict him after this (blessing).

(Surely, he is exultant and boastful (ungrateful to Allah).) This means that he is pleased with what he has in his hand and ungrateful (to Allah). At the same time he is boastful towards others. Allah, the Exalted, then says,

(Except those who show patience) meaning, those who show patience during times of hardship and adversity. In reference to Allah's statement,

(and do righteous good deeds) This means that they perform the good deeds in times of ease and good health. Concerning the statement,

(those, theirs will be forgiveness) meaning, that they will be forgiven due to the calamities that afflicted them. Concerning Allah's statement,

(and a great reward.) This great reward is due to them because of what they sent forth (of good deeds) in their times of ease. This is similar to what is mentioned in the Hadith,

«وَالَّذِي نَفْسِي بِيَدِهِ لَا يُصِيبُ الْمُؤْمِنَ هَمٌّ وَلَا غَمٌّ وَلَا نَصَبٌ وَلَا وَصَبٌ وَلَا حَزَنٌ، حَتَّى الشَّوْكَةُ يُشَاكُهَا إِلَّا كَفَّرَ اللهُ عَنْهُ بِهَا مِنْ خَطَايَاهُ»

(By He in Whose Hand is my soul! No worry, calamity, distress, illness, or grief strikes a believer, even the prick of a thorn, except that Allah will expiate his sins for him because of it.) In the Sahih it is recorded that the Prophet said,

«وَالَّذِي نَفْسِي بِيَدِهِ لَا يَقْضِي اللهُ لِلْمُؤْمِنِ قَضَاءً إِلَّا كَانَ خَيْرًا لَهُ، إِنْ أَصَابَتْهُ سَرَّاءُ فَشَكَرَ كَانَ خَيْرًا لَهُ، وَإِنْ أَصَابَتْهُ ضَرَّاءُ فَصَبَرَ كَانَ خَيْرًا لَهُ، وَلَيْسَ ذَلِكَ لِأَحَدٍ غَيْرِ الْمُؤْمِنِ»

(By He in Whose Hand is my soul! Allah does not decree any matter for the believer except that it is good for him. If any blessing befalls him, he is thankful (to Allah) and that is good for him. If any harm comes to him, he is patient and that is also good for him. This is (a bounty) exclusively for the believer.) For this reason, Allah, the Exalted, says,

(By Al-`Asr (the time). Verily, man is in loss. Except those who believe and do righteous good deeds. And recommend one another to the truth and recommend one another to patience.) (103:1-3) Allah also says,

(Verily, man was created very impatient.) (70:19)

## Surah: 11 Ayah: 12, Ayah: 13 & Ayah: 14

﴿ فَلَعَلَّكَ تَارِكٌ بَعْضَ مَا يُوحَىٰ إِلَيْكَ وَضَآئِقٌ بِهِۦ صَدْرُكَ أَن يَقُولُواْ لَوْلَآ أُنزِلَ عَلَيْهِ كَنزٌ أَوْ جَآءَ مَعَهُۥ مَلَكٌ إِنَّمَآ أَنتَ نَذِيرٌ وَٱللَّهُ عَلَىٰ كُلِّ شَىْءٍ وَكِيلٌ ﴾

47. So perchance you (Muhammad (peace be upon him)) may give up a part of what is revealed unto you, and that your breast feels straitened for it because they say, "Why has not a treasure been sent down unto him, or an angel has come with him?" But you are only a warner. And Allâh is a Wakîl (Disposer of affairs, Trustee, Guardian) over all things.

﴿ أَمْ يَقُولُونَ ٱفْتَرَىٰهُ قُلْ فَأْتُواْ بِعَشْرِ سُوَرٍ مِّثْلِهِۦ مُفْتَرَيَاتٍ وَٱدْعُواْ مَنِ ٱسْتَطَعْتُم مِّن دُونِ ٱللَّهِ إِن كُنتُمْ صَادِقِينَ ﴾

48. Or they say, "He (Prophet Muhammad (peace be upon him)) forged it (the Qur'an)." Say: "Bring you then ten forged Sûrahs (chapters) like unto it, and call whomsoever you can, other than Allâh (to your help), if you speak the truth!"

﴿ فَإِلَّمْ يَسْتَجِيبُواْ لَكُمْ فَٱعْلَمُوٓاْ أَنَّمَآ أُنزِلَ بِعِلْمِ ٱللَّهِ وَأَن لَّآ إِلَـٰهَ إِلَّا هُوَ فَهَلْ أَنتُم مُّسْلِمُونَ ﴾

49. If then they answer you not, know then that it is (the Revelation (this Qur'ân)) is sent down with the Knowledge of Allâh and that Lâ ilâha illa Huwa: (none has the right to be worshipped but He)! Will you then be Muslims (those who submit to Islâm)?

### Transliteration

12. FalaAAallaka tarikun baAAda ma yooha ilayka wada-iqun bihi sadruka an yaqooloo lawla onzila AAalayhi kanzun aw jaa maAAahu malakun innama anta natheerun waAllahu AAala kulli shay-in wakeelun   13. Am yaqooloona iftarahu qul fa/too biAAashri suwarin mithlihi muftarayatin waodAAoo mani istataAAtum min dooni Allahi in kuntum sadiqeena   14. Fa-illam yastajeeboo lakum faiAAlamoo annama onzila biAAilmi Allahi waan la ilaha illa huwa fahal antum muslimoona

### Tafsir Ibn Kathir

## The Messenger grieving by the Statements of the Polytheists, and His Gratification

This statement of Allah, the Exalted, to His Messenger comforted the worries that the polytheists were causing him due to their statements directed towards him. This is just as Allah says about them,

Chapter 11: Hud (Hud), Verses 006-123

(And they say: "Why does this Messenger eat food, and walk about in the markets. Why is not an angel sent down to him to be a warner with him" Or; "(why) has not a treasure been granted to him, or why has he not a garden whereof he may eat" And the wrongdoers say: "You follow none but a man bewitched.") (25:7-8) Thus, Allah commanded His Messenger and guided him to not let these statements of theirs grieve his heart. Allah directed him to not let these statements prevent him, or deter him from calling them to Allah, both day and night. This is as Allah said,

(Indeed, We know that your breast is straitened at what they say.) (15:97) Allah says in this verse,

(So perchance you may give up a part of what is revealed unto you, and that your breast feels straitened for it because they say...) The meaning here is that he (the Prophet ) may be compelled to give up the Message due to what they (the polytheists) say about him. However, Allah goes on to explain: "You (Muhammad) are only a warner and you have an example in your brothers of the Messengers who came before you. For verily, the previous Messengers were rejected and harmed, yet they were patient until the help of Allah came to them."

### An Explanation concerning the Miracle of the Qur'an

Then Allah, the Exalted, explains the miracle of the Qur'an, and that no one is able to produce its like, or even bring ten chapters, or one chapter like it. The reason for this is that the Speech of the Lord of all that exists is not like the speech of the created beings, just as His attributes are not like the attributes of the creation. Nothing resembles His existence. Exalted is He, the Most Holy, and the Sublime. There is no deity worthy of worship except He and there is no true Lord other than He. Then Allah goes on to say,

(If then they answer you not,) Meaning, that if they do not come with a reply to that which you have challenged them with (to the reproduction of ten chapters like the Qur'an), then know that it is due to their inability to do so. Know (that this is a proof) that this is the speech revealed from Allah. It contains His knowledge, His commands and His prohibitions. Then Allah continues by saying,

(and that there is no God besides Him! Will you then be Muslims)

### Surah: 11 Ayah: 15 & Ayah: 16

﴿ مَن كَانَ يُرِيدُ ٱلْحَيَوٰةَ ٱلدُّنْيَا وَزِينَتَهَا نُوَفِّ إِلَيْهِمْ أَعْمَٰلَهُمْ فِيهَا وَهُمْ فِيهَا لَا يُبْخَسُونَ ۝ ﴾

50. Whosoever desires the life of the world and its glitter; to them We shall pay in full (the wages of) their deeds therein, and they will have no diminution therein.

$$\text{﴿ أُوْلَٰٓئِكَ ٱلَّذِينَ لَيْسَ لَهُمْ فِى ٱلْءَاخِرَةِ إِلَّا ٱلنَّارُ ۖ وَحَبِطَ مَا صَنَعُواْ فِيهَا وَبَٰطِلٌ مَّا كَانُواْ يَعْمَلُونَ ۞ ﴾}$$

51. They are those for whom there is nothing in the Hereafter but Fire, and vain are the deeds they did therein. And of no effect is that which they used to do.

### Transliteration

15. Man kana yureedu alhayata alddunya wazeenataha nuwaffi ilayhim aAAmalahum feeha wahum feeha la yubkhasoona 16. Ola-ika allatheena laysa lahum fee al-akhirati illa alnnaru wahabita ma sanaAAoo feeha wabatilun ma kanoo yaAAmaloona

### Tafsir Ibn Kathir

## Whoever wants the Worldly Life, then He will have no Share of the Hereafter

Al-`Awfi reported that Ibn `Abbas said concerning this verse, "Verily those who show off, will be given their reward for their good deeds in this life. This will be so that they are not wronged, even the amount equivalent to the size of the speck on a date-stone." Ibn `Abbas continued saying, "Therefore, whoever does a good deed seeking to acquire worldly gain - like fasting, prayer, or standing for prayer at night - and he does so in order to acquire worldly benefit, then Allah says, `Give him the reward of that which he sought in the worldly life,' and his deed that he did is wasted because he was only seeking the life of this world. In the Hereafter he will be of the losers." A similar narration has been reported from Mujahid, Ad-Dahhak and many others. Anas bin Malik and Al-Hasan both said, "This verse was revealed concerning the Jews and the Christians." Mujahid and others said, "This verse was revealed concerning the people who perform deeds to be seen." Qatadah said, "Whoever's concern, intention and goal is this worldly life, then Allah will reward him for his good deeds in this life. Then, when reaches the next life, he will not have any good deeds that will be rewarded. However, concerning the believer, he will be rewarded for his good deeds in this life and in the Hereafter as well." Allah, the Exalted, says,

(Whoever desires the quick-passing (transitory enjoyment of this world), We readily grant him what We will for whom We like. Then, afterwards, We have appointed for him Hell; he will burn therein disgraced and rejected. And whoever desires the Hereafter and strives for it, with the necessary effort due for it while he is a believer - then such are the ones whose striving shall be appreciated. On each - these as well as those - We bestow from the bounties of your Lord. And the bounties of your Lord can never be forbidden. See how We prefer one above another, and verily, the Hereafter will be greater in degrees and greater in intricacy.) (17:18-21) Allah, the Exalted, says,

(Whosoever desires the reward of the Hereafter, We give him increase in his reward, and whosoever desires the reward of this world, We give him thereof, and he has no portion in the Hereafter.) (42:20)

## Surah: 11 Ayah: 17

﴿ أَفَمَن كَانَ عَلَىٰ بَيِّنَةٍ مِّن رَّبِّهِ وَيَتْلُوهُ شَاهِدٌ مِّنْهُ وَمِن قَبْلِهِ كِتَٰبُ مُوسَىٰٓ إِمَامًا وَرَحْمَةً ۚ أُو۟لَٰٓئِكَ يُؤْمِنُونَ بِهِ ۚ وَمَن يَكْفُرْ بِهِ مِنَ ٱلْأَحْزَابِ فَٱلنَّارُ مَوْعِدُهُۥ ۚ فَلَا تَكُ فِى مِرْيَةٍ مِّنْهُ ۚ إِنَّهُ ٱلْحَقُّ مِن رَّبِّكَ وَلَٰكِنَّ أَكْثَرَ ٱلنَّاسِ لَا يُؤْمِنُونَ ۝ ﴾

52. Can they (Muslims) who rely on a clear proof (the Qur'ân) from their Lord, and whom a witness (Jibril (Gabriel (peace be upon him))) from Him recites (follows) it (can they be equal with the disbelievers); and before it, came the Book of Mûsâ (Moses), a guidance and a mercy, they believe therein, but those of the sects (Jews, Christians and all the other non-Muslim nations) that reject it (the Qur'ân), the Fire will be their promised meeting-place. So be not in doubt about it (i.e. those who denied Prophet Muhammad (peace be upon him) and also denied all that which he brought from Allâh. Surely, they will enter Hell). Verily, it is the truth from your Lord, but most of the mankind believe not.

### Transliteration

17. Afaman kana AAala bayyinatin min rabbihi wayatloohu shahidun minhu wamin qablihi kitabu moosa imaman warahmatan ola-ika yu/minoona bihi waman yakfur bihi mina al-ahzabi faalnnaru mawAAiduhu fala taku fee miryatin minhu innahu alhaqqu min rabbika walakinna akthara alnnasi la yu/minoona

### Tafsir Ibn Kathir

#### The One Who believes in the Qur'an is upon Clear Proof from His Lord

Allah, the Exalted, informs of the condition of the believers who are upon the natural religion of Allah, which He made inherent in His creatures. This is based upon their confession to Him that there is none worthy of worship except He. This is similar to Allah's statement,

(So set you your face towards the religion, Hanifan. Allah's Fitrah with which He has created mankind.) (30:30), In the Two Sahihs it is recorded that Abu Hurayrah said that the Messenger of Allah said,

« كُلُّ مَوْلُودٍ يُولَدُ عَلَى الْفِطْرَةِ فَأَبَوَاهُ يُهَوِّدَانِهِ أَوْ يُنَصِّرَانِهِ أَوْ يُمَجِّسَانِهِ كَمَا تُولَدُ الْبَهِيمَةُ بَهِيمَةً جَمْعَاءَ هَلْ تُحِسُّونَ فِيهَا مِنْ جَدْعَاءَ؟ »

(Every child is born upon the Fitrah, but his parents make him a Jew, Christian, or Magian. This is just as the calf that is born whole. Have you noticed any calves that are born mutilated) In Sahih Muslim it is recorded that `Iyad bin Himar said that the Messenger of Allah said,

«يَقُولُ اللهُ تَعَالَى: إِنِّي خَلَقْتُ عِبَادِي حُنَفَاءَ فَجَاءَتْهُمُ الشَّيَاطِينُ فَاجْتَالَتْهُمْ عَنْ دِينِهِمْ وَحَرَّمَتْ عَلَيْهِمْ مَا أَحْلَلْتُ لَهُمْ، وَأَمَرَتْهُمْ أَنْ يُشْرِكُوا بِي مَا لَمْ أُنْزِلْ بِهِ سُلْطَانًا»

(Allah, the Exalted, says, `Verily, I created my servants Hunafa', but the devils came to them and distracted them from their religion. They made unlawful for them what I had made lawful for them and they commanded them to associate partners with Me, concerning which no authority has been revealed.) Therefore, the believer is one who remains upon this Fitrah. Concerning Allah's statement,

(and whom a witness from Him recites (follows) it;) This means that a witness comes to him from Allah. That witness is the pure, perfect and magnificent legislation that Allah revealed to the Prophets. These legislations were finalized with the legislation (Shari`ah) of Muhammad . The believer has the natural disposition that bears witness to (the truth of) the general legislation, and accepts that specific laws are taken from the general legislation. The Fitrah accepts the Shari`ah and believes in it. For this reason Allah, the Exalted, says,

(Can they who rely on a clear proof from their Lord, and whom a witness from Him recites (follows) it;) This clear proof which is recited is the Qur'an, which Jibril conveyed to the Prophet and the Prophet Muhammad conveyed it to his Ummah. Then Allah says,

(and before it, came the Book of Musa,) This means that before the Qur'an, there was the Book of Musa, the Tawrah.

(a guidance and a mercy) This means that Allah, the Exalted, revealed it to that Ummah as a leader for them and a guide for them to follow, as a mercy from Allah upon them. Therefore, whoever believed in it with true faith, then it would lead him to believe in the Qur'an as well. For this reason Allah said,

(they believe therein) Then Allah, the Exalted, threatens those who reject the Qur'an, or any part of it, by saying,

(but those of the sects that reject it, the Fire will be their promised meeting place.) This is directed towards everyone on the face of the earth who disbelieves in the Qur'an, whether they are idolators, disbelievers, People of the Scripture, or other sects from the descendants of Adam. This applies to all whom the Qur'an reaches, regardless of their differences in color, appearance, or nationality. As Allah says,

(that I may therewith warn you and whomsoever it may reach. ) (6:19) Allah, the Exalted, said,

(Say: "O mankind! Verily, I am sent to you all as the Messenger of Allah.") Allah says, (but those of the sects that reject it, the Fire will be their promised meeting place.) In Sahih Muslim it is recorded that Abu Musa Al-Ash`ari, may Allah be pleased with him, said that the Messenger of Allah said,

«وَالَّذِي نَفْسِي بِيَدِهِ لَا يَسْمَعُ بِي أَحَدٌ مِنْ هَذِهِ الْأُمَّةِ يَهُودِيٌّ (أَوْ) نَصْرَانِيٌّ ثُمَّ لَا يُؤْمِنُ بِي إِلَّا دَخَلَ النَّارَ»

(By He in Whose Hand is my soul! there is no one of this Ummah, whether he be a Jew or Christian, who hears of me and does not believe in me, except that he will enter the Hell-fire.)

## Every Hadith is confirmed by the Qur'an

Ayyub As-Sakhtiyani reported from Sa`id bin Jubayr that he said, "I did not hear any Hadith of the Prophet , substantiated as he stated it, except that I found its confirmation in the Qur'an. (The narrator said, "Or he said, `I found its verification in the Qur'an.'") Thus, it reached me that the Prophet said,

«لَا يَسْمَعُ بِي أَحَدٌ مِنْ هَذِهِ الْأُمَّةِ يَهُودِيٌّ وَلَا نَصْرَانِيٌّ ثُمَّ لَا يُؤْمِنُ بِي إِلَّا دَخَلَ النَّارَ»

(There is no one of this Ummah, whether he be a Jew or Christian, who hears of me and does not believe in me, except that he will enter the Hellfire.) Therefore, I said, `Where is its verification in the Book of Allah Most of what I have heard reported from the Messenger of Allah , I have found its verification in the Qur'an.' Then I found this verse,

(but those of the sects that reject it (the Qur`an), the Fire will be their promised meeting place.) And this means from all religions." Then Allah says,

(So be not in doubt about it. Verily, it is the truth from your Lord,) This means that the Qur'an is the truth from Allah and there is no doubt or suspicion concerning it. This is as Allah says,

(Alif Lam Mim. The revelations of the Book in which there is no doubt, is from the Lord of all that exists!)(32:1-2) Allah, the Exalted, says,

(Alif Lam Mim. This is the Book in which there is no doubt.) (2:1-2) The Ayah;

(but most of mankind believe not.) is similar to Allah's statement,

(And most of mankind will not believe even if you desire it eagerly.)(12:103) Likewise, Allah says,

(And if you obey most of those on the earth, they will mislead you far away from Allah's path.) Allah also says,

(And indeed Iblis did prove true his thought about them: and they followed him, all except a group of true believers.)(34:20)

### Surah: 11 Ayah: 18, Ayah: 19, Ayah: 20, Ayah: 21 & Ayah: 22

﴿ وَمَنْ أَظْلَمُ مِمَّنِ ٱفْتَرَىٰ عَلَى ٱللَّهِ كَذِبًا ۚ أُوْلَٰٓئِكَ يُعْرَضُونَ عَلَىٰ رَبِّهِمْ وَيَقُولُ ٱلْأَشْهَٰدُ هَٰٓؤُلَآءِ ٱلَّذِينَ كَذَبُواْ عَلَىٰ رَبِّهِمْ ۚ أَلَا لَعْنَةُ ٱللَّهِ عَلَى ٱلظَّٰلِمِينَ ﴾ ۝

53. And who does more wrong than he who invents a lie against Allâh. Such will be brought before their Lord, and the witnesses will say, "These are the ones who lied against their Lord!" No doubt! the curse of Allâh is on the Zâlimûn (polytheists, wrong-doers, oppressors).

﴿ ٱلَّذِينَ يَصُدُّونَ عَن سَبِيلِ ٱللَّهِ وَيَبْغُونَهَا عِوَجًا وَهُم بِٱلْأَخِرَةِ هُمْ كَٰفِرُونَ ﴾ ۝

54. Those who hinder (others) from the Path of Allâh (Islâmic Monotheism), and seek a crookedness therein, while they are disbelievers in the Hereafter.

﴿ أُوْلَٰٓئِكَ لَمْ يَكُونُواْ مُعْجِزِينَ فِى ٱلْأَرْضِ وَمَا كَانَ لَهُم مِّن دُونِ ٱللَّهِ مِنْ أَوْلِيَآءَ ۘ يُضَٰعَفُ لَهُمُ ٱلْعَذَابُ ۚ مَا كَانُواْ يَسْتَطِيعُونَ ٱلسَّمْعَ وَمَا كَانُواْ يُبْصِرُونَ ﴾ ۝

55. By no means will they escape (from Allâh's Torment) on earth, nor have they protectors besides Allâh! Their torment will be doubled! They could not bear to hear (the preachers of the truth) and they used not to see (the truth because of their severe aversion, in spite of the fact that they had the sense of hearing and sight).

﴿ أُوْلَٰٓئِكَ ٱلَّذِينَ خَسِرُوٓاْ أَنفُسَهُمْ وَضَلَّ عَنْهُم مَّا كَانُواْ يَفْتَرُونَ ﴾ ۝

56. They are those who have lost their own selves, and their invented false deities will vanish from them.

﴿ لَا جَرَمَ أَنَّهُمْ فِى ٱلْأَخِرَةِ هُمُ ٱلْأَخْسَرُونَ ﴾ ۝

57. Certainly, they are those who will be the greatest losers in the Hereafter.

## Transliteration

18. Waman athlamu mimmani iftara AAala Allahi kathiban ola-ika yuAAradoona AAala rabbihim wayaqoolu al-ashhadu haola-i allatheena kathaboo AAala rabbihim ala laAAnatu Allahi AAala alththalimeena  19. Allatheena yasuddoona AAan sabeeli Allahi wayabghoonaha AAiwajan wahum bial-akhirati hum kafiroona  20. Ola-ika lam yakoonoo muAAjizeena fee al-ardi wama kana lahum min dooni Allahi min awliyaa yudaAAafu lahumu alAAathabu ma kanoo yastateeAAoona alssamAAa wama kanoo yubsiroona  21. Ola-ika allatheena khasiroo anfusahum wadalla AAanhum ma kanoo yaftaroona  22. La jarama annahum fee al-akhirati humu al-akhsaroona

## Tafsir Ibn Kathir

### Those Who invent Lies against Allah and hinder Others from His Path are the Greatest Losers

Allah, the Exalted, explains the condition of those who lie against Him and that their scandal in the Hereafter will be presented before the heads of creation (for testimony) from the angels, Messengers, Prophets and the rest of mankind and Jinns. This is just as Imam Ahmad recorded from Safwan bin Muhriz. Safwan said, "I was holding the hand of Ibn `Umar when a man was brought to him. The man said, `How did you hear the Messenger of Allah describe An-Najwa (secret counsel or confidential talk) on the Day of Resurrection' Ibn `Umar said, `I heard him say,

«إِنَّ اللهَلَلَهَعَزَّ وَجَلَّ يُدْنِي الْمُؤْمِنَ فَيَضَعُ عَلَيْهِ كَنَفَهُ، وَيَسْتُرُهُ مِنَ النَّاسِ، وَيُقَرِّرُهُ بِذُنُوبِهِ وَيَقُولُ لَهُ: أَتَعْرِفُ ذَنْبَ كَذَا؟ أَتَعْرِفُ ذَنْبَ كَذَا؟ أَتَعْرِفُ ذَنْبَ كَذَا؟ حَتَّى إِذَا قَرَّرَهُ بِذُنُوبِهِ وَرَأَى فِي نَفْسِهِ أَنَّهُ قَدْ هَلَكَ قَالَ: فَإِنِّي قَدْ سَتَرْتُهَا عَلَيْكَ فِي الدُّنْيَا وَإِنِّي أَغْفِرُهَا لَكَ الْيَوْمَ»

(Verily, Allah, the Mighty and Sublime, will draw near the believer and He will place His shade over him. He will conceal him from the people and make him confess to his sins. He will say to him, "Do you recognize this sin Do you recognize that sin Do you recognize such and such sin" This will continue until He makes him confess to all of his sins and he (the believer) will think to himself that he is about to be destroyed. Then Allah will say, "Verily, I have concealed these sins for you in the worldly life and I have forgiven you for them today." Then he (the believer) will be given his Book of good deeds. As for the disbelievers and the hypocrites, the witnesses will say,)

(These are the ones who lied against their Lord! No doubt! The curse of Allah is on the wrongdoers)." Both Al-Bukhari and Muslim recorded this narration in the Two Sahihs. Concerning Allah's statement,

(Those who hinder (others) from the path of Allah, and seek a crookedness therein,) This means that they prevent the people from following the truth and traversing upon the path of guidance that leads to Allah, the Mighty and Sublime. In doing so they also keep the people away from Paradise itself. Allah's statement,

(and seek a crookedness therein,) This means that they want their path to be crooked and uneven. Then, Allah's statement,

(while they are disbelievers in the Hereafter.) This means that they deny the Hereafter and they reject the idea that any of its events will occur, or any of it exists at all. Concerning Allah's statement,

(By no means will they escape on earth, nor have they protectors besides Allah!) This means that these disbelievers are under the power of Allah and His force. They are in His grasp and are subject to His authority. He is Most Able to exact vengeance against them in this life before the coming of the Hereafter. This is like Allah's statement,

(but He gives them respite up to a Day when the eyes will stare in horror.)(14:42) In the Two Sahihs it is recorded that the Prophet said,

«إِنَّ اللهَ لَيُمْلِي لِلظَّالِمِ حَتَّى إِذَا أَخَذَهُ لَمْ يُفْلِتْهُ»

(Verily Allah gives respite to the oppressor until He seizes him, then he will not be able to escape Him.) For this reason Allah says,

(Their torment will be doubled!) This means that the torment will be doubled upon them, because Allah gave them hearing, vision and hearts, but these things did not benefit them. Rather, they were deaf from hearing the truth and blinded away from following it. This is just as Allah has mentioned concerning them when they enter into the Hellfire. Allah says,

(And they will say: "Had we but listened or used our intelligence, we would not have been among the dwellers of the blazing Fire!") Allah also says,

(Those who disbelieved and hinder (men) from the path of Allah, for them We will add torment to the torment.)(16:88) For this reason they will be punished for every command that they abandoned and every prohibition that they indulged in. Then Allah continues by saying,

(They are those who have lost their own selves, and that which they invented eluded them.) They lost themselves, meaning that they be made to enter a blazing Fire, where they will be punished, and its torment will not be lifted from them for even the blinking of an eye. This is as Allah said,

(Whenever it abates, We shall increase for them the fierceness of the Fire.)(17:97) Concerning the statement,

(eluded them.) meaning that it has left them.

(that which they invented) besides Allah, such as rivals and idols. Yet, these things did not avail them in the slightest. In fact, these things actually caused them great harm. This is as Allah says,

(And when mankind are gathered, they will become their enemies and will deny their worshipping.)(46:6) Allah says,

(When those who were followed disown those who followed (them), and they see the torment, then all their relations will be cut off from them.)(2:166) Likewise, there are many other verses that prove this loss of theirs and their destruction. For this reason Allah says,

(Certainly, they are those who will be the greatest losers in the Hearafter.) (11:22) In this verse Allah informs about the direction of their end. He explains that they are the greatest losers among mankind in their transaction for the abode of the Hereafter. That is because they exchanged the highest levels (of Paradise) for the lowest levels (of Hell) and they substituted the pleasure of Gardens (of Paradise) for the fierce boiling water (of Hell). They exchanged the drink of sealed nectar with the fierce hot wind, boiling water, and a shade of black smoke. They chose food from the filth of dirty wounds instead of wide-eyed lovely maidens. They preferred Hawiyah (a pit in Hell) instead of lofty castles. They chose the anger of Allah and His punishment over nearness to Him and the blessing of gazing at Him. Therefore, it is no injustice that such people should be the greatest losers in the Hereafter.

## Surah: 11 Ayah: 23 & Ayah: 24

﴿ إِنَّ ٱلَّذِينَ ءَامَنُواْ وَعَمِلُواْ ٱلصَّٰلِحَٰتِ وَأَخْبَتُوٓاْ إِلَىٰ رَبِّهِمْ أُوْلَٰٓئِكَ أَصْحَٰبُ ٱلْجَنَّةِ هُمْ فِيهَا خَٰلِدُونَ ﴿٢٣﴾ ﴾

58. Verily, those who believe (in the Oneness of Allâh - Islâmic Monotheism) and do righteous good deeds, and humble themselves (in repentance and obedience) before their Lord, they will be dwellers of Paradise to dwell therein forever.

﴿ ۞ مَثَلُ ٱلْفَرِيقَيْنِ كَٱلْأَعْمَىٰ وَٱلْأَصَمِّ وَٱلْبَصِيرِ وَٱلسَّمِيعِ هَلْ يَسْتَوِيَانِ مَثَلًا أَفَلَا تَذَكَّرُونَ ﴿٢٤﴾ ﴾

59. The likeness of the two parties is as the blind and the deaf and the seer and the hearer. Are they equal when compared? Will you not then take heed?

### Transliteration

23. Inna allatheena amanoo waAAamiloo alsalihati waakhbatoo ila rabbihim ola-ika as-habu aljannati hum feeha khalidoona  24. Mathalu alfareeqayni kaal-aAAma waal-asammi waalbaseeri waalssameeAAi hal yastawiyani mathalan afala tathakkaroona

## Tafsir Ibn Kathir

### Rewarding the People of Faith

When Allah, the Exalted, mentioned the condition of the wretched, He also commended the people of delight (the believers). They are those who believe and work righteous deeds. Thus, their hearts believed and their limbs worked righteous deeds, both in statements and actions. This includes their performance of deeds of obedience and their abandonment of evils. In this way they are the inheritors of Gardens (of Paradise), which contain lofty rooms and seats arranged in rows. Therein they will find bunches of fruit near to them, elevated couches, fair and beautiful wives, various types of fruit, desired kinds of food and delicious drinks. They also will be allowed to see the Creator of the heavens and the earth and they will be in this state of pleasure forever. They will not die, nor will they grow old. They will not experience sickness, nor will they sleep. They will not have excrement, nor will they spit or snot. Their sweat will be the perfume of musk.

### The Parable of the Believers and the Disbelievers

Then, Allah, the Exalted, makes a parable of the disbelievers and the believers. He says,

(The likeness of the two parties) This refers to those disbelievers whom Allah first described as wretched, and then those believers whom He described with delightfulness. The first group is like one who is blind and deaf, while the second group is like he who sees and hears. Thus, the disbeliever is blind from the truth in this life and in the Hereafter. He is not guided to goodness, nor does he recognize it. He is deaf from hearing the proofs, thus he does not hear that which would benefit him. As Allah says,

(Had Allah known of any good in them, He would indeed have made them listen.)(8:23) The believer is smart, bright and clever. He sees the truth and distinguishes between the truth and falsehood. Thus, he follows the good and abandons the evil. He hears and distinguishes between the proof and scepticism. Therefore, falsehood does not overcome him. Are these two types of people alike

(Will you not then take heed) This statement means, "Will you not consider, so that you may distinguish between these two categories of people." This is as Allah mentions in another verse,

(Not equal are the dwellers of the Fire and the dwellers of the Paradise. It is the dwellers of Paradise that will be successful.)(59:20) Allah also says,

(Not alike are the blind and the seeing. Nor are (alike) darkness and light. Nor are (alike) the shade and the sun's heat. Nor are (alike) the living and the dead. Verily, Allah makes whom He wills to hear, but you cannot make hear those who are in graves. You are only a warner. Verily, We have sent you with the truth, a bearer of glad tidings and a warner. And there never was a nation but a warner had passed among them.)(35:19-24)

# Chapter 11: Hud (Hud), Verses 006-123

### Surah: 11 Ayah: 25, Ayah: 26 & Ayah: 27

﴿ وَلَقَدْ أَرْسَلْنَا نُوحًا إِلَىٰ قَوْمِهِۦٓ إِنِّى لَكُمْ نَذِيرٌ مُّبِينٌ ﴾ ۝

60. And indeed We sent Nûh (Noah) to his people (and he said): "I have come to you as a plain warner."

﴿ أَن لَّا تَعْبُدُوٓاْ إِلَّا ٱللَّهَ إِنِّىٓ أَخَافُ عَلَيْكُمْ عَذَابَ يَوْمٍ أَلِيمٍ ﴾ ۝

61. "That you worship none but Allâh; surely, I fear for you the torment of a painful Day."

﴿ فَقَالَ ٱلْمَلَأُ ٱلَّذِينَ كَفَرُواْ مِن قَوْمِهِۦ مَا نَرَىٰكَ إِلَّا بَشَرًا مِّثْلَنَا وَمَا نَرَىٰكَ ٱتَّبَعَكَ إِلَّا ٱلَّذِينَ هُمْ أَرَاذِلُنَا بَادِىَ ٱلرَّأْىِ وَمَا نَرَىٰ لَكُمْ عَلَيْنَا مِن فَضْلٍ بَلْ نَظُنُّكُمْ كَٰذِبِينَ ﴾ ۝

62. The chiefs who disbelieved among his people said: "We see you but a man like ourselves, nor do we see any follow you but the meanest among us and they (too) followed you without thinking. And we do not see in you any merit above us, in fact we think you are liars."

### Transliteration

25. Walaqad arsalna noohan ila qawmihi innee lakum natheerun mubeenun 26. An la taAAbudoo illa Allaha innee akhafu AAalaykum AAathaba yawmin aleemin 27. Faqala almalao allatheena kafaroo min qawmihi ma naraka illa basharan mithlana wama naraka ittabaAAaka illa allatheena hum arathiluna badiya alrra/yi wama nara lakum AAalayna min fadlin bal nathunnukum kathibeena

### Tafsir Ibn Kathir

#### The Story of Nuh and His Conversation with His People

Allah, the Exalted, informs about Prophet Nuh. He was the first Messenger whom Allah sent to the people of the earth who were polytheists involved in worshipping idols. Allah mentions that he (Nuh) said to his people,

(I have come to you as a plain warner.) meaning, to openly warn you against facing Allah's punishment if you continue worshipping other than Allah. Thus, Nuh said,

(That you worship none but Allah;) This can also be seen in his statement,

(surely, I fear for you the torment of a painful Day.) This means, "If you all continue doing this, then Allah will punish you with a severe punishment in the Hereafter." Then Allah says,

(The chiefs who disbelieved among his people said;) The word `chiefs' (Al-Mala'u) here means the leaders and the heads of the disbelievers. They said,

(We see you but a man like ourselves,) This means, "You are not an angel. You are only a human being, so how can revelation come to you over us We do not see anyone following you except the lowliest people among us, like the merchants, weavers and similar people. No people of nobility, or rulers among us follow you. These people who follow you are not known for their intelligence, wit, or sharp thinking. Rather, you merely invited them (to this Islam) and they responded to your call and followed you (ignorantly)." This is the meaning of their statement,

(nor do we see any follow you but the meanest among us and they (too) followed you without thinking.) The statement, "without thinking," means that they merely followed the first thing that came to their minds. Concerning the statement,

(And we do not see in you any merit above us, in fact we think you are liars.) In this they are saying, "We do not see that you (and your followers) have any virtuous status above us in your physical appearance, your character, your provisions, or your condition, since you accepted this (new) religion of yours."

s(in fact we think you are liars. ) This means, "We think you are lying about that which you are claiming for yourselves of righteousness, piety, worship and happiness in the abode of the Hereafter when you arrive there." This was the response of the disbelievers to Nuh and his followers. This is a proof of their ignorance and their deficiency in knowledge and intelligence. For verily, the truth is not to be rejected because of the lowly status of those who follow it. Verily, the truth is correct in itself, regardless of whether its followers are of low status, or nobility. Actually, the reality concerning which there is no doubt, is that the followers of the truth are the noble ones, even though they may be poor. On the other hand, those who reject the truth are the lowly wretches, even though they may be wealthy. Thus, we see that usually the weakest of people are the ones who follow the truth, while the nobility and high-class people usually are opposed to the truth. This is as Allah says,

(And similarly, We sent not a warner before you to any town (people) but the luxurious ones among them said: "We found our fathers following a cerain way and religion, and we will indeed follow their footsteps.")(43:23) When Heraclius, the emperor of Rome, asked Abu Sufyan Sakhr bin Harb about the qualities of the Prophet , he said to him, "Are his followers the noble people, or the weak" Abu Sufyan said, "They are the weakest of them." Then Heraclius said, "They (weak ones) are the followers of the Messengers." Concerning their statement,

(without thinking. ) In reality this is not objectionable, or something derogatory, because the truth when it is made clear, does not leave room for second-guessing, or excessive thinking. Rather, it is mandatory that it should be followed and this is the condition of every pious, intelligent person. No one continues doubtfully pondering the truth (after it is made clear) except one who is ignorant and excessively critical. The Messengers - Allah's peace and blessings be upon them all - only delivered what was obvious and clear. Concerning Allah's statement,

(And we do not see in you any merit above us,) They did not see this (the virtue of accepting Islam) because they were blind from the truth. They could not see, nor could they hear. Rather, they were wavering in their skepticism. They were wandering blindly in the darknesses of their ignorance. They, in reality, were the slanderers and liars, lowly and despicable. Therefore, in the Hereafter they will be the greatest losers.

### Surah: 11 Ayah: 28

﴿ قَالَ يَٰقَوْمِ أَرَءَيْتُمْ إِن كُنتُ عَلَىٰ بَيِّنَةٍ مِّن رَّبِّى وَءَاتَىٰنِى رَحْمَةً مِّنْ عِندِهِۦ فَعُمِّيَتْ عَلَيْكُمْ أَنُلْزِمُكُمُوهَا وَأَنتُمْ لَهَا كَٰرِهُونَ ۞ ﴾

63. He said: "O my people! Tell me, if I have a clear proof from my Lord, and a Mercy (Prophethood) has come to me from Him, but that (Mercy) has been obscured from your sight. Shall we compel you to accept it (Islâmic Monotheism) when you have a strong hatred for it?

### Translation

28. He said: "O my people! Tell me, if I have a clear proof from my Lord, and a Mercy (Prophethood, etc.) has come to me from Him, but that (Mercy) has been obscured from your sight. Shall we compel you to accept it (Islâmic Monotheism) when you have a strong hatred for it?

### Tafsir Ibn Kathir

**The Response of Nuh**

Allah says, informing about the response of Nuh to his people,

(Tell me, if I have a clear proof from my Lord,) Bayyinah means certainty, a clear matter, and truthful prophethood. That is the greatest mercy from Allah upon him (Nuh) and them (his people).

(but that (mercy) has been obscured from your sight.) "Obscured from your sight" in this verse means, `it was hidden from you and you are not guided to it. Thus, you (people) did not know its importance so you hastily rejected and denied it.'

(Shall we compel you (to accept) it) This means, "Should we force you to accept it, while you actually detest it."

### Surah: 11 Ayah: 29 & Ayah: 30

﴿ وَيَٰقَوْمِ لَآ أَسْـَٔلُكُمْ عَلَيْهِ مَالًا ۖ إِنْ أَجْرِىَ إِلَّا عَلَى ٱللَّهِ ۚ وَمَآ أَنَا۠ بِطَارِدِ ٱلَّذِينَ ءَامَنُوٓا۟ ۚ إِنَّهُم مُّلَٰقُوا۟ رَبِّهِمْ وَلَٰكِنِّىٓ أَرَىٰكُمْ قَوْمًا تَجْهَلُونَ ۞ ﴾

64. "And O my people! I ask of you no wealth for it, my reward is from none but Allâh. I am not going to drive away those who have believed. Surely, they are going to meet their Lord, but I see that you are a people that are ignorant.

﴿ وَيَـٰقَوْمِ مَن يَنصُرُنِى مِنَ ٱللَّهِ إِن طَرَدتُّهُمْ ۚ أَفَلَا تَذَكَّرُونَ ۝ ﴾

65. "And O my people! Who will help me against Allâh, if I drove them away? Will you not then give a thought?

### Transliteration

29. Waya qawmi la as-alukum AAalayhi malan in ajriya illa AAala Allahi wama ana bitaridi allatheena amanoo innahum mulaqoo rabbihim walakinnee arakum qawman tajhaloona   30. Waya qawmi man yansurunee mina Allahi in taradtuhum afala tathakkaroona

### Tafsir Ibn Kathir

Nuh says to his people, "I do not ask you for any wealth in return for my sincere advice to you." Wealth (Mal) here means, "payment that I take from you." Nuh means, "I am only seeking the reward from Allah, the Mighty and Sublime." Concerning the statement,

(I am not going to drive away those who have believed.) This alludes to the fact that they (the disbelievers) requested Nuh to disassociate himself from the believers, because they were averse to them and felt themselves too important to sit with them. This is similar to the request of disbelievers to the seal of the Messengers to disassociate himself from a group of the people who were considered weak in their social status. They wanted the Prophet to sit with them in a special gathering of the elite. Therefore, Allah revealed,

(And turn not away those who invoke their Lord, morning and afternoon.) Allah also says,

(Thus We have tried some of them with others, that they might say: "Is it these (poor believers) whom Allah has favored from among us" Does not Allah know best those who are grateful)(6:53)

### Surah: 11 Ayah: 31

﴿ وَلَا أَقُولُ لَكُمْ عِندِى خَزَآئِنُ ٱللَّهِ وَلَا أَعْلَمُ ٱلْغَيْبَ وَلَا أَقُولُ إِنِّى مَلَكٌ وَلَا أَقُولُ لِلَّذِينَ تَزْدَرِىٓ أَعْيُنُكُمْ لَن يُؤْتِيَهُمُ ٱللَّهُ خَيْرًا ۖ ٱللَّهُ أَعْلَمُ بِمَا فِىٓ أَنفُسِهِمْ ۖ إِنِّىٓ إِذًا لَّمِنَ ٱلظَّـٰلِمِينَ ۝ ﴾

66. "And I do not say to you that with me are the Treasures of Allâh, nor that I know the Ghaib (unseen), nor do I say I am an angel, and I do not say of those whom your eyes look down upon that Allâh will not bestow any good on them. Allâh knows what is in their inner-selves (as regards belief, etc.). In that case, I should, indeed be one of the Zâlimûn (wrong-doers, oppressors)."

# Chapter 11: Hud (Hud), Verses 006-123

### Transliteration

31. Wala aqoolu lakum AAindee khaza-inu Allahi wala aAAlamu alghayba wala aqoolu innee malakun wala aqoolu lillatheena tazdaree aAAyunukum lan yu/tiyahumu Allahu khayran Allahu aAAlamu bima fee anfusihim innee ithan lamina aththalimeena

### Tafsir Ibn Kathir

Nuh is informing them that he is a Messenger from Allah, calling to the worship of Allah alone, without any partners and he is doing this by the permission of Allah. At the same time, he is not asking them for any reward for this work. He invites whomever he meets, whether of nobility or low class. Therefore, whoever responds favorably, then he has achieved salvation. He also explains that he has no power to manipulate the hidden treasures of Allah, nor does he have any knowledge of the Unseen, except what Allah has allowed him to know. Likewise, he is not an angel, rather, he is merely a human Messenger aided with miracles. Nuh goes on to say, "I do not say about these people whom you (disbelievers) detest and look down upon, that Allah will not reward them for their deeds. Allah knows best what is in their souls. If they are believers in their hearts, as their condition appears to be outwardly, then they will have a good reward. If anyone behaves evilly with them after they have believed, then he is a wrongdoer who speaks what he has no knowledge of.

### Surah: 11 Ayah: 32, Ayah: 33 & Ayah: 34

﴿ قَالُواْ يَـٰنُوحُ قَدْ جَـٰدَلْتَنَا فَأَكْثَرْتَ جِدَٰلَنَا فَأْتِنَا بِمَا تَعِدُنَآ إِن كُنتَ مِنَ ٱلصَّـٰدِقِينَ ﴾

67. They said: "O Nûh (Noah)! You have disputed with us and much have you prolonged the dispute with us, now bring upon us what you threaten us with, if you are of the truthful."

﴿ قَالَ إِنَّمَا يَأْتِيكُم بِهِ ٱللَّهُ إِن شَآءَ وَمَآ أَنتُم بِمُعْجِزِينَ ﴾

68. He said: "Only Allâh will bring it (the punishment) on you, if He will, and then you will escape not.

﴿ وَلَا يَنفَعُكُمْ نُصْحِىٓ إِنْ أَرَدتُّ أَنْ أَنصَحَ لَكُمْ إِن كَانَ ٱللَّهُ يُرِيدُ أَن يُغْوِيَكُمْ هُوَ رَبُّكُمْ وَإِلَيْهِ تُرْجَعُونَ ﴾

69. "And my advice will not profit you, even if I wish to give you good counsel, if Allâh's Will is to keep you astray. He is your Lord! and to Him you shall return."

### Transliteration

32. Qaloo ya noohu qad jadaltana faaktharta jidalana fa/tina bima taAAiduna in kunta mina alssadiqeena   33. Qala innama ya/teekum bihi Allahu in shaa wama antum

bimuAAjizeena 34. Wala yanfaAAukum nushee in aradtu an ansaha lakum in kana Allahu yureedu an yughwiyakum huwa rabbukum wa-ilayhi turjaAAoona

### Tafsir Ibn Kathir

### The People's Request of Nuh to bring the Torment and His Response to Them

Allah, the Exalted, informs that the people of Nuh sought to hasten Allah's vengeance, torment, anger and the trial (His punishment). This is based on their saying,

(They said: "O Nuh! You have disputed with us and much have you prolonged the dispute with us...") They meant by this, "You (Nuh) have argued with us long enough, and we are still not going to follow you."

(now bring upon us what you threaten us with,) What he (Nuh) promised is referring to the vengeance and torment (from Allah). They were actually saying, "Supplicate against us however you wish, and let whatever you have supplicated come to us."

("...if you are of the truthful." (In reply to this,) He said: "Only Allah will bring it (the punishment) on you, if He wills, and then you will escape not.)(11:32-33) This means, `It is only Allah Who can punish you and hasten your punishment for you. He is the One from Whom nothing escapes. '

(And my advice will not profit you, even if I wish to give you good counsel, if Allah's will is to keep you astray.) This means: something that could be useful to you (in acceptance) of my preaching to you, warning you and advising you.

(if Allah's will is to keep you astray.) This means: your deception and your ultimate destruction.

(He is your Lord! and to Him you shall return.) He is the Owner of the finality of all matters. He is the Controller, the Judge, the Most Just and He does not do any injustice. Unto Him belongs the creation and the command. He is the Originator and the Repeater (of the creation). He is the Owner of this life and the Hereafter.

### Surah: 11 Ayah: 35

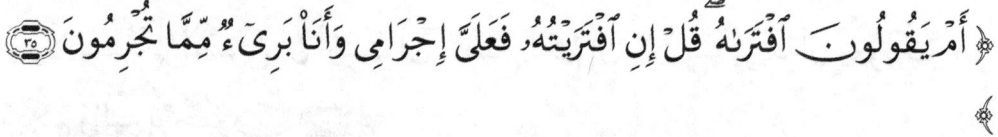

70. Or they (the pagans of Makkah) say: "He (Muhammad (peace be upon him)) has fabricated it (the Qur'ân)." Say: "If I have fabricated it, upon me be my crimes, but I am innocent of (all) those crimes which you commit."

### Transliteration

35. Am yaqooloona iftarahu qul ini iftaraytuhu faAAalayya ijramee waana baree-on mimma tujrimoona

# Chapter 11: Hud (Hud), Verses 006-123

## Tafsir Ibn Kathir

### An Interruption to verify the Truthfulness of the Prophet

This is presented in the middle of the story to affirm the story itself. It is as if Allah, the Exalted, is saying to Muhammad , "Or do these obstinate disbelievers say that he fabricated this and invented it himself"

(Say: "If I have fabricated it, upon me be my crimes...") This means: such sin would be mine alone.

(but I am innocent of (all) those crimes which you commit.) This story is not invented, or fabricated falsely. Because he (the Prophet) knows better the punishment of Allah for one who lies on Allah.

### Surah: 11 Ayah: 36, Ayah: 37, Ayah: 38 & Ayah: 39

﴿ وَأُوحِيَ إِلَىٰ نُوحٍ أَنَّهُ لَن يُؤْمِنَ مِن قَوْمِكَ إِلَّا مَن قَدْ ءَامَنَ فَلَا تَبْتَئِسْ بِمَا كَانُوا۟ يَفْعَلُونَ ﴾

71. And it was revealed to Nûh (Noah): "None of your people will believe except those who have believed already. So be not sad because of what they used to do.

﴿ وَٱصْنَعِ ٱلْفُلْكَ بِأَعْيُنِنَا وَوَحْيِنَا وَلَا تُخَٰطِبْنِى فِى ٱلَّذِينَ ظَلَمُوٓا۟ إِنَّهُم مُّغْرَقُونَ ﴾

72. "And construct the ship under Our Eyes and with Our Revelation, and call not upon Me on behalf of those who did wrong; they are surely to be drowned."

﴿ وَيَصْنَعُ ٱلْفُلْكَ وَكُلَّمَا مَرَّ عَلَيْهِ مَلَأٌ مِّن قَوْمِهِۦ سَخِرُوا۟ مِنْهُ قَالَ إِن تَسْخَرُوا۟ مِنَّا فَإِنَّا نَسْخَرُ مِنكُمْ كَمَا تَسْخَرُونَ ﴾

73. And as he was constructing the ship, whenever the chiefs of his people passed by him, they mocked at him. He said: "If you mock at us, so do we mock at you likewise for your mocking.

﴿ فَسَوْفَ تَعْلَمُونَ مَن يَأْتِيهِ عَذَابٌ يُخْزِيهِ وَيَحِلُّ عَلَيْهِ عَذَابٌ مُّقِيمٌ ﴾

74. "And you will know who it is on whom will come a torment that will cover him with disgrace and on whom will fall a lasting torment."

### Transliteration

36. Waoohiya ila noohin annahu lan yu/mina min qawmika illa man qad amana fala tabta-is bima kanoo yafAAaloona    37. WaisnaAAi alfulka bi-aAAyunina wawahyina

wala tukhatibnee fee allatheena thalamoo innahum mughraqoona 38. WayasnaAAu alfulka wakullama marra AAalayhi malaon min qawmihi sakhiroo minhu qala in taskharoo minna fa-inna naskharu minkum kama taskharoona 39. Fasawfa taAAlamoona man ya/teehi AAathabun yukhzeehi wayahillu AAalayhi AAathabun muqeemun

## Tafsir Ibn Kathir

### The Revelation to Nuh concerning what would happen to the People and the Command to prepare for It

Allah, the Exalted, sent revelation to Nuh when his people hastened the vengeance and punishment of Allah upon themselves. Then, Nuh supplicated against them, as Allah mentioned, when He said;

(My Lord! Leave not one of the disbelievers inhabiting the earth!) (71:26) And he said,

(Then he invoked his Lord (saying): "I have been overcome, so help (me)!")(54:10) At this point Allah revealed to him,

(None of your people will believe except those who have believed already.) Therefore, do not grieve over them and do not be concerned with their affair.

(And construct the ship.) The word Fulk here means ship.

(under Our Eyes) This means under Our vision.

(and with Our revelation,) This means, "We will teach you (Nuh) what to do."

(and address Me not on behalf of those who did wrong; they are surely to be drowned.) Muhammad bin Ishaq mentioned from the Tawrah, "Allah commanded him (Nuh) to make it (the ship) from Indian oak wood. Then He commanded him to make its length eighty cubits and its width fifty cubits. Allah then commanded him to coat its interior and exterior with tar and to make it with a slanted bow to part the water (as it sailed). Its height was thirty cubits into the sky. It had three levels and each level was ten cubits high. The lowest level was for the animals, both tame and wild, the second level was for the human beings and the highest level was for the birds. Its door was in the center of it and it had a cover on top of it that covered the entire ship. Concerning Allah's statement,

(And as he was constructing the ship, whenever the chiefs of his people passed by him, they mocked at him.) This means that they teased him and rejected his threat that they would drown (in the forthcoming flood).

(He said: "If you mock at us, so do we mock at you likewise...") This is a severe threat and a serious warning.

(who it is on whom will come a torment that will cover him with disgrace) This means that it (the torment) will humiliate him in this life.

(and on whom will fall a lasting torment.) that is continuous and everlasting.

Chapter 11: Hud (Hud), Verses 006-123

### Surah: 11 Ayah: 40

﴿ حَتَّىٰٓ إِذَا جَآءَ أَمْرُنَا وَفَارَ ٱلتَّنُّورُ قُلْنَا ٱحْمِلْ فِيهَا مِن كُلٍّ زَوْجَيْنِ ٱثْنَيْنِ وَأَهْلَكَ إِلَّا مَن سَبَقَ عَلَيْهِ ٱلْقَوْلُ وَمَنْ ءَامَنَ ۚ وَمَآ ءَامَنَ مَعَهُۥٓ إِلَّا قَلِيلٌ ﴾

75. (So it was) till when Our Command came and the oven gushed forth (water like fountains from the earth). We said: "Embark therein, of each kind two (male and female), and your family - except him against whom the Word has already gone forth - and those who believe. And none believed with him except a few."

### Transliteration

40. Hatta itha jaa amruna wafara alttannooru qulna ihmil feeha min kullin zawjayni ithnayni waahlaka illa man sabaqa AAalayhi alqawlu waman amana wama amana maAAahu illa qaleelun

### Tafsir Ibn Kathir

### The beginning of the Flood and Nuh loads Every Creature in Pairs upon the Ship

This was the promise of Allah to Nuh, when the command of Allah came, the rain was continuous and there was a severe storm which did not slacken or subside, as Allah said,

(So We opened the gates of the heaven with water pouring forth. And We caused springs to gush forth from the earth. So the waters (of the heaven and the earth) met for a matter predestined. And We carried him on a (ship) made of planks and nails. Floating under Our Eyes: a reward for him who had been rejected!)(54:11-14) In reference to Allah's statement,

(and the oven gushed forth.) It is related from Ibn `Abbas that he said, "At-Tannur is the face of the earth." This verse means that the face of the earth became gushing water springs. This continued until the water gushed forth from the Tananir, which are places of fire. Therefore, water even gushed from the places where fire normally would be. This is the opinion of the majority of the Salaf (predecessors) and the scholars of the Khalaf (later generations). At this point, Allah commanded Nuh to select one pair from every kind of creature possessing a soul, and load them on the ship. Some said that this included other creatures as well, such as pairs of plants, male and female. It has also been said that the first of the birds to enter the ship was the parrot, and the last of the animals to enter was the donkey. Concerning Allah's statement,

(and your family -- except him against whom the Word has already gone forth) This means, "Load your family upon the ship." This is referring to the members of his household and his relatives, except him against whom the Word has already gone forth, for they did not believe in Allah. Among them was the son of Nuh, Yam, who went in hermitage. Among them was the wife of Nuh who was a disbeliever in Allah and His Messenger. Concerning Allah's statement, (and those who believe.) from your people.

(And none believed with him, except a few.) This means that only a very small number believed, even after the long period of time that he (Nuh) was among them -- nine hundred and fifty years. It is reported from Ibn `Abbas that he said, "They were eighty people including their women."

### Surah: 11 Ayah: 41, Ayah: 42 & Ayah: 43

﴿ ۞ وَقَالَ ٱرْكَبُوا۟ فِيهَا بِسْمِ ٱللَّهِ مَجْرٜىٰهَا وَمُرْسَىٰهَآ إِنَّ رَبِّى لَغَفُورٌ رَّحِيمٌ ۝ ﴾

76. And he (Nûh (Noah) (peace be upon him)) said: "Embark therein: in the Name of Allâh will be its (moving) course and its (resting) anchorage. Surely, my Lord is Oft-Forgiving, Most Merciful." (Tafsir At-Tabarî)

﴿ وَهِىَ تَجْرِى بِهِمْ فِى مَوْجٍ كَٱلْجِبَالِ وَنَادَىٰ نُوحٌ ٱبْنَهُۥ وَكَانَ فِى مَعْزِلٍ يَٰبُنَىَّ ٱرْكَب مَّعَنَا وَلَا تَكُن مَّعَ ٱلْكَٰفِرِينَ ۝ ﴾

77. So it (the ship) sailed with them amidst waves like mountains, and Nûh (Noah) called out to his son, who had separated himself (apart), "O my son! Embark with us and be not with the disbelievers."

﴿ قَالَ سَـَٔاوِىٓ إِلَىٰ جَبَلٍ يَعْصِمُنِى مِنَ ٱلْمَآءِ ۚ قَالَ لَا عَاصِمَ ٱلْيَوْمَ مِنْ أَمْرِ ٱللَّهِ إِلَّا مَن رَّحِمَ ۚ وَحَالَ بَيْنَهُمَا ٱلْمَوْجُ فَكَانَ مِنَ ٱلْمُغْرَقِينَ ۝ ﴾

78. (The son) replied: "I will betake myself to some mountain; it will save me from the water." Nûh (Noah) said: "This day there is no savior from the Decree of Allâh except him on whom He has mercy." And waves came in between them, so he (the son) was among the drowned.

### Transliteration

41. Waqala irkaboo feeha bismi Allahi majraha wamursaha inna rabbee laghafoorun raheemun 42. Wahiya tajree bihim fee mawjin kaaljibali wanada noohunu ibnahu wakana fee maAAzilin ya bunayya irkab maAAana wala takun maAAa alkafireena 43. Qala saawee ila jabalin yaAAsimunee mina alma-i qala la AAasima alyawma min amri Allahi illa man rahima wahala baynahuma almawju fakana mina almughraqeena

### Tafsir Ibn Kathir

#### The riding upon the Ship and Its sailing through the huge Waves

Allah, the Exalted, says concerning Nuh, that he said to those whom he was commanded to carry them with him in the ship,

(Embark therein: in the Name of Allah will be its (moving) course and its (resting) anchorage.) This means that its sailing upon the surface of the water, the end of its journeying and its anchoring, would all be with the Name of Allah. Abu Raja' Al-

`Utaridi recited it, (وَمُرْسِيهَا مُجرِيهَا اللهِ بِسْمِ) "In the Name of Allah, Who will be the One Who moves its course, and rests its anchor." Allah, the Exalted, said,

(And when you have embarked on the ship, you and whoever is with you, then say: "All the praises and thanks are to Allah, Who has saved us from the people who are wrongdoers. And say: "My Lord! Cause me to land at a blessed landing place, for You are the Best of those who bring to land.")(23:28-29) For this reason, it is preferred to mention the Name of Allah (Bismillah) at the beginning of all affairs. The Name of Allah should be mentioned when boarding a ship, or when mounting an animal. This is as Allah, the Exalted, says,

(And Who has created all the pairs and has appointed for you ships and cattle on which you ride, in order that you may mount on their backs.)(43:12-13) This practice (mentioning Allah's Name) has been encouraged in the Sunnah and is considered a preferred act. A discussion concerning this is forthcoming in the explanation of Surat Az-Zukhruf (43), if Allah wills. In reference to Allah's statement,

(Surely, my Lord is Oft-Forgiving, Most Merciful.) Such statement is suitable while mentioning (His) vengeance upon the disbelievers by drowning all of them. Therefore, he (Nuh) mentions that His Lord is Oft Forgiving, Most Merciful. This is similar to Allah's statement,

(Surely, your Lord is swift in retribution, and certainly He is Oft-Forgiving, Most Merciful.) (7:167) He also says,

(But verily, your Lord is full of forgiveness for mankind inspite of their wrongdoing. And verily, your Lord is (also) severe in punishment.) (13:6) Likewise, there are many other verses that combine Allah's mercy and His vengeance. Concerning Allah's statement,

(So it sailed with them amidst waves like mountains,) This means that the ship sailed with them upon the surface of the water, which had completely covered the earth until it encompassed the tops of the mountains and even rose over them by a height of fifteen cubits. It was also said that the waves rose over the mountains by a height of eighty miles. Yet, this ship continued to move upon the water, sailing by the permission of Allah. It moved under His shade, His help, His protection and His blessing. This is as Allah, the Exalted, said,

(Verily, when the water rose beyond its limits, We carried you in the ship. That We might make it an admonition for you and it might be retained by the retaining ears.)(69:11-12) Allah also said,

(And We carried him on a (ship) made of planks and nails, floating under Our Eyes: a reward for him who had been rejected! And indeed, We have left this as a sign. Then is there any that will remember (or receive admonition))(54:13-15)

## The Story of the drowning of Nuh's Disbelieving Son

Allah continues the story, saying,

(and Nuh called out to his son,) This was the fourth son of Nuh. His name was Yam and he was a disbeliever. His father, Nuh, called him at the time of boarding the ship, that he might believe and embark with them. If he did so, he would be saved from drowning like the other disbelievers.

(The son replied: "I will betake myself to some mountain, it will save me from the water.") He believed, in his ignorance, that the flood would not reach the tops of the mountains and that if he clung to the top of a mountain, he would be saved from drowning. His father, Nuh, said to him,

(This day there is no savior from the decree of Allah except him on whom He has mercy.) This means that nothing will be saved today from the command of Allah.

(And waves came in between them, so he (the son) was among the drowned.)

### Surah: 11 Ayah: 44

﴿ وَقِيلَ يَٰأَرْضُ ٱبْلَعِى مَآءَكِ وَيَٰسَمَآءُ أَقْلِعِى وَغِيضَ ٱلْمَآءُ وَقُضِىَ ٱلْأَمْرُ وَٱسْتَوَتْ عَلَى ٱلْجُودِىِّ وَقِيلَ بُعْدًا لِّلْقَوْمِ ٱلظَّٰلِمِينَ ﴾

79. And it was said: "O earth! Swallow up your water, and O sky! Withhold (your rain)." And the water was made to subside and the Decree (of Allâh) was fulfilled (i.e. the destruction of the people of Nûh (Noah). And it (the ship) rested on Mount Jûdî, and it was said: "Away with the people who are Zalimûn (polytheists and wrong-doing)!"

### Transliteration

44. Waqeela ya ardu iblaAAee maaki waya samao aqliAAee wagheeda almao waqudiya al-amru waistawat AAala aljoodiyyi waqeela buAAdan lilqawmi alththalimeena

### Tafsir Ibn Kathir

**The End of the Flood**

Allah, the Exalted, informs that when the people of the earth were all drowned, except for the people on the ship, He commanded the earth to swallow its water, which had sprang from it and gathered upon it. Then He commanded the sky to cease raining.

(And the water was made to subside) This means that it (the water) began to decrease.

(and the decree was fulfilled.) This means that all of those who disbelieved in Allah were removed from the people of the earth. Not a single one of them remained upon the earth.

(And it (the ship) rested) This is referring to the ship and those who were in it.

# Chapter 11: Hud (Hud), Verses 006-123

(on (Mount) Judi.) Mujahid said, "Judi is a mountain in Al-Jazirah (Northwest Mesopotamia) where the mountains sought to tower above each other on the day of the drowning. On that day of destruction, all the mountains sought to be higher (to avoid being overcome by the water). However, this mountain (Judi) humbled itself for Allah, the Mighty and Sublime, and therefore it was not drowned. This is why Nuh's ship anchored upon it." Qatadah said, "The ship rested upon it (Mount Judi) for a month before they (the people) came down from it. " Qatadah also said, "Allah made Nuh's ship remain on Mount Judi in the land of Al-Jazirah, as a lesson and a sign." Even the early generations of this Ummah saw it. How many ships are there that have come after it and have been destroyed and became dust

(and it was said: "Away with the people who are wrongdoing!") means destruction and loss for them. The term "away with" here implies being far away from the mercy of Allah. For verily, they were destroyed to the last of them, and none of them survived.

## Surah: 11 Ayah: 45, Ayah: 46 & Ayah: 47

﴿ وَنَادَىٰ نُوحٌ رَّبَّهُۥ فَقَالَ رَبِّ إِنَّ ٱبۡنِي مِنۡ أَهۡلِي وَإِنَّ وَعۡدَكَ ٱلۡحَقُّ وَأَنتَ أَحۡكَمُ ٱلۡحَٰكِمِينَ ﴾

80. And Nûh (Noah) called upon his Lord and said, "O my Lord! Verily, my son is of my family! And certainly, Your Promise is true, and You are the Most Just of the judges."

﴿ قَالَ يَٰنُوحُ إِنَّهُۥ لَيۡسَ مِنۡ أَهۡلِكَ إِنَّهُۥ عَمَلٌ غَيۡرُ صَٰلِحٍ فَلَا تَسۡـَٔلۡنِ مَا لَيۡسَ لَكَ بِهِۦ عِلۡمٌ إِنِّيٓ أَعِظُكَ أَن تَكُونَ مِنَ ٱلۡجَٰهِلِينَ ﴾

81. He said: "O Nûh (Noah)! Surely, he is not of your family; verily, his work is unrighteous, so ask not of Me that of which you have no knowledge! I admonish you, lest you be one of the ignorant."

﴿ قَالَ رَبِّ إِنِّيٓ أَعُوذُ بِكَ أَنۡ أَسۡـَٔلَكَ مَا لَيۡسَ لِي بِهِۦ عِلۡمٌ وَإِلَّا تَغۡفِرۡ لِي وَتَرۡحَمۡنِيٓ أَكُن مِّنَ ٱلۡخَٰسِرِينَ ﴾

82. Nûh (Noah) said: "O my Lord! I seek refuge with You from asking You that of which I have no knowledge. And unless You forgive me and have Mercy on me, I would indeed be one of the losers."

### Transliteration

45. Wanada noohun rabbahu faqala rabbi inna ibnee min ahlee wa-inna waAAdaka alhaqqu waanta ahkamu alhakimeena  46. Qala ya noohu innahu laysa min ahlika innahu AAamalun ghayru salihin fala tas-alni ma laysa laka bihi AAilmun innee aAAithuka an takoona mina aljahileena  47. Qala rabbi innee aAAoothu bika an as-

alaka ma laysa lee bihi AAilmun wa-illa taghfir lee watarhamnee akun mina alkhasireena

### Tafsir Ibn Kathir

### A Return to the Story of the Son of Nuh and mentioning what transpired between Nuh and Allah concerning Him

This was a request for information and an inquiry from Nuh concerning the cirumstances of his son's drowning.

(and said, "O my Lord! Verily, my son is of my family!") This means, "Verily, You promised to save my family and Your promise is the truth that does not fail. Therefore, how can he (my son) be drowned and You are the Most Just of the judges"

(He (Allah) said: "O Nuh! Surely, he is not of your family...") This means, "He (your son) is not of those whom I promised to save. I only promised you that I would save those of your family who believe." For this reason Allah said,

I(and your family except him against whom the Word has already gone forth.) (11:40) Thus, for his son, it had already been decreed that he would be drowned due to his disbelief and his opposition to his father, the Prophet of Allah, Nuh peace be upon him. Concerning Allah's statement,

(Surely, he is not of your family;) meaning that he (Nuh's son) was not among those whom Allah promised to save. `Abdur-Razzaq recorded that Ibn `Abbas said, "He was the son of Nuh, but he opposed him in deeds and intention." `Ikrimah said in some of the modes of recitation it said here, "Verily, he (Nuh's son) worked deeds that were not righteous."

### Surah: 11 Ayah: 48

﴿ قِيلَ يَـٰنُوحُ ٱهْبِطْ بِسَلَـٰمٍ مِّنَّا وَبَرَكَـٰتٍ عَلَيْكَ وَعَلَىٰٓ أُمَمٍ مِّمَّن مَّعَكَ وَأُمَمٌ سَنُمَتِّعُهُمْ ثُمَّ يَمَسُّهُم مِّنَّا عَذَابٌ أَلِيمٌ ﴾

83. It was said: "O Nûh (Noah)! Come down (from the ship) with peace from Us and blessings on you and on the people who are with you (and on some of their off-spring), but (there will be other) people to whom We shall grant their pleasures (for a time), but in the end a painful torment will reach them from Us."

### Transliteration

48. Qeela ya noohu ihbit bisalamin minna wabarakatin AAalayka waAAala omamin mimman maAAaka waomamun sanumattiAAuhum thumma yamassuhum minna AAathabun aleemun

## Tafsir Ibn Kathir

### The Command to descend from the Ship with Peace and Blessings

Allah, the Exalted, informs of what was said to Nuh when the ship anchored on Mount Judi, peace be upon him, peace were sent upon him and the believers with him. This salutation was also for every believer from his progeny until the Day of Resurrection. Muhammad bin Ka`b said, "Every male and female believer until the Day of Resurrection is included in this salutation of peace. Likewise, every male and female disbeliever until the Day of Resurrection is included in this promise of torment and pleasure. Muhammad bin Ishaq said, "When Allah wanted to stop the flood, He sent a wind upon the face of the earth that caused the water to be still. Then the springs of the earth were closed off from the great flooding and the pouring (rain) from the sky halted. Allah, the Exalted, says,

(And it was said: "O earth! Swallow up your water...") (11:44) Thus, the water began decreasing and subsiding until the ship settled on Mount Judi. The People of the Tawrah (the Jews) claim that this occurred during the seventh month (of the year) and it lasted for seventeen nights. Then, on the first day of the tenth month, he (Nuh) saw the mountain tops. Then after forty more days, Nuh opened the small window in the roof of the ship and he sent a raven out to see what the water had done. However, the raven did not return to him. Then, he sent a pigeon out but it returned to him without finding any place (land) to put its two feet down. He extended his hand out of the ship and the pigeon grabbed his hand so that Nuh could pull it back into the ship. Then, after seven more days passed, he sent the pigeon out again to investigate for him. The pigeon returned in the evening with a leaf from an olive tree in its mouth. From this, Nuh knew that the water had decreased from the face of the earth. He remained in the ship for seven more days before he sent the pigeon out again. This time the pigeon did not return to him, so he knew that the earth had appeared. Thus, a year was completed from the time that Allah sent the flood, until the time of Nuh sending the pigeon. The first day of the first month of the second year began when the face of the earth appeared and land became visible. This is when Nuh uncovered the opening of the ship. During the second month of the second year, after twenty six nights,

(It was said: "O Nuh! Come down (from the ship) with peace from Us)

### Surah: 11 Ayah: 49

﴿تِلْكَ مِنْ أَنۢبَآءِ ٱلْغَيْبِ نُوحِيهَآ إِلَيْكَ مَا كُنتَ تَعْلَمُهَآ أَنتَ وَلَا قَوْمُكَ مِن قَبْلِ هَـٰذَا ۖ فَٱصْبِرْ ۖ إِنَّ ٱلْعَـٰقِبَةَ لِلْمُتَّقِينَ ۞﴾

84. This is of the news of the Unseen which We reveal unto you (O Muhammad (peace be upon him)) neither you nor your people knew it before this. So be patient. Surely, the (good) end is for the Muttaqûn (pious - see V.2:2)

### Transliteration

49. Tilka min anba-i alghaybi nooheeha ilayka ma kunta taAAlamuha anta wala qawmuka min qabli hatha faisbir inna alAAaqibata lilmuttaqeena

### Tafsir Ibn Kathir

## The Explanation of These Stories is a Proof of the Revelation of Allah to His Messenger

Allah, the Exalted, says to His Prophet concerning these stories and their like,

(of the news of the Unseen) from the information of the unseen of the past. Allah revealed it to you (the Prophet ) in the way that it occurred, as if he witnessed it himself.

(which We reveal unto you;) This means, "We teach it to you (Muhammad) as revelation from Us to you."

(neither you nor your people knew it before this.) This means that neither you (Muhammad ) nor anyone of your people, have any knowledge of this. This is so that no one who rejects you can say that you learned it from him. Rather, it was Allah Who informed you of it in conformity with the true situation (of the story), just as the Books of the Prophets who were before you testify to. Therefore, you should be patient with the rejection of your people and their harming you. For verily, We shall help you and surround you with Our aid. Then, We will make the (good) end for you and those who follow you in this life and the Hereafter. This is what We did with the Messengers when We helped them against their enemies.

(Verily, We will indeed make victorious Our Messengers and those who believe.) Allah also said,

(And, verily, Our Word has gone forth of old for Our servants, the Messengers, that they verily, would be made triumphant.) (37:171-172) Then, Allah says,

(So be patient. Surely, the (good) end is for those who have Taqwa.)

### Surah: 11 Ayah: 50, Ayah: 51 & Ayah: 52

﴿ وَإِلَىٰ عَادٍ أَخَاهُمْ هُودًا ۚ قَالَ يَـٰقَوْمِ ٱعْبُدُواْ ٱللَّهَ مَا لَكُم مِّنْ إِلَـٰهٍ غَيْرُهُۥٓ ۖ إِنْ أَنتُمْ إِلَّا مُفْتَرُونَ ﴿٥٠﴾ ﴾

85. And to 'Ad (people We sent) their brother Hûd. He said, "O my people! Worship Allâh! You have no other Ilâh (god) but Him. Certainly, you do nothing but invent lies!

$$\text{﴿ يَـٰقَوْمِ لَآ أَسْـَٔلُكُمْ عَلَيْهِ أَجْرًا ۖ إِنْ أَجْرِىَ إِلَّا عَلَى ٱلَّذِى فَطَرَنِىٓ ۚ أَفَلَا تَعْقِلُونَ ﴾}$$

86. "O my people I ask of you no reward for it (the Message). My reward is only from Him Who created me. Will you not then understand?

$$\text{﴿ وَيَـٰقَوْمِ ٱسْتَغْفِرُوا۟ رَبَّكُمْ ثُمَّ تُوبُوٓا۟ إِلَيْهِ يُرْسِلِ ٱلسَّمَآءَ عَلَيْكُم مِّدْرَارًا وَيَزِدْكُمْ قُوَّةً إِلَىٰ قُوَّتِكُمْ وَلَا تَتَوَلَّوْا۟ مُجْرِمِينَ ﴾}$$

87. "And O my people! Ask forgiveness of your Lord and then repent to Him, He will send you (from the sky) abundant rain, and add strength to your strength, so do not turn away as Mujrimûn (criminals, disbelievers in the Oneness of Allâh)."

### Transliteration

50. Wa-ila AAadin akhahum hoodan qala ya qawmi oAAbudoo Allaha ma lakum min ilahin ghayruhu in antum illa muftaroona 51. Ya qawmi la as-alukum AAalayhi ajran in ajriya illa AAala allathee fataranee afala taAAqiloona 52. Waya qawmi istaghfiroo rabbakum thumma tooboo ilayhi yursili alssamaa AAalaykum midraran wayazidkum quwwatan ila quwwatikum wala tatawallaw mujrimeena

### Tafsir Ibn Kathir

### The Story of Prophet Hud and the People of `Ad

Allah, the Exalted, says, (And) This is an introductory to what is implied: "Verily, We sent."

(to the `Ad (people) their brother Hud.) Hud came to them commanding them to worship Allah alone, without any associates. He forbade them from worshipping the idols which they made up, inventing names as gods. He informed them that he did not want any reward from them for his sincere advising and conveying of Allah's Message. He only sought his reward from Allah, the One Who created him.

(Will you not then understand) Someone has come calling you to what will benefit your situation in this life and the Hereafter without asking for any wage (from them). Then he commanded them to seek the forgiveness of the One Who is capable of expiating previous sins. He also commanded them to repent for that which they may do in the future. Whoever has these characteristics, Allah will make his sustenance easy for him, grant him ease in his affairs and guard over his situation. For this reason Allah says,

(He will send you (from the sky) abundant rain,)

## Surah: 11 Ayah: 53, Ayah: 54, Ayah: 55 & Ayah: 56

﴿ قَالُواْ يَـٰهُودُ مَا جِئْتَنَا بِبَيِّنَةٍ وَمَا نَحْنُ بِتَارِكِى ءَالِهَتِنَا عَن قَوْلِكَ وَمَا نَحْنُ لَكَ بِمُؤْمِنِينَ ۝ ﴾

88. They said: "O Hûd! No evidence have you brought us, and we shall not leave our gods for your (mere) saying! And we are not believers in you.

﴿ إِن نَّقُولُ إِلَّا ٱعْتَرَىٰكَ بَعْضُ ءَالِهَتِنَا بِسُوٓءٍ ۗ قَالَ إِنِّىٓ أُشْهِدُ ٱللَّهَ وَٱشْهَدُوٓاْ أَنِّى بَرِىٓءٌ مِّمَّا تُشْرِكُونَ ۝ ﴾

89. "All that we say is that some of our gods (false deities) have seized you with evil (madness)." He said: "I call Allâh to witness and bear you witness that I am free from that which you ascribe as partners in worship,

﴿ مِن دُونِهِۦ ۖ فَكِيدُونِى جَمِيعًا ثُمَّ لَا تُنظِرُونِ ۝ ﴾

90. With Him (Allâh). So plot against me, all of you, and give me no respite.

﴿ إِنِّى تَوَكَّلْتُ عَلَى ٱللَّهِ رَبِّى وَرَبِّكُمْ ۚ مَّا مِن دَآبَّةٍ إِلَّا هُوَ ءَاخِذٌۢ بِنَاصِيَتِهَآ ۚ إِنَّ رَبِّى عَلَىٰ صِرَٰطٍ مُّسْتَقِيمٍ ۝ ﴾

91. "I put my trust in Allâh, my Lord and your Lord! There is not a moving (living) creature but He has grasp of its forelock. Verily, my Lord is on the Straight Path (the truth).

### Transliteration

53. Qaloo ya hoodu ma ji/tana bibayyinatin wama nahnu bitarikee alihatina AAan qawlika wama nahnu laka bimu/mineena  54. In naqoolu illa iAAtaraka baAAdu alihatina bisoo-in qala innee oshhidu Allaha waishhadoo annee baree-on mimma tushrikoona  55. Min doonihi fakeedoonee jameeAAan thumma la tunthirooni  56. Innee tawakkaltu AAala Allahi rabbee warabbikum ma min dabbatin illa huwa akhithun binasiyatiha inna rabbee AAala siratin mustaqeemin

### Tafsir Ibn Kathir

#### The Conversation between (the People of) `Ad and Hud

Allah, the Exalted, informs that they said to their Prophet,

(No evidence have you brought us.) This means that they claimed that Hud had not brought them any proof or evidence for what he claimed.

Chapter 11: Hud (Hud), Verses 006-123                                                                    49

(and we shall not leave our gods for your (mere) saying!) They were saying how could his mere statement, "Leave these gods," be sufficient proof for them to leave their idols

(and we are not believers in you.) This means that they did not believe what he was saying was true.

(All that we say is that some of our gods have seized you with evil.) They were saying, "We think that some of our idols have afflicted you with madness and insanity in your intellect because you are trying to stop them from being worshipped and defame them."

(He said: "I call Allah to witness and bear you witness, that I am free from that which you ascribe as partners in worship besides Him (Allah).)(11:54-55) Here, he is saying, "Verily, I am innocent of all of the rivals and idols (that you associate with Allah).

(So plot against me, all of you,) you and your gods if they are true."

(and give me no respite.) the blinking of an eye." Then, Allah says,

(I put my trust in Allah, my Lord and your Lord! There is not a moving creature but He has the grasp of its forelock.) Every creature is under His (Allah's) power and His authority. He is the Best Judge, the Most Just, Who does not do any injustice in His ruling. For verily, He is upon the straight path. Verily, this argument contains a far-reaching proof and absolute evidence of the truthfulness of what Hud had come to them with. It also proves the falsehood of them worshipping idols that could not benefit nor harm them. Rather, these idols were inanimate objects that could not hear, see, befriend, or make enmity. The only One Who is worthy of having worship directed solely towards Him is Allah alone, without any partners. He is the One in Whose Hand is the sovereignty and He is in control of all things. There is nothing except that it is under His owner- ship, power and authority. Thus, there is no deity worthy of worship except Him and there is no Lord other than Him.

### Surah: 11 Ayah: 57, Ayah: 58, Ayah: 59 & Ayah: 60

﴿ فَإِن تَوَلَّوْاْ فَقَدْ أَبْلَغْتُكُم مَّآ أُرْسِلْتُ بِهِۦٓ إِلَيْكُمْۚ وَيَسْتَخْلِفُ رَبِّى قَوْمًا غَيْرَكُمْ وَلَا تَضُرُّونَهُۥ شَيْـًٔاۚ إِنَّ رَبِّى عَلَىٰ كُلِّ شَىْءٍ حَفِيظٌ ۝ ﴾

92. "So if you turn away, still I have conveyed the Message with which I was sent to you. My Lord will make another people succeed you, and you will not harm Him in the least. Surely, my Lord is Guardian over all things."

﴿ وَلَمَّا جَآءَ أَمْرُنَا نَجَّيْنَا هُودًا وَٱلَّذِينَ ءَامَنُواْ مَعَهُۥ بِرَحْمَةٍ مِّنَّا وَنَجَّيْنَٰهُم مِّنْ عَذَابٍ غَلِيظٍ ۝ ﴾

93. And when Our Commandment came, We saved Hûd and those who believed with him by a Mercy from Us, and We saved them from a severe torment.

﴿ وَتِلْكَ عَادٌ ۖ جَحَدُواْ بِـَٔايَـٰتِ رَبِّهِمْ وَعَصَوْاْ رُسُلَهُۥ وَٱتَّبَعُوٓاْ أَمْرَ كُلِّ جَبَّارٍ عَنِيدٍ ۝ ﴾

94. Such were 'Ad (people). They rejected the Ayât (proofs, evidences, verses, lessons, signs, revelations, etc.) of their Lord and disobeyed His Messengers, and followed the command of every proud obstinate (oppressor of the truth, from their leaders).

﴿ وَأُتْبِعُواْ فِى هَـٰذِهِ ٱلدُّنْيَا لَعْنَةً وَيَوْمَ ٱلْقِيَـٰمَةِ ۗ أَلَآ إِنَّ عَادًا كَفَرُواْ رَبَّهُمْ ۗ أَلَا بُعْدًا لِّعَادٍ قَوْمِ هُودٍ ۝ ﴾

95. And they were pursued by a curse in this world and (so they will be) on the Day of Resurrection. No doubt! Verily, 'Ad disbelieved in their Lord. So away with 'Ad, the people of Hûd.

### Transliteration

57. Fa-in tawallaw faqad ablaghtukum ma orsiltu bihi ilaykum wayastakhlifu rabbee qawman ghayrakum wala tadurroonahu shay-an inna rabbee AAala kulli shay-in hafeethun 58. Walamma jaa amruna najjayna hoodan waallatheena amanoo maAAahu birahmatin minna wanajjaynahum min AAathabin ghaleethin 59. Watilka AAadun jahadoo bi-ayati rabbihim waAAasaw rusulahu waittabaAAoo amra kulli jabbarin AAaneedin 60. WaotbiAAoo fee hathihi alddunya laAAnatan wayawma alqiyamati ala inna AAadan kafaroo rabbahum ala buAAdan liAAadin qawmi hoodin

### Tafsir Ibn Kathir

Hud says to them, "If you turn away from that which I have brought to you in reference to worship of Allah, Who is your Lord alone, without any partners, then the proof has been established against you. This is because I have conveyed the Message of Allah to you, which He has sent me with."

(My Lord will make another people succeed you, ) This refers to a group of people who will worship Allah alone, without associating anything with Him. This also implies that the polytheists do not bother Allah and they do not harm Him in the least with their disbelief. To the contrary, their disbelief merely harms their own selves.

(Surely, my Lord is Guardian over all things.) This means that Allah is a Witness and Guardian over the statements of His servants and their actions. He will give them due recompense for their actions. If they do good deeds, He will reward them with good. If they do evil, He will punish them with evil.

Chapter 11: Hud (Hud), Verses 006-123                                              51

## The Destruction of the People of `Ad and the Salvation of Those among Them Who believed

(And when Our commandment came,) This is referring to the barren wind with which Allah destroyed them, to the very last of them. The mercy and kindness of Allah, the Exalted saved Hud and his followers from this terrible punishment.

g(Such were `Ad (people). They rejected the Ayat of their Lord) This means they disbelieved in the proofs and revelations (of Allah) and they disobeyed the Messengers of Allah. This is due to the fact that whoever disbelieves in a Prophet, then verily, he has disbelieved in all of the Prophets, peace be upon them. There is no difference between any one of them, in the sense that it is necessary to believe in all of them. Therefore, `Ad disbelieved in Hud and their disbelief was considered disbelief in all of the Messengers.

(and followed the command of every proud, obstinate.) This means that they abandoned following their rightly guided Messenger and they followed the command of every proud, obstinate person. Thus, they were followed in this life by a curse from Allah and His believing servants whenever they are mentioned. On the Day of Resurrection a call will be made against them in front of witnesses.

(Verily, `Ad disbelieved in their Lord.)

### Surah: 11 Ayah: 61

﴿ ۞ وَإِلَىٰ ثَمُودَ أَخَاهُمْ صَـٰلِحًا ۚ قَالَ يَـٰقَوْمِ ٱعْبُدُوا۟ ٱللَّهَ مَا لَكُم مِّنْ إِلَـٰهٍ غَيْرُهُۥ ۖ هُوَ أَنشَأَكُم مِّنَ ٱلْأَرْضِ وَٱسْتَعْمَرَكُمْ فِيهَا فَٱسْتَغْفِرُوهُ ثُمَّ تُوبُوٓا۟ إِلَيْهِ ۚ إِنَّ رَبِّى قَرِيبٌ مُّجِيبٌ ﴿٦١﴾ ﴾

96. And to Thamûd (people We sent) their brother Sâlih. He said: "O my people! Worship Allâh, you have no other Ilâh (god) but Him. He brought you forth from the earth and settled you therein, then ask forgiveness of Him and turn to Him in repentance. Certainly, my Lord is Near (to all by His Knowledge), Responsive."

### Transliteration

61. Wa-ila thamooda akhahum salihan qala ya qawmi oAAbudoo Allaha ma lakum min ilahin ghayruhu huwa anshaakum mina al-ardi waistaAAmarakum feeha faistaghfiroohu thumma tooboo ilayhi inna rabbee qareebun mujeebun

### Tafsir Ibn Kathir

### The Story of Salih and the People of Thamud

Allah, the Exalted, says, (And) This is an introduction to that which is implied, "Verily, We sent."

(to Thamud) They were a group of people who were living in cities carved from the rocks, between Tabuk and Al-Madinah (in Arabia). They lived after the people of `Ad, so Allah sent to them,

(their brother Salih.) He (Salih) commanded them to worship Allah alone. He said to them,

(He brought you forth from the earth) This means: `He began your creation from it (the earth). From it He created your father, Adam.'

(and settled you therein,) This means: `He made you prosperous in the earth. You are settled in it and you treasure it.'

(then ask forgiveness) `This is in reference to your previous sins. '

(and turn to Him in repentance.) `This is in reference to the future.'

(Certainly, my Lord is Near (to all by His knowledge), Responsive.) This is similar to Allah's statement,

(And when My servants ask you concerning Me, then (answer them), I am indeed Near (to them by My knowledge). I respond to the invocations of the supplicant when he calls on Me.) (2:186)

### Surah: 11 Ayah: 62 & Ayah: 63

﴿ قَالُوا۟ يَـٰصَـٰلِحُ قَدْ كُنتَ فِينَا مَرْجُوًّا قَبْلَ هَـٰذَآ أَتَنْهَىٰنَآ أَن نَّعْبُدَ مَا يَعْبُدُ ءَابَآؤُنَا وَإِنَّنَا لَفِى شَكٍّ مِّمَّا تَدْعُونَآ إِلَيْهِ مُرِيبٍ ﴾

97. They said: "O Sâlih! You have been among us as a figure of good hope (and we wished for you to be our chief) till this (new thing which you have brought that we leave our gods and worship your God (Allâh) Alone)! Do you (now) forbid us the worship of what our fathers have worshipped? But we are really in grave doubt as to that which you invite us to (monotheism)."

﴿ قَالَ يَـٰقَوْمِ أَرَءَيْتُمْ إِن كُنتُ عَلَىٰ بَيِّنَةٍ مِّن رَّبِّى وَءَاتَىٰنِى مِنْهُ رَحْمَةً فَمَن يَنصُرُنِى مِنَ ٱللَّهِ إِنْ عَصَيْتُهُۥ فَمَا تَزِيدُونَنِى غَيْرَ تَخْسِيرٍ ﴾

98. He said: "O my people! Tell me, if I have a clear proof from my Lord, and there has come to me a Mercy (Prophethood) from Him, who then can help me against Allâh, if I were to disobey Him? Then you increase me not but in loss.

### Transliteration

62. Qaloo ya salihu qad kunta feena marjuwwan qabla hatha atanhana an naAAbuda ma yaAAbudu abaona wa-innana lafee shakkin mimma tadAAoona ilayhi mureebun
63. Qala ya qawmi araaytum in kuntu AAala bayyinatin min rabbee waatanee minhu

rahmatan faman yansurunee mina Allahi in AAasaytuhu fama tazeedoonanee ghayra takhseerin

### Tafsir Ibn Kathir

### The Conversation between Salih and the People of Thamud

Allah, the Exalted, mentions what transpired in the discussion between Salih and his people. Allah informs of their ignorance and obstinacy in their statement,

(You have been among us as a figure of good hope till this!) They were saying in this, "We had hope in your strong intellect before you began saying what you have said."

(Do you (now) forbid us the worship of what our fathers have worshipped) "what those who were before us were upon."

(But we are really in grave doubt as to that which you invite us.) This alludes to the great amount of doubt that they had.

(He said: "O my people! Tell me, if I have a clear proof from my Lord...") `In reference to what He (Allah) has sent me with to you, I am upon conviction and sure evidence.'

(and there has come to me a mercy from Him, who then can help me against Allah, if I were to disobey Him) `and abandon calling you to the truth and the worship of Allah alone. If I did so, you would not be able to bring me any benefit, nor increase me

(but in loss.)' This means loss and ruin.

### Surah: 11 Ayah: 64, Ayah: 65, Ayah: 66, Ayah: 67 & Ayah: 68

﴿ وَيَـٰقَوْمِ هَـٰذِهِۦ نَاقَةُ ٱللَّهِ لَكُمْ ءَايَةً فَذَرُوهَا تَأْكُلْ فِىٓ أَرْضِ ٱللَّهِ وَلَا تَمَسُّوهَا بِسُوٓءٍ فَيَأْخُذَكُمْ عَذَابٌ قَرِيبٌ ۝ ﴾

99. "And O my people! This she-camel of Allâh is a sign to you, so leave her to feed (graze) on Allâh's land, and touch her not with evil, lest a near torment should seize you."

﴿ فَعَقَرُوهَا فَقَالَ تَمَتَّعُوا۟ فِى دَارِكُمْ ثَلَـٰثَةَ أَيَّامٍ ذَٰلِكَ وَعْدٌ غَيْرُ مَكْذُوبٍ ۝ ﴾

100. But they killed her. So he said: "Enjoy yourselves in your homes for three days. This is a promise (i.e. a threat) that will not be belied."

﴿ فَلَمَّا جَآءَ أَمْرُنَا نَجَّيْنَا صَٰلِحًا وَٱلَّذِينَ ءَامَنُوا۟ مَعَهُۥ بِرَحْمَةٍ مِّنَّا وَمِنْ خِزْىِ يَوْمِئِذٍ إِنَّ رَبَّكَ هُوَ ٱلْقَوِىُّ ٱلْعَزِيزُ ۝ ﴾

101. So when Our Commandment came, We saved Sâlih and those who believed with him by a Mercy from Us, and from the disgrace of that Day. Verily, your Lord - He is the All-Strong, the All-Mighty.

﴿ وَأَخَذَ ٱلَّذِينَ ظَلَمُوا۟ ٱلصَّيْحَةُ فَأَصْبَحُوا۟ فِى دِيَٰرِهِمْ جَٰثِمِينَ ۝ ﴾

102. And As-Saîhah (torment - awful cry) overtook the wrong-doers, so they lay (dead), prostrate in their homes,

﴿ كَأَن لَّمْ يَغْنَوْا۟ فِيهَآ أَلَآ إِنَّ ثَمُودَا۟ كَفَرُوا۟ رَبَّهُمْ أَلَا بُعْدًا لِّثَمُودَ ۝ ﴾

103. As if they had never lived there. No doubt! Verily, Thamûd disbelieved in their Lord. So away with Thamûd!

### Transliteration

64. Waya qawmi hathihi naqatu Allahi lakum ayatan fatharooha ta/kul fee ardi Allahi wala tamassooha bisoo-in faya/khuthakum AAathabun qareebun 65. FaAAaqarooha faqala tamattaAAoo fee darikum thalathata ayyamin thalika waAAdun ghayru makthoobin 66. Falamma jaa amruna najjayna salihan waallatheena amanoo maAAahu birahmatin minna wamin khizyi yawmi-ithin inna rabbaka huwa alqawiyyu alAAazeezu 67. Waakhatha allatheena thalamoo alssayhatu faasbahoo fee diyarihim jathimeena 68. Kaan lam yaghnaw feeha ala inna thamooda kafaroo rabbahum ala buAAdan lithamooda

### Tafsir Ibn Kathir

A discussion of this story has already preceded in Surat Al-A`raf and it is sufficient without having to be repeated here. Allah is the Giver of success.

### Surah: 11 Ayah: 69, Ayah: 70, Ayah: 71, Ayah: 72 & Ayah: 73

﴿ وَلَقَدْ جَآءَتْ رُسُلُنَآ إِبْرَٰهِيمَ بِٱلْبُشْرَىٰ قَالُوا۟ سَلَٰمًا قَالَ سَلَٰمٌ فَمَا لَبِثَ أَن جَآءَ بِعِجْلٍ حَنِيذٍ ۝ ﴾

104. And verily, there came Our Messengers to Ibrâhîm (Abraham) with glad tidings. They said: Salâm (greetings or peace!) He answered, Salâm (greetings or peace!) and he hastened to entertain them with a roasted calf.

﴿ فَلَمَّا رَءَآ أَيْدِيَهُمْ لَا تَصِلُ إِلَيْهِ نَكِرَهُمْ وَأَوْجَسَ مِنْهُمْ خِيفَةً قَالُوا۟ لَا تَخَفْ إِنَّآ أُرْسِلْنَآ إِلَىٰ قَوْمِ لُوطٍ ۝ ﴾

105. But when he saw their hands went not towards it (the meal), he mistrusted them, and conceived a fear of them. They said: "Fear not, we have been sent against the people of Lût (Lot)."

﴿ وَٱمْرَأَتُهُۥ قَآئِمَةٌ فَضَحِكَتْ فَبَشَّرْنَٰهَا بِإِسْحَٰقَ وَمِن وَرَآءِ إِسْحَٰقَ يَعْقُوبَ ۝ ﴾

106. And his wife was standing (there), and she laughed (either, because the messengers did not eat their food or for being glad for the destruction of the people of Lût (Lot)) But We gave her glad tidings of Ishâq (Isaac), and after Ishâq, of Ya'qûb (Jacob).

﴿ قَالَتْ يَٰوَيْلَتَىٰٓ ءَأَلِدُ وَأَنَا۠ عَجُوزٌ وَهَٰذَا بَعْلِى شَيْخًا إِنَّ هَٰذَا لَشَىْءٌ عَجِيبٌ ۝ ﴾

107. She said (in astonishment): "Woe unto me! Shall I bear a child while I am an old woman, and here is my husband an old man? Verily! This is a strange thing!"

﴿ قَالُوٓا۟ أَتَعْجَبِينَ مِنْ أَمْرِ ٱللَّهِ ۖ رَحْمَتُ ٱللَّهِ وَبَرَكَٰتُهُۥ عَلَيْكُمْ أَهْلَ ٱلْبَيْتِ إِنَّهُۥ حَمِيدٌ مَّجِيدٌ ۝ ﴾

108. They said: "Do you wonder at the Decree of Allâh? The Mercy of Allâh and His Blessings be on you, O the family (of Ibrahîm (Abraham)) Surely, He (Allâh) is All-Praiseworthy, All-Glorious."

### Transliteration

69. Walaqad jaat rusuluna ibraheema bialbushra qaloo salaman qala salamun fama labitha an jaa biAAijlin haneethin   70. Falamma raa aydiyahum la tasilu ilayhi nakirahum waawjasa minhum kheefatan qaloo la takhaf inna orsilna ila qawmi lootin   71. Waimraatuhu qa-imatun fadahikat fabashsharnaha bi-ishaqa wamin wara-i ishaqa yaAAqooba   72. Qalat ya waylata aalidu waana AAajoozun wahatha baAAlee shaykhan inna hatha lashay-on AAajeebun   73. Qaloo ataAAjabeena min amri Allahi rahmatu Allahi wabarakatuhu AAalaykum ahla albayti innahu hameedun majeedun

### Tafsir Ibn Kathir

### The Coming of the Angels to Ibrahim and Their Glad Tidings to Him of Ishaq and Ya`qub

Allah, the Exalted, says,

(And verily, there came Our messengers) The word "messengers" here means angels.

(to Ibrahim with the glad tidings.) It has been said that the word "the glad tidings" means, "Receive the glad tidings of Ishaq." Others have said that it means, "The destruction of the people of Prophet Lut." The proof of the correctness of the first view is in Allah's statement,

(Then when the fear had gone away from (the mind of) Ibrahim, and the glad tidings had reached him, he began to plead with Us for the people of Lut.)(11:74)

(They said: "Salaman." He answered, "Salamun.") This means, "Upon you." The scholars of explanation have said, "Ibrahim's reply of `Salamun' was better than that with which they had greeted him with, because the subjective case (Salamun instead of Salaman) alludes to affirmation and eternity. "

(and he hastened to entertain them with a roasted calf.) This means that he (Ibrahim) left with haste in order to bring them food, as a host. The food that he brought was a calf. The word Hanidh means roasted upon heated stones. This meaning has been reported from Ibn `Abbas, Qatadah and others. This is as Allah has said in another verse,

(Then he turned to his household, and brought out a roasted calf. And placed it before them (saying): "Will you not eat")(51:26-27) This verse contains many aspects of the etiquettes of hosting guests.

(But when he saw their hands went not towards it (the meal), he mistrusted them,) This means that he felt estranged from them.

(and conceived a fear of them.) This is because angels are not concerned with food. They do not desire it, nor do they eat it. Therefore, when Ibrahim saw them reject the food that he had brought them, without tasting any of it at all, he felt a mistrust of them.

(and conceived a fear of them. ) As-Suddi said, "When Allah sent the angels to the people of Lut, they set out walking in the form of young men, until they came to Ibrahim and they were hosted by him. When Ibrahim saw them, he rushed to host them.

(Then he turned to his household, and brought out a roasted calf.)(51:26) He slaughtered it (the calf), roasted it on hot stones and brought it to them. Then, he sat down with them. when he placed it before them. (saying): `Will you not eat' They said, `O Ibrahim! Verily, we do not eat food without a price.' Ibrahim then said, `Verily, this food has a price.' They said, `What is its price' He said, `You must mention the Name of Allah over it before eating it and praise Allah upon finishing it.' Jibril then looked at Mika'il and said, `This man has the right that his Lord should take him as an intimate friend.'

(But when he saw their hands went not towards it (the meal), he mistrusted them,) When Ibrahim saw that they were not eating, he became scared and frightened by them. Then, when Sarah looked and saw that he was honoring them, she began to serve them and she was laughing. She said, `What amazing guests we have. We serve them ourselves, showing them respect and they do not eat our food.'" Then, concerning Allah's statement about the angels,

(They said: "Fear not,") They were saying, "Do not be afraid of us. Verily, we are angels sent to the people of Lut in order to destroy them." Then, Sarah laughed in delight of the good news of their destruction. This is because they had caused much corruption and their disbelief was severe. For this reason, she was rewarded with the glad tidings of a son, even after her despair. Concerning Allah's statement,

(and after Ishaq, of Ya`qub.) This means that the son that she was going to have would have a son (her grandson) who would succeed him and beget many children. For verily, Ya`qub was the son of Ishaq, just as Allah says in Surat Al-Baqarah,

(Or were you witnesses when death approached Ya'qub When he said unto his sons, "What will you worship after me" They said, "We shall worship your God, the God of your fathers, Ibrahim, Isma`il, Ishaq, One God, and to him we submit.") (2:133) From this point in this verse there is an evidence for those who say that Isma`il was the son of Ibrahim who was to be sacrificed. It could not have been Ishaq, because the glad tidings were given that he would have a son born to him named Ya`qub. So how could Ibrahim be commanded to sacrifice him when he was a small child and there had not been born to him a child yet, named Ya`qub, who was promised The promise of Allah is true and there is no breaking of Allah's promise. Therefore, it is not possible that Ibrahim was to sacrifice this child (Ishaq) with the condition being as it was. This makes it clear that Isma`il was the son that was to be sacrificed and this is the best, most correct and clearest evidence of that. And all praise is due to Allah. 9

(She said (in astonishment): "Woe unto me! Shall I bear a child while I am an old woman, and here is my husband an old man") Allah speaks of her statement in this verse, just as He spoke of her action in another verse.

(Then his wife came forward with a loud voice: she smote her face, and said: "A barren old woman!")(51:29) This was the custom of the women in their speech and actions when they were expressing amazement.

(Then said: "Do you wonder at the decree of Allah") This means that the angels were saying to her, "Do not be amazed at the command of Allah, for verily, whenever He wants something, He merely says `Be' and it is. So do not be amazed at this, even though you are old and barren and your husband is a very old man. Verily, Allah is able to do whatever He wills."

(The mercy of Allah and His blessing be on you, O the family (of Ibrahim). Surely, He (Allah) is All-Praiseworthy, All-Glorious.) This means that He is the Most Praiseworthy in all of His actions and statements. He is praised and glorified in His Attributes and His Self. For this reason, it is confirmed in the two Sahihs that they (the Prophet's Companions) said, "Verily, we already know how to greet you with Salam (peace), but how do we send Salah (prayer) upon you, O Messenger of Allah" He said,

«قُولُوا: اللَّهُمَّ صَلِّ عَلَى مُحَمَّدٍ وَعَلَى آلِ مُحَمَّدٍ كَمَا صَلَّيْتَ عَلَى إِبْرَاهِيمَ وَآلِ إِبْرَاهِيمَ، وَبَارِكْ عَلَى مُحَمَّدٍ وَعَلَى آلِ مُحَمَّدٍ كَمَا بَارَكْتَ عَلَى آلِ إِبْرَاهِيمَ إِنَّكَ حَمِيدٌ مَجِيدٌ»

(Say, "O Allah, send prayers upon Muhammad and the family of Muhammad, just as You have sent prayers upon Ibrahim and the family of Ibrahim. And bless Muhammad and the family of Muhammad, just as You have blessed the family of Ibrahim. Truly, You are the All-Praiseworthy, All-Glorious.")

### Surah: 11 Ayah: 74, Ayah: 75 & Ayah: 76

﴿ فَلَمَّا ذَهَبَ عَنْ إِبْرَٰهِيمَ ٱلرَّوْعُ وَجَآءَتْهُ ٱلْبُشْرَىٰ يُجَٰدِلُنَا فِى قَوْمِ لُوطٍ ۝ ﴾

109. Then when the fear had gone away from (the mind of) Ibrahîm (Abraham), and the glad tidings had reached him, he began to plead with Us (Our messengers) for the people of Lût (Lot).

﴿ إِنَّ إِبْرَٰهِيمَ لَحَلِيمٌ أَوَّٰهٌ مُّنِيبٌ ۝ ﴾

110. Verily, Ibrahîm (Abraham) was, without doubt, forbearing, used to invoking Allâh with humility, and was repentant (to Allâh all the time, again and again).

﴿ يَٰٓإِبْرَٰهِيمُ أَعْرِضْ عَنْ هَٰذَآ إِنَّهُۥ قَدْ جَآءَ أَمْرُ رَبِّكَ وَإِنَّهُمْ ءَاتِيهِمْ عَذَابٌ غَيْرُ مَرْدُودٍ ۝ ﴾

111. "O Ibrahîm (Abraham)! Forsake this. Indeed, the Commandment of your Lord has gone forth. Verily, there will come a torment for them which cannot be turned back."

### Transliteration

74. Falamma thahaba AAan ibraheema alrrawAAu wajaat-hu albushra yujadiluna fee qawmi lootin 75. Inna ibraheema lahaleemun awwahun muneebun 76. Ya ibraheemu aAArid AAan hatha innahu qad jaa amru rabbika wa-innahum ateehim AAathabun ghayru mardoodin

### Tafsir Ibn Kathir

**The Dispute of Ibrahim over the People of Lut**

Allah, the Exalted, informs of what happened after the fright of Ibrahim left him and he felt no more fear of the angels when they refused to eat. After this, they gave him the glad tidings of the birth of a son and the destruction of the people of Lut. When they told him of this, he spoke to them as Sa`id bin Jubayr narrated concerning this verse. Sa`id said: When Jibril and the other angels who were with him came to Ibrahim, they said,

(Verily, we are going to destroy the people of this town.) Ibrahim said to them, "Will you destroy a town that has three hundred believers in it" They said, "No." He then said, "Will you destroy a town that has two hundred believers in it" They said, "No." He said, "Will you destroy a town that has forty believers in it" They said, "No." He then said, "Thirty" They still replied, "No." This continued until he said, "Five" They

## Chapter 11: Hud (Hud), Verses 006-123

said, "No." Then he said, "What do you think if there is one Muslim man in the town, would you destroy it" They said, "No." With this, Ibrahim said,

(But there is Lut in it. They said: "We know better who is there. We will verily, save him and his family except his wife.") Therefore, Ibrahim remained silent and his soul was at rest. Concerning Allah's statement,

(Verily, Ibrahim was, without doubt, forbearing, used to invoke Alllah with humility, and was repentant (to Allah).) (11:75) This is a commendation for Ibrahim because of these beautiful characteristics. Then Allah says,

(O Ibrahim! Forsake this. Indeed, the commandment of your Lord has gone forth.) This means the decree was settled concerning them and the Word was already given that they should be destroyed. The evil torment was coming to them, that cannot be averted from wicked people.

### Surah: 11 Ayah: 77, Ayah: 78 & Ayah: 79

﴿ وَلَمَّا جَاءَتْ رُسُلُنَا لُوطًا سِيءَ بِهِمْ وَضَاقَ بِهِمْ ذَرْعًا وَقَالَ هَـٰذَا يَوْمٌ عَصِيبٌ ﴾ ۷۷

112. And when Our messengers came to Lût (Lot), he was grieved on account of them and felt himself straitened for them (lest the town people should approach them to commit sodomy with them). He said: "This is a distressful day."

﴿ وَجَاءَهُ قَوْمُهُ يُهْرَعُونَ إِلَيْهِ وَمِن قَبْلُ كَانُوا يَعْمَلُونَ ٱلسَّيِّئَاتِ ۚ قَالَ يَـٰقَوْمِ هَـٰؤُلَاءِ بَنَاتِي هُنَّ أَطْهَرُ لَكُمْ ۖ فَٱتَّقُوا ٱللَّهَ وَلَا تُخْزُونِ فِي ضَيْفِي ۖ أَلَيْسَ مِنكُمْ رَجُلٌ رَّشِيدٌ ﴾ ۷۸

113. And his people came rushing towards him, and since aforetime they used to commit crimes (sodomy), he said: "O my people! Here are my daughters (i.e. the women of the nation), they are purer for you (if you marry them lawfully). So fear Allâh and disgrace me not with regard to my guests! Is there not among you a single right-minded man?"

﴿ قَالُوا لَقَدْ عَلِمْتَ مَا لَنَا فِي بَنَاتِكَ مِنْ حَقٍّ وَإِنَّكَ لَتَعْلَمُ مَا نُرِيدُ ﴾ ۷۹

114. They said: "Surely you know that we have neither any desire nor in need of your daughters, and indeed you know well what we want!"

### Transliteration

77. Walamma jaat rusuluna lootan see-a bihim wadaqa bihim tharAAan waqala hatha yawmun AAaseebun  78. Wajaahu qawmuhu yuhraAAoona ilayhi wamin qablu kanoo yaAAmaloona alssayyi-ati qala ya qawmi haola-i banatee hunna atharu lakum faittaqoo Allaha wala tukhzooni fee dayfee alaysa minkum rajulun rasheedun  79.

Qaloo laqad AAalimta ma lana fee banatika min haqqin wa-innaka lataAAlamu ma nureedu

## Tafsir Ibn Kathir

### The Coming of the Angels to Lut, His Grief, and His Discussion with His People

Allah, the Exalted, informs about the coming of His messenger angels. After they informed Ibrahim of their mission to destroy the people of Lut, they left him and set out to destroy Lut's people that very night. After leaving Ibrahim, they came to Lut. Some say that they came to him while he was on a piece of land that belonged to him. Others say that they came to him while he was in his home. They approached him while they were in the most handsome of forms. They appeared in the forms of young men with handsome faces. This was a test from Allah that contained much wisdom and a firm evidence. Their appearance saddened him (Lut) and he felt grief in his soul because of them. He was afraid that if he did not host them as his guests, someone else of his people would host them and harm them.

(He said: "This is a distressful day.") Ibn `Abbas and others said that this means, "A severe test for him." This was because he knew that he would have to defend them and it would cause great problems for him. Qatadah said, "They came to him while he was on a piece of land that belonged to him. They requested him to host them. He agreed, but he was shy of them and he walked in front of them. On the way to his home he said to them in attempt to convince them to go away, `By Allah, I do not know any people on the face of the earth more wicked and disgusting than these people of this town.' Then he walked on a little further. Then he repeated the same statement to them. He continued doing this until he had repeated the same thing four times." Then Qatadah said, "They were ordered not to destroy them until their Prophet testified against them of this." Concerning Allah's statement,

(rushing towards him.) meaning, they made haste and rushed due to their delight of this (new young men). Concerning the statement,

(and since aforetime they used to commit crimes.) This means that this did not cease being their behavior until they were seized (by Allah's torment) and they were still in the same condition.

(He said: "O my people! Here are my daughters (the women of the nation), they are purer for you...") This was his attempt to direct them to their women, for verily the Prophet is like a father for his nation. Therefore, he tries to guide them to that which is better for them in this life and the Hereafter. This is similar to his statement to them in another verse,

(Go you in unto the males of the nation, and leave those whom Allah has created for you to be your wives Nay, you are a trespassing people!)(26:165-166) Allah said in another verse,

(They (the people of the city) said: "Did we not forbid you from entertaining any of the `Alamin")(15:70) This means, "Didn't we forbid you from hosting men (male) guests"

((Lut) said: "These (the girls of the nation) are my daughters, if you must act (so)." Verily, by your life, in their wild intoxication, they were wandering blindly.)(15:71-72) Then, Allah said, in this noble verse,

(Here are my daughters, they are purer for you.) Mujahid said, "Actually, they were not his daughters, but they were from among his nation. Every Prophet is like a father to his nation." A similar statement has been reported from Qatadah and others. Concerning the statement,

(So have Taqwa of Allah and disgrace me not with regard to my guests!) This means, "Accept what I command you by limiting the fulfillment of your desires to your women."

(Is there not among you a single right-minded man) This means, "Is there not a good man among you who will accept what I am enjoining upon you and abandon what I have forbidden for you"

(They said: "Surely, you know that we have no need of your daughters...") This means, "Verily, you know that we do not want our women, nor do we desire them."

(and indeed you know well what we want!) This means, "We only want males and you know that. So what need is there for you to continue speaking to us about this"

### Surah: 11 Ayah: 80 & Ayah: 81

﴿ قَالَ لَوْ أَنَّ لِى بِكُمْ قُوَّةً أَوْ ءَاوِىٓ إِلَىٰ رُكْنٍ شَدِيدٍ ۝ ﴾

115. He said: "Would that I had strength (men) to overpower you, or that I could betake myself to some powerful support (to resist you)."

﴿ قَالُوا۟ يَٰلُوطُ إِنَّا رُسُلُ رَبِّكَ لَن يَصِلُوٓا۟ إِلَيْكَ ۖ فَأَسْرِ بِأَهْلِكَ بِقِطْعٍ مِّنَ ٱلَّيْلِ وَلَا يَلْتَفِتْ مِنكُمْ أَحَدٌ إِلَّا ٱمْرَأَتَكَ ۖ إِنَّهُۥ مُصِيبُهَا مَآ أَصَابَهُمْ ۚ إِنَّ مَوْعِدَهُمُ ٱلصُّبْحُ ۚ أَلَيْسَ ٱلصُّبْحُ بِقَرِيبٍ ۝ ﴾

116. They (messengers) said: "O Lût (Lot)! Verily, we are the messengers from your Lord! They shall not reach you! So travel with your family in a part of the night, and let not any of you look back; but your wife (will remain behind), verily, the punishment which will afflict them, will afflict her. Indeed, morning is their appointed time. Is not the morning near?"

### Transliteration

80. Qala law anna lee bikum quwwatan aw awee ila ruknin shadeedin 81. Qaloo ya lootu inna rusulu rabbika lan yasiloo ilayka faasri bi-ahlika biqitAAin mina allayli wala yaltafit minkum ahadun illa imraataka innahu museebuha ma asabahum inna mawAAidahumu alssubhu alaysa alssubhu biqareebin

### Tafsir Ibn Kathir

### Lut's Inability, His Desire for Strength and the Angels' Informing Him of the Reality

Allah, the Exalted says that Lut was threatening them with his statement,

(Would that I had strength (men) to overpower you,) meaning, `I would surely have made an example of you and done (harm) to you from myself and my family.' In this regard, there is a Hadith which is reported from Abu Hurayrah that the Messenger of Allah said,

«رَحْمَةُ اللهِ عَلَى لُوطٍ لَقَدْ كَانَ يَأْوِي إِلَى رُكْنٍ شَدِيد»

(May Allah's mercy be upon Lut, for verily, he betook himself to a powerful support -- (meaning Allah, the Mighty and Sublime.)

«فَمَا بَعَثَ اللهُ بَعْدَهُ مِنْ نَبِيَ إِلَّا فِي ثَرْوَةٍ مِنْ قَوْمِه»

Allah did not send any Prophet after him, except amidst (an influential family) among his people.) With this, the angels informed him that they were the messengers of Allah sent to them. They also told him that his people would not be able to reach him (with any harm).

(They (messengers said): "O Lut! Verily, we are the messengers from your Lord! They shall not reach you!) They commanded him to travel with his family during the last part of night and that he should follow them from behind. In this way it would be as though he were driving his family (as a cattle herder).

(and let not any of you look back;) This means, "If you hear the sound of what (torment) befalls them (the people of the village), do not rush towards that disturbing noise. Rather, continue leaving."

(but your wife,) Most of the scholars said that this means that she would not travel at night and she did not go with Lut. Rather, she stayed in her house and was destroyed. Others said that it means that she looked back (during the travel). This later group says that she left with them and when she heard the inevitable destruction, she turned and looked back. When she looked she said, "O my people!" Thus, a stone came down from the sky and killed her. Then they (the angels) brought close to him the destruction of his people as good news for him, because he said to them, "Destroy them in this very hour." They replied,

Chapter 11: Hud (Hud), Verses 006-123

(Indeed, morning is their appointed time. Is not the morning near) They were saying this while Luts people were standing at his door. They tried to rush his door from all sides and Lut was standing at the door repelling them, deterring them and trying to prevent them from what they were doing. Yet, they would not listen to him. Instead, they threatened him and sought to intimidate him. At this point, Jibril came out to them and struck them in their faces with his wing. This blow blinded their eyes and they retreated, unable to see their way. This is as Allah said,

(And they indeed sought to shame his guest (asking to commit sodomy with them). So We blinded their eyes (saying), "Then taste you My torment and My warnings.")(54:37)

### Surah: 11 Ayah: 82 & Ayah: 83

﴿ فَلَمَّا جَاءَ أَمْرُنَا جَعَلْنَا عَٰلِيَهَا سَافِلَهَا وَأَمْطَرْنَا عَلَيْهَا حِجَارَةً مِّن سِجِّيلٍ مَّنضُودٍ ﴾

117. So when Our Commandment came, We turned (the towns of Sodom in Palestine) upside down, and rained on them stones of baked clay, in a well-arranged manner one after another;

﴿ مُّسَوَّمَةً عِندَ رَبِّكَ وَمَا هِيَ مِنَ ٱلظَّٰلِمِينَ بِبَعِيدٍ ﴾

118. Marked from your Lord, and they are not ever far from the Zâlimûn (polytheists, evil-doers).

### Transliteration

82. Falamma jaa amruna jaAAalna AAaliyaha safilaha waamtarna AAalayha hijaratan min sijjeelin mandoodin  83. Musawwamatan AAinda rabbika wama hiya mina alththalimeena bibaAAeedin

### Tafsir Ibn Kathir

### The Town of Lut's People is overturned and Their Destruction

Allah, the Exalted, says,

(So when Our commandment came,) This happened at sunrise.

(We (turned it)...) The city of Sadum (Sodom)

(upside down,) This is similar to Allah's statement,

(So there covered them that which did cover (torment with stones).)(53:54) This means, "We rained upon it with stones made of Sijjil." Sijjil is a Persian word meaning stones made of clay. This definition has been mentioned by Ibn `Abbas and others. Some of the scholars said that it (Sijjil) derived from the word Sang, which means a stone. Some others said it means Wakil, which is clay. In another verse Allah says, (the stones of clay,) This means clay made into strong, hard stone. Some of the scholars said it means baked clay. Al-Bukhari said, "Sijjil means that which is big and strong." Concerning Allah's statement,

(in an array. ) Some of the scholars said that Mandud means the stones were arranged in the heavens and prepared for that (destruction). Others said,

(in an array.) This word means that some of them (the stones) followed others in their descent upon the people of Lut. Concerning the statement,

(Marked) meaning the stones were marked and sealed, all of them having the names of their victims written on them. Qatadah and `Ikrimah both said, "Musawwamah means each stone was encompassed by a sprinkling of red coloring." The commentators have mentioned that it (the shower of stones) descended upon the people of the town and upon the various villages around it. One of them would be speaking with some people when a stone would strike him from the sky and kill him while he was among the people. Thus, the stones followed them, striking the people in the entire land until they destroyed them all. Not a single one of them remained. Concerning Allah's statement,

(and they are not ever far from the wrongdoers.) This means that this vengeance (of Allah) is not far from similar wrongdoers. Verily, it has been reported in a Hadith of the Sunan collections, from Ibn `Abbas, which he attributed to the Prophet ,

«مَنْ وَجَدْتُمُوهُ يَعْمَلُ عَمَلَ قَوْمِ لُوطٍ فَاقْتُلُوا الْفَاعِلَ وَالْمَفْعُولَ بِهِ»

(Whoever you find doing the deed of Lut's people (homosexuality), then kill the doer and the one who allows it to be done to him (both partners).)

### Surah: 11 Ayah: 84

﴿ ۞ وَإِلَىٰ مَدْيَنَ أَخَاهُمْ شُعَيْبًا ۚ قَالَ يَٰقَوْمِ ٱعْبُدُوا۟ ٱللَّهَ مَا لَكُم مِّنْ إِلَٰهٍ غَيْرُهُۥ ۖ وَلَا تَنقُصُوا۟ ٱلْمِكْيَالَ وَٱلْمِيزَانَ ۚ إِنِّىٓ أَرَىٰكُم بِخَيْرٍ وَإِنِّىٓ أَخَافُ عَلَيْكُمْ عَذَابَ يَوْمٍ مُّحِيطٍ ﴾

119. And to the Madyan (Midian) people (We sent) their brother Shu'aib. He said: "O my people! Worship Allâh, you have no other Ilâh (god) but Him, and give not short measure or weight, I see you in prosperity and verily I fear for you the torment of a Day encompassing.

### Transliteration

84. Wa-ila madyana akhahum shuAAayban qala ya qawmi oAAbudoo Allaha ma lakum min ilahin ghayruhu wala tanqusoo almikyala waalmeezana innee arakum bikhayrin wa-innee akhafu AAalaykum AAathaba yawmin muheetin

### Tafsir Ibn Kathir

### The Story of the People of Madyan and the Call of Shu`ayb

Allah, the Exalted, says, `We sent a Messenger to the people of Madyan.' They were a tribe of Arabs who lived between the land of the Al-Hijaz and Ash-Sham, close to the land of Ma`an. Their land was known by the name of their tribe and was thus, called Madyan. Allah sent unto them the Prophet Shu`ayb and he was of the noblest of them in lineage. For this reason, Allah said,

(their brother Shu`ayb.) Shu`ayb commanded them to worship Allah alone without associating any partners with him. He also prohibited them from cheating in their weights and measures (for business transactions).

(I see you in prosperity) meaning, `in your livelihood and your provisions. And verily, I fear that you will be deprived of this bounty that you are enjoying by violating Allah's prohibitions.'

(and verily, I fear for you the torment of a Day encompassing.) This means the abode of the Hereafter.

### Surah: 11 Ayah: 85 & Ayah: 86

﴿ وَيَٰقَوْمِ أَوْفُوا۟ ٱلْمِكْيَالَ وَٱلْمِيزَانَ بِٱلْقِسْطِ ۖ وَلَا تَبْخَسُوا۟ ٱلنَّاسَ أَشْيَآءَهُمْ وَلَا تَعْثَوْا۟ فِى ٱلْأَرْضِ مُفْسِدِينَ ۝ ﴾

120. "And O my people! Give full measure and weight in justice and reduce not the things that are due to the people, and do not commit mischief in the land, causing corruption.

﴿ بَقِيَّتُ ٱللَّهِ خَيْرٌ لَّكُمْ إِن كُنتُم مُّؤْمِنِينَ ۚ وَمَآ أَنَا۠ عَلَيْكُم بِحَفِيظٍ ۝ ﴾

121. "That which is left by Allâh for you (after giving the rights of the people) is better for you, if you are believers. And I am not a guardian over you.

### Transliteration

85. Waya qawmi awfoo almikyala waalmeezana bialqisti wala tabkhasoo alnnasa ashyaahum wala taAAthaw fee al-ardi mufsideena  86. Baqiyyatu Allahi khayrun lakum in kuntum mu/mineena wama ana AAalaykum bihafeethin

### Tafsir Ibn Kathir

First, he (Shu`ayb) prohibited them from cheating in business by decreasing the weights whenever they gave (products) to people.

He commanded them to give just measure and weight whether they were giving or receiving (in transactions). He also forbade them from causing mischief and corruption in the land. This was due to their practice of highway robbery along the roads. Abu Ja`far bin Jarir said,

(That which is left by Allah (after giving the rights of the people) is better for you,) "This means what you gain from your successful business dealings in which you have given just measure, is better for you than wrongfully taking the wealth of the people." Ibn Jarir said that this statement has been reported from Ibn `Abbas and I say it is similar to Allah's statement,

(Say: "Not equal are Khabith (all that is evil) and Tayyib (all that is good), even though the abundance of Khabith may please you.")(5:100) Allah then says,

(And I am not a guardian over you.) This means a watcher over you people. In other words, "Do this for Allah and not to be seen by the people."

### Surah: 11 Ayah: 87

﴿ قَالُواْ يَـٰشُعَيْبُ أَصَلَوٰتُكَ تَأْمُرُكَ أَن نَّتْرُكَ مَا يَعْبُدُ ءَابَآؤُنَآ أَوْ أَن نَّفْعَلَ فِىٓ أَمْوَٰلِنَا مَا نَشَـٰٓؤُاْ إِنَّكَ لَأَنتَ ٱلْحَلِيمُ ٱلرَّشِيدُ ۝ ﴾

122. They said: "O Shu'aib! Does your Salât (prayer) command that we give up what our fathers used to worship, or that we give up doing what we like with our property? Verily, you are the forbearer, right-minded!" (They said this sarcastically).

### Transliteration

87. Qaloo ya shuAAaybu asalatuka ta/muruka an natruka ma yaAAbudu abaona aw an nafAAala fee amwalina ma nashao innaka laanta alhaleemu alrrasheedu

### Tafsir Ibn Kathir

#### The Response of Shu`ayb's People

They said to Shu`ayb, in mockery, (Does your Salah) Al-A`mash said, "This means your reading." (command you that we give up what our fathers used to worship,) meaning the idols and statues.

(or that we give up doing what we like with our property) This means, "Should we abandon our practice of lightening the scales because of your statement This is our wealth and we will do with it as we please." Al-Hasan said concerning Allah's statement,

(Does your Salah command you that we give up what our fathers used to worship,)(11:87) "By Allah, this means that his prayer commanded them to abandon what their fathers used to worship." At-Thawri said concerning Allah's statement,

(or that we give up doing what we like with our property) "They were speaking in reference to the paying of Zakah (charity). "

(Verily, you are the forbearer right-minded!) Ibn `Abbas, Maymun bin Mihran, Ibn Jurayj, Ibn Aslam, and Ibn Jarir all said, "These enemies of Allah were only saying this

# Chapter 11: Hud (Hud), Verses 006-123

in mockery. May Allah disfigure them and curse them from ever receiving His mercy. And verily, He did so."

## Surah: 11 Ayah: 88

﴿ قَالَ يَـٰقَوْمِ أَرَءَيْتُمْ إِن كُنتُ عَلَىٰ بَيِّنَةٍ مِّن رَّبِّى وَرَزَقَنِى مِنْهُ رِزْقًا حَسَنًا وَمَا أُرِيدُ أَنْ أُخَالِفَكُمْ إِلَىٰ مَا أَنْهَـٰكُمْ عَنْهُ إِنْ أُرِيدُ إِلَّا ٱلْإِصْلَـٰحَ مَا ٱسْتَطَعْتُ وَمَا تَوْفِيقِى إِلَّا بِٱللَّهِ عَلَيْهِ تَوَكَّلْتُ وَإِلَيْهِ أُنِيبُ ﴾

123. He said: "O my people! Tell me if I have a clear evidence from my Lord and He has given me a good sustenance from Himself (shall I corrupt it by mixing it with the unlawfully earned money). I wish not, in contradiction to you, to do that which I forbid you. I only desire reform to the best of my power. And my guidance cannot come except from Allâh, in Him I trust and unto Him I repent.

### Transliteration

88. Qala ya qawmi araaytum in kuntu AAala bayyinatin min rabbee warazaqanee minhu rizqan hasanan wama oreedu an okhalifakum ila ma anhakum AAanhu in oreedu illa al-islaha ma istataAAtu wama tawfeeqee illa biAllahi AAalayhi tawakkaltu wa-ilayhi oneebu

### Tafsir Ibn Kathir

**Shu`ayb's Refutation of His People**

He said to them: Do you see O my people, that if I

(have a clear evidence from my Lord) meaning, upon clear guidance in that which I am calling to.

(and He has given me a good sustenance from Himself.) It has been said that he meant the prophethood. It has also been said that he meant the lawful provisions. It seems that the verse carries both meanings. Ath-Thawri said,

(I wish not, in contradiction to you, to do that which I forbid you.) meaning, `do not forbid you from something and at the same time I contradict my prohibitions in secret behind your backs, doing what I have forbidden.' This is similar to what Qatadah said concerning Allah's statement,

(I wish not, in contradiction to you, to do that which I forbid you.) "He is saying, `I do not forbid you all from something while I do it myself.'"

(I only desire reform to the best of my power.) This means, "In that which I command and forbid you, I only want to correct your affair as much as I am able."

(And my guidance cannot come) This means, "In whatever I intend that agrees with the truth."

(except from Allah, in Him I put my trust) This means in all of my affairs.

(and unto Him I repent.) meaning; "I return." This has been said by Mujahid and others.

### Surah: 11 Ayah: 89 & Ayah: 90

﴿ وَيَـٰقَوْمِ لَا يَجْرِمَنَّكُمْ شِقَاقِى أَن يُصِيبَكُم مِّثْلُ مَا أَصَابَ قَوْمَ نُوحٍ أَوْ قَوْمَ هُودٍ أَوْ قَوْمَ صَـٰلِحٍ وَمَا قَوْمُ لُوطٍ مِّنكُم بِبَعِيدٍ ﴾

124. "And O my people! Let not my Shiqâq cause you to suffer the fate similar to that of the people of Nûh (Noah) or of Hûd or of Sâlih, and the people of Lût (Lot) are not far off from you!

﴿ وَاسْتَغْفِرُواْ رَبَّكُمْ ثُمَّ تُوبُواْ إِلَيْهِ إِنَّ رَبِّى رَحِيمٌ وَدُودٌ ﴾

125. "And ask forgiveness of your Lord and turn unto Him in repentance. Verily, my Lord is Most Merciful, Most Loving."

### Transliteration

89. Waya qawmi la yajrimannakum shiqaqee an yuseebakum mithlu ma asaba qawma noohin aw qawma hoodin aw qawma salihin wama qawmu lootin minkum bibaAAeedin 90. Waistaghfiroo rabbakum thumma tooboo ilayhi inna rabbee raheemun wadoodun

### Tafsir Ibn Kathir

He (Shu`ayb) said to them,

(And O my people! Let not my Shiqaq cause you) This means, "Do not let your hatred and enmity of me cause you to persist in your corruption and disbelief. If you continue this way, you will suffer the same vengeance and torment that overcame Nuh's people, Hud's people, Salih's people and Lut's people." Qatadah said,

(And O my people! Let not my Shiqaq cause you) "He is saying, `Do not be influenced by your differing with me.'" As-Suddi said, "This means your enmity of me should not lead you to continue in misguidance and disbelief, or else you will be afflicted by what afflicted them." Concerning His statement,

(and the people of Lut are not far off from you!) It has been said that this refers to the period of time. Qatadah said, "This means that they were only destroyed before you yesterday." It has also been said that it refers to place. Actually, the verse carries both meanings.

(And ask forgiveness of your Lord) from the previous sins.

(and turn unto Him in repentance.) In whatever evil actions you may encounter in the future. Concerning his statement,

(Verily, my Lord is Most Merciful, Most Loving.) to those who repent.

### Surah: 11 Ayah: 91 & Ayah: 92

﴿ قَالُواْ يَـٰشُعَيْبُ مَا نَفْقَهُ كَثِيرًا مِّمَّا تَقُولُ وَإِنَّا لَنَرَاكَ فِينَا ضَعِيفًا وَلَوْلَا رَهْطُكَ لَرَجَمْنَـٰكَ وَمَآ أَنتَ عَلَيْنَا بِعَزِيزٍ ۝ ﴾

126. They said: "O Shu'aib! We do not understand much of what you say, and we see you a weak (man, it is said that he was a blind man) among us. Were it not for your family, we should certainly have stoned you and you are not powerful against us."

﴿ قَالَ يَـٰقَوْمِ أَرَهْطِى أَعَزُّ عَلَيْكُم مِّنَ ٱللَّهِ وَٱتَّخَذْتُمُوهُ وَرَآءَكُمْ ظِهْرِيًّا إِنَّ رَبِّى بِمَا تَعْمَلُونَ مُحِيطٌ ۝ ﴾

127. He said: "O my people! Is then my family of more weight with you than Allâh? And you have cast Him away behind your backs. Verily, my Lord is surrounding all that you do.

### Transliteration

91. Qaloo ya shuAAaybu ma nafqahu katheeran mimma taqoolu wa-inna lanaraka feena daAAeefan walawla rahtuka larajamnaka wama anta AAalayna biAAazeezin  92. Qala ya qawmi arahtee aAAazzu AAalaykum mina Allahi waittakhathtumoohu waraakum thihriyyan inna rabbee bima taAAmaloona muheetun

### Tafsir Ibn Kathir

#### The Response of Shu`ayb's People

They said,

(O Shu`ayb! We do not understand) This means that we do not comprehend.

(much) `most of what you say'. Ath-Thawri said, "He (Shu`ayb) was called the orator of the Prophets." As-Suddi said,

(and we see you weak among us.) "They meant, `You are only one person.'" Abu Rawq said, "They meant, `You are despised, because your tribe is not upon your religion.'"

(Were it not for your family, you would have been stoned,) This means, your people. Were it not for their powerful position over the people of Madyan, they would have stoned him to death. Some said that this means with rocks. It has also been said that this means that they would have cursed and insulted him verbally.

(and you are not powerful against us.) This means, "You have no position of power over us."

## Shu`ayb's Refutation of His People

(He said: "O my people! Is then my family of more weight with you than Allah")( He says: You would leave me alone out of respect for my people but not out of respect for the greatness of the Lord, the Most Blessed and Exalted Does not your awe of Allah prevent you from harming His Prophet Indeed you have placed the fear of Allah,

(behind your backs.) This means that you have thrown it behind you. You do not obey it, nor do you respect it.

(Verily, my Lord is surrounding all that you do.) This means that He knows all of your actions and He will reward you according to them.

### Surah: 11 Ayah: 93, Ayah: 94 & Ayah: 95

﴿ وَيَـٰقَوْمِ ٱعْمَلُواْ عَلَىٰ مَكَانَتِكُمْ إِنِّى عَـٰمِلٌ سَوْفَ تَعْلَمُونَ مَن يَأْتِيهِ عَذَابٌ يُخْزِيهِ وَمَنْ هُوَ كَـٰذِبٌ وَٱرْتَقِبُوٓاْ إِنِّى مَعَكُمْ رَقِيبٌ ﴿٩٣﴾ ﴾

128. "And O my people! Act according to your ability and way, and I am acting (on my way). You will come to know who it is on whom descends the torment that will cover him with ignominy, and who is a liar! And watch you! Verily, I too am watching with you."

﴿ وَلَمَّا جَآءَ أَمْرُنَا نَجَّيْنَا شُعَيْبًا وَٱلَّذِينَ ءَامَنُواْ مَعَهُ بِرَحْمَةٍ مِّنَّا وَأَخَذَتِ ٱلَّذِينَ ظَلَمُواْ ٱلصَّيْحَةُ فَأَصْبَحُواْ فِى دِيَـٰرِهِمْ جَـٰثِمِينَ ﴿٩٤﴾ ﴾

129. And when Our Commandment came, We saved Shu'aib and those who believed with him by a Mercy from Us. And As-Saîhah (torment - awful cry) seized the wrong-doers, and they lay (dead) prostrate in their homes.

﴿ كَأَن لَّمْ يَغْنَوْاْ فِيهَآ أَلَا بُعْدًا لِّمَدْيَنَ كَمَا بَعِدَتْ ثَمُودُ ﴿٩٥﴾ ﴾

130. As if they had never lived there! So away with Madyan (Midian)! As away with Thamud! (All these nations were destroyed).

### Transliteration

93. Waya qawmi iAAmaloo AAala makanatikum innee AAamilun sawfa taAAlamoona man ya/teehi AAathabun yukhzeehi waman huwa kathibun wairtaqiboo inne maAAakum raqeebun   94. Walamma jaa amruna najjayna shuAAayban waallatheena amanoo maAAahu birahmatin minna waakhathati allatheena thalamoo alssayhatu faasbahoo fee diyarihim jathimeena   95. Kaan lam yaghnaw feeha ala buAAdan limadyana kama baAAidat thamoodu

## Tafsir Ibn Kathir

**Shu`ayb's threatening of His People When the Prophet of Allah, Shu`ayb, despaired of their response to him, he said, "O my people,**

(Act according to your ability,) This means, "Act according to your current ways." This is actually a severe threat.

(I am acting.) according to my way.

(You will come to know who it is on whom descends the torment that will cover him with ignominy, and who is a liar!) meaning, between me and you.

(And watch you!) This means to wait.

(I too am watching with you.) Allah then says,

(And when Our commandment came, We saved Shu`ayb and those who believed with him by a mercy from Us. And As-Sayhah (awful cry) seized the wrongdoers, and they lay (Jathimin) in their homes.) His saying Jathimin means extinct and lifeless without any movement. Here Allah mentions that a loud cry (Sayhah) came to them. In Surat Al-A`raf He says a severe quake (Rajfah) came to them. In Surat Ash-Shu`ara', He said it was a torment of a cloudy day. They were one nation upon which all of these punishments were gathered on the day of their destruction. In each context, Allah only mentioned that which was suitable. In Surat Al-A`raf when they said,

(We shall certainly drive you out, O Shu`ayb, and those who have believed with you from our town.)(7:88) In this verse it was suitable to mention a tremor, or quake (Rajfah). The earth in which they practiced their wrongdoing and they wanted to expel their Prophet from it, shook them. Here, due to their disrespectful manners in speaking to their Prophet, Allah mentioned the awful cry (Sayhah) which overcame them and killed them. In Surat Ash-Shu`ara' when they said,

(So cause a piece of the heaven to fall on us, if you are of the truthful!)(26:187) Allah said in response,

(So the torment of the day of Shadow seized them. Indeed that was the torment of a Great Day.)(26:189) This is from the intricate secrets and to Allah belongs all praise and much bounty forever. Concerning the statement,

(As if they had never lived there!) This means it was as if they had not lived in their homes before that.

(So away with Madyan as just as Thamud went away!) They (Thamud) were their neighbors and they did not live far from the homes of the people of Madyan. They were similar in their disbelief and their highway robbery. They were also both Arabs.

**Surah: 11 Ayah: 96, Ayah: 97, Ayah: 98 & Ayah: 99**

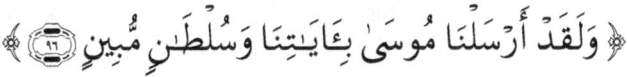

131. And indeed We sent Mûsâ (Moses) with Our Ayât (proofs, evidences, verses, lessons, signs, revelations, etc.) and a manifest authority.

﴿ إِلَىٰ فِرْعَوْنَ وَمَلَإِيْهِۦ فَٱتَّبَعُوٓاْ أَمْرَ فِرْعَوْنَ وَمَآ أَمْرُ فِرْعَوْنَ بِرَشِيدٍ ۝ ﴾

132. To Fir'aun (Pharaoh) and his chiefs, but they followed the command of Fir'aun (Pharaoh), and the command of Fir'aun (Pharaoh) was no right guide.

﴿ يَقْدُمُ قَوْمَهُۥ يَوْمَ ٱلْقِيَـٰمَةِ فَأَوْرَدَهُمُ ٱلنَّارَ وَبِئْسَ ٱلْوِرْدُ ٱلْمَوْرُودُ ۝ ﴾

133. He will go ahead of his people on the Day of Resurrection, and will lead them into the Fire, and evil indeed is the place to which they are led.

﴿ وَأُتْبِعُواْ فِى هَـٰذِهِۦ لَعْنَةً وَيَوْمَ ٱلْقِيَـٰمَةِ بِئْسَ ٱلرِّفْدُ ٱلْمَرْفُودُ ۝ ﴾

134. They were pursued by a curse in this (deceiving life of this world) and (so they will be pursued by a curse) on the Day of Resurrection. Evil indeed is the gifted gift (i.e. the curse (in this world) pursued by another curse (in the Hereafter).

### Transliteration

96. Walaqad arsalna moosa bi-ayatina wasultanin mubeenin  97. Ila firAAawna wamala-ihi faittabaAAoo amra firAAawna wama amru firAAawna birasheedin  98. Yaqdumu qawmahu yawma alqiyamati faawradahumu alnnara wabi/sa alwirdu almawroodu  99. WaotbiAAoo fee hathihi laAAnatan wayawma alqiyamati bi/sa alrrifdu almarfoodu

### Tafsir Ibn Kathir

### The Story of Musa and Fir`awn

In these verses Allah informs of His sending Musa with His signs and clear proofs to Fir'awn, the king of the Coptic people, and his chiefs.

(but they followed the command of Fir`awn.) This means that they followed his path, way and methodology in transgression.

(and the command of Fir`awn was no right guide.) This means there was no right guidance in it. It was only ignorance, misguidance, disbelief and stubbornness. Just as they followed him in this life and he was their leader and chief, likewise he will lead them to the Hellfire on the Day of Resurrection. He will lead them directly to it and they will drink from springs of destruction. Fir`awn will have a great share in that awful punishment. This is as Allah, the Exalted, said,

(But Fir`awn disobeyed the Messenger; so We seized him with a severe punishment.)(73:16) Allah also said,

(But Fir`awn belied and disobeyed. Then he turned his back, striving (against Allah). Then he gathered (his people) and cried aloud, Saying: "I am your lord, most high." So Allah, seized him with exemplary punishment for his last and first transgression.

Verily, in this is an instructive admonition for whosoever fears Allah.)(79:21-26) Allah also said,

(He will go ahead of his people on the Day of Resurrection, and will lead them into the Fire, and evil indeed is the place to which they are led.) This will be the condition of those who were followed. They will have a great share of the punishment on the Day of Resurrection. This is as Allah says,

(For each one there is double (torment), but you know not.) (7:38) Allah also says that the disbelievers will say while they are in the Hellfire,

("Our Lord! Verily, we obeyed our chiefs and our great ones, and they misled us from the (right) way. Our Lord! Give them double torment.") (33:67-68) Concerning the statement,

(They were pursued by a curse in this (deceiving life of this world) and (so they will be pursued by a curse) on the Day of Resurrection. ) meaning, `We have made them to be followed by something more than the punishment of the Fire and that is their being cursed in this life.'

(and on the Day of Resurrection, evil is the gift granted.) Mujahid said, "Another curse will be added to them on the Day of Resurrection, so these are two curses." `Ali bin Abi Talhah said that Ibn `Abbas said,

(evil indeed is the gift granted.) "The curse of this life and the Hereafter." Ad-Dahhak and Qatadah both said the same thing. This is similar to Allah's statement,

(And We made them leaders inviting to the Fire: and on the Day of Resurrection, they will not be helped. And We made a curse to follow them in this world, and on the Day of Resurrection, they will be among the despised.)(28:41-42) Allah also says,

(The Fire, they are exposed to it, morning and afternoon. And on the Day when the Hour will be established (it will be said to the angels): "Cause Fir`awn's people to enter the severest torment!")(40:46)

### Surah: 11 Ayah: 100 & Ayah: 101

﴿ ذَٰلِكَ مِنْ أَنۢبَآءِ ٱلْقُرَىٰ نَقُصُّهُۥ عَلَيْكَ ۖ مِنْهَا قَآئِمٌ وَحَصِيدٌ ۝ ﴾

135. These are some of the news of the (population of) towns which We relate unto you (O Muhammad (peace be upon him)) of them, some are (still) standing, and some have been (already) reaped.

﴿ وَمَا ظَلَمْنَٰهُمْ وَلَٰكِن ظَلَمُوٓا۟ أَنفُسَهُمْ ۖ فَمَآ أَغْنَتْ عَنْهُمْ ءَالِهَتُهُمُ ٱلَّتِى يَدْعُونَ مِن دُونِ ٱللَّهِ مِن شَىْءٍ لَّمَّا جَآءَ أَمْرُ رَبِّكَ ۖ وَمَا زَادُوهُمْ غَيْرَ تَتْبِيبٍ ۝ ﴾

136. We wronged them not, but they wronged themselves. So their âlihah (gods), other than Allâh, whom they invoked, profited them naught when there came the Command of your Lord, nor did they add aught to them but destruction.

### Transliteration

100. Thalika min anba-i alqura naqussuhu AAalayka minha qa-imun wahaseedun 101. Wama thalamnahum walakin thalamoo anfusahum fama aghnat AAanhum alihatuhumu allatee yadAAoona min dooni Allahi min shay-in lamma jaa amru rabbika wama zadoohum ghayra tatbeebin

### Tafsir Ibn Kathir

### The Lesson taken from the Destroyed Towns

When Allah mentioned the story of the Prophets and what happened with them and their nations -- how He destroyed the disbelievers and saved the believers -- He goes on to say,

(That is some of the news of the (population of ) towns) meaning, news of them

(which We relate unto you; of them, some are (still) standing,) This means still remaining.

(and some have been (already) reaped.) This means totally destroyed.

(We wronged them not,) This means, "When We destroyed them."

(but they wronged themselves.) their rejecting their Messengers and disbelieving in them.

(So their gods, profited them (not)...) This is referring to their idols that they used to worship and invoke.

(other than Allah naught) the idols did not benefit them, nor did they save them when Allah's com- mand came for their destruction.

(nor did they add aught to them but destruction.) Mujahid, Qatadah and others said, "This means loss. Because the reason for their destruction and their ruin was that they followed those false gods. Therefore, they were losers in this life and the Hereafter."

### Surah: 11 Ayah: 102

﴿وَكَذَلِكَ أَخْذُ رَبِّكَ إِذَا أَخَذَ ٱلْقُرَىٰ وَهِىَ ظَٰلِمَةٌ إِنَّ أَخْذَهُۥ أَلِيمٌ شَدِيدٌ﴾

137. Such is the Seizure of your Lord when He seizes the (population of) the towns while they are doing wrong. Verily, His Seizure is painful, (and) severe.

### Transliteration

102. Wakathalika akhthu rabbika itha akhatha alqura wahiya thalimatun inna akhthahu aleemun shadeedun

### Tafsir Ibn Kathir

It is as though Allah is saying, "Just as We have destroyed these wicked generations who rejected their Messengers, We will do the same to any who are like them."

(Verily, His punishment is painful (and) severe.) In the Two Sahihs, it is recorded that Abu Musa said that the Messenger of Allah said,

«إِنَّ اللهَ لَيُمْلِي لِلظَّالِمِ حَتَّى إِذَا أَخَذَهُ لَمْ يُفْلِتْه»

(Verily, Allah gives respite to a wrongdoer until He seizes him and he cannot escape.) Then the Messenger of Allah recited,

(Such is the punishment of your Lord when He seizes the towns while they are doing wrong.)

### Surah: 11 Ayah: 103, Ayah: 104 & Ayah: 105

﴿ إِنَّ فِى ذَٰلِكَ لَءَايَةً لِّمَنْ خَافَ عَذَابَ ٱلْءَاخِرَةِ ذَٰلِكَ يَوْمٌ مَّجْمُوعٌ لَّهُ ٱلنَّاسُ وَذَٰلِكَ يَوْمٌ مَّشْهُودٌ ﴾

138. Indeed in that (there) is a sure lesson for those who fear the torment of the Hereafter. That is a Day whereon mankind will be gathered together, and that is a Day when all (the dwellers of the heavens and the earth) will be present.

﴿ وَمَا نُؤَخِّرُهُ إِلَّا لِأَجَلٍ مَّعْدُودٍ ﴾

139. And We delay it only for a term (already) fixed.

﴿ يَوْمَ يَأْتِ لَا تَكَلَّمُ نَفْسٌ إِلَّا بِإِذْنِهِ فَمِنْهُمْ شَقِىٌّ وَسَعِيدٌ ﴾

140. On the Day when it comes, no person shall speak except by His (Allâh's) Leave. Some among them will be wretched and (others) blessed.

### Transliteration

103. Inna fee thalika laayatan liman khafa AAathaba al-akhirati thalika yawmun majmooAAun lahu alnnasu wathalika yawmun mashhoodun 104. Wama nu-akhkhiruhu illa li-ajalin maAAdoodin 105. Yawma ya/ti la takallamu nafsun illa bi-ithnihi faminhum shaqiyyun wasaAAeedin

## Tafsir Ibn Kathir

### The Destruction of the Towns is a Proof of the Establishment of the Hour (Judgement)

Allah, the Exalted, is saying that in the destruction of the disbelievers and the salvation of the believers by us is,

(a sure lesson). This means an admonition and lesson concerning the truthfulness of that which We are promised in the Hereafter.

.(Verily, We will indeed make victorious Our Messengers and those who believe in this world's life and on the Day when the witnesses will stand forth.)(40:51) Allah, the Exalted, also says,

(So their Lord revealed to them: "Truly, We shall destroy the wrongdoers.) (14:13) Concerning Allah's statement,

(That is a Day whereon mankind will be gathered together,) This means the first of them and the last of them. This is similar to Allah's statement,

(And We shall gather them all together so as to leave not one of them behind.) (18: 47)

(and that is a Day when all will be present.) This means a day that is great. The angels will be present, the Messengers will gather and all of the creation will be gathered with their families. The humans, Jinns, birds, wild beasts and domesticated riding animals will all be gathered. Then the Most Just, Who does not wrong anyone even an atom's weight, will judge between them and He will increase their good deeds in reward. Concerning the statement,

(And We delay it only for a term (already) fixed.) This means for a fixed period of time than cannot be increased or decreased. Then He says,

(On the Day when it comes, no person shall speak except by His (Allah's) leave.) This means that on the Day of Judgement no one will speak except with the permission of Allah. This is similar to another verse, which says,

(they will not speak except him whom the Most Gracious (Allah) allows, and he will speak what is right.) (78:38) Allah also says,

(And all the voices will be humbled for the Most Gracious (Allah). ) (20:108) In the Hadith about the intercession, which is recorded in the Two Sahihs, the Messenger of Allah said,

«وَلَا يَتَكَلَّمُ يَوْمَئِذٍ إِلَّا الرُّسُلُ، وَدَعْوَى الرُّسُلِ يَوْمَئِذٍ اللَّهُمَّ سَلِّمْ سَلِّمْ»

(No one will speak on that day except the Messengers, and the call of the Messengers will be, "O Allah, save us, save us.") Concerning Allah's statement,

# Chapter 11: Hud (Hud), Verses 006-123

(Some among them will be wretched and (others) blessed.) This means that from the people of the gathering (on Judgement Day), some will be miserable and some will be happy. This is as Allah said,

(When a party will be in Paradise and a party in the blazing Fire) (42:7) Al-Hafiz Abu Ya`la recorded in his Musnad on the authority of Ibn `Umar that `Umar said, "When this verse was revealed,

(Some among them will be wretched and (others) blessed.) I asked the Prophet , `O Messenger of Allah, will there be a sign for us to know (which party we are from) Will it be because of something that a person did, or something that he did not do' He said,

«عَلَى شَيْءٍ قَدْ فُرِغَ مِنْهُ يَا عُمَرُ وَجَرَتْ بِهِ الْأَقْلَامُ،وَلَكِنْ كُلٌّ مُيَسَّرٌ لِمَا خُلِقَ لَه»

(O `Umar, it will be due to something that he did and the pens wrote it down. But every easy deed was created for its purpose (to be carried out).) Then Allah explains the situation of the wretched people and the happy people. He, the Exalted, says,

### Surah: 11 Ayah: 106 & Ayah: 107

﴿ فَأَمَّا ٱلَّذِينَ شَقُوا۟ فَفِى ٱلنَّارِ لَهُمْ فِيهَا زَفِيرٌ وَشَهِيقٌ ﴾

141. As for those who are wretched, they will be in the Fire, sighing in a high and low tone.

﴿ خَٰلِدِينَ فِيهَا مَا دَامَتِ ٱلسَّمَٰوَٰتُ وَٱلْأَرْضُ إِلَّا مَا شَآءَ رَبُّكَ إِنَّ رَبَّكَ فَعَّالٌ لِّمَا يُرِيدُ ﴾

142. They will dwell therein for all the time that the heavens and the earth endure, except as your Lord wills. Verily, your Lord is the doer of what He intends (or wills).

### Transliteration

106. Faamma allatheena shaqoo fafee alnnari lahum feeha zafeerun washaheequn
107. Khalideena feeha ma damati alssamawatu waal-ardu illa ma shaa rabbuka inna rabbaka faAAAAalun lima yureedu

### Tafsir Ibn Kathir

### The Condition of the Wretched People and their Destination

Allah, the Exalted, says,

(in it they will experience Zafir and Shahiq.) Ibn `Abbas said, "Az-Zafir is a sound in the throat and Ash-Shahiq is a sound in the chest. This means that their exhaling will be Zafir and their inhaling will Shahiq." This will be due to the torment that they will be experiencing. We seek refuge with Allah from such evil.

(They will dwell therein for all the time that the heavens and the earth endure,) Imam Abu Ja`far bin Jarir said, "It was from the customs of the Arabs that when they wanted to describe something that would last forever, they would say, `This is as enduring as the heavens and the earth.' Or, `It will last as until the night and day separate.' They would say, `As long as talkers at night continue to chat.' They meant by these statements the condition of eternity. Therefore, Allah addressed them in a manner that they were familiar with among themselves. Thus, He said,

(They will dwell therein for all the time that the heavens and the earth endure,) The literal meaning is also intended with; "for all the time that the heavens and the earth endure." This is due to the fact that there will be heavens and earth in the life of the next world, just as Allah said,

(On the Day when the earth will be changed to another earth and so will be the heavens.) (14:48) For this reason, Al-Hasan Al-Basri said concerning the statement of Allah,

(the heavens and the earth endure.) "Allah is referring to a heaven other than this heaven (which we see now) and an earth other than this earth. That (new) heaven and earth will be eternal." Concerning Allah's statement,

(except as your Lord wills. Verily, your Lord is the doer of whatsoever He intends.) This is similar to His statement,

(The Fire be your dwelling place, you will dwell therein forever, except as Allah may will. Certainly your Lord is All-Wise, All-Knowing.) (6:128) It has been said that the exception mentioned in this verse refers to the disobedient among the people of Tawhid. It is these whom Allah will bring out of the Fire by the intercession of the interceders. Those who will be allowed to intercede are the angels, the Prophets and the believers. They will intercede even on behalf of those who committed major sins. Then, the generous mercy of Allah will remove from the Fire those who have never done any good, except for saying La ilaha illallah one day of their life. This has been mentioned in numerous authentic reports from the Messenger of Allah , including narrations from Anas bin Malik, Jabir bin `Abdullah, Abu Sa`id Al-Khudri, Abu Hurayrah and other Companions. No one remains in the Fire after this final intercession, except those who will remain there forever without escape. This is the opinion held by many of the scholars, both past and present, concerning the explanation of this verse.

# Chapter 11: Hud (Hud), Verses 006-123

**Surah: 11 Ayah: 108**

﴿ ۞ وَأَمَّا ٱلَّذِينَ سُعِدُواْ فَفِى ٱلْجَنَّةِ خَٰلِدِينَ فِيهَا مَا دَامَتِ ٱلسَّمَٰوَٰتُ وَٱلْأَرْضُ إِلَّا مَا شَآءَ رَبُّكَ عَطَآءً غَيْرَ مَجْذُوذٍ ۝ ﴾

143. And those who are blessed, they will be in Paradise, abiding therein for all the time that the heavens and the earth endure, except as your Lord wills; a gift without an end.

## Transliteration

108. Waamma allatheena suAAidoo fafee aljannati khalideena feeha ma damati alssamawatu waalardu illa ma shaa rabbuka AAataan ghayra majthoothin

## Tafsir Ibn Kathir

### The Condition of the Happy People and their Destination

Allah, the Exalted, says,

(And those who are blessed.) These are the followers of the Messengers.

(they will be in Paradise,) This means that their final abode will be Paradise.

(abiding therein for all the time) This means that they will remain there forever.

(that the heavens and the earth endure, except as your Lord wills:) The meaning of the exception that is made here is that the condition of eternal pleasure that they will experience therein is something that is not mandatory by itself. Rather, it is something that is dependent upon the will of Allah. Unto Him belongs the favor of immortality upon them. For this reason they are inspired to glorify and praise Him, just as they are inspired to breathe. Ad-Dahhak and Al-Hasan Al-Basri both said, "It is about the right of the disobedient people of Tawhid who were in the Fire and then brought out of it." Then Allah finished this statement by saying,

(a gift without an end.) This means that it will never be cut off. This has been mentioned by Mujahid, Ibn `Abbas, Abu Al-`Aliyah and others. This has been mentioned so that the suspicious person will not doubt after the mention of the will of Allah. Someone may think that the mention of Allah's will here means that the pleasure of Paradise may end or change. To the contrary, it has been decreed that this pleasure will truly be forever and will never end. Likewise, Allah has clarified here that the eternal torment of the people of the Fire in Hell also is due to His will. He explains that He punishes them due to His justness and wisdom. This is why He says,

(Verily, your Lord is the doer of whatsoever He intends.) Similarly, Allah says,

(He cannot be questioned as to what He does, while they will be questioned.)(21:23) Here, Allah soothes the hearts and affirms the intent, by His saying, (a gift without an end.) It has been recorded in the Two Sahihs that the Messenger of Allah said,

«يُؤْتَى بِالْمَوْتِ فِي صُورَةِ كَبْشٍ أَمْلَحَ فَيُذْبَحُ بَيْنَ الْجَنَّةِ وَالنَّارِ، ثُمَّ يُقَالُ: يَا أَهْلَ الْجَنَّةِ خُلُودٌ فَلَا مَوْتَ، وَيَا أَهْلَ النَّارِ خُلُودٌ فَلَا مَوْتَ»

(Death will be brought in the form of a handsome ram (on the Day of Judgement) and it will be slaughtered between Paradise and the Hellfire. Then, it will be said, "O people of Paradise! Eternity and no death! O people of Hellfire! Eternity and no death!") In the Sahih it is recorded that the Messenger of Allah said,

«فَيُقَالُ: يَا أَهْلَ الْجَنَّةِ إِنَّ لَكُمْ أَنْ تَعِيشُوا فَلَا تَمُوتُوا أَبَدًا، وَإِنَّ لَكُمْ أَنْ تَشِبُّوا فَلَا تَهْرَمُوا أَبَدًا، وَإِنَّ لَكُمْ أَنْ تَصِحُّوا فَلَا تَسْقَمُوا أَبَدًا، وَإِنَّ لَكُمْ أَنْ تَنْعَمُوا فَلَا تَبْأَسُوا أَبَدًا»

(It will be said, `O people of Paradise, verily you will live and you will never die. You will remain young and you will never grow old. You will remain healthy and you will never become ill. You will be happy and you will never grieve.)

### Surah: 11 Ayah: 109, Ayah: 110 & Ayah: 111

﴿ فَلَا تَكُ فِي مِرْيَةٍ مِّمَّا يَعْبُدُ هَـٰٓؤُلَاءِ ۚ مَا يَعْبُدُونَ إِلَّا كَمَا يَعْبُدُ ءَابَآؤُهُم مِّن قَبْلُ ۚ وَإِنَّا لَمُوَفُّوهُمْ نَصِيبَهُمْ غَيْرَ مَنقُوصٍ ﴾

144. So be not in doubt (O Muhammad (peace be upon him)) as to what these people (pagans and polytheists) worship. They worship nothing but what their fathers worshipped before (them). And verily, We shall repay them in full their portion without diminution.

﴿ وَلَقَدْ ءَاتَيْنَا مُوسَى ٱلْكِتَـٰبَ فَٱخْتُلِفَ فِيهِ ۚ وَلَوْلَا كَلِمَةٌ سَبَقَتْ مِن رَّبِّكَ لَقُضِىَ بَيْنَهُمْ ۚ وَإِنَّهُمْ لَفِى شَكٍّ مِّنْهُ مُرِيبٍ ﴾

145. Indeed, We gave the Book to Mûsa (Moses), but differences arose therein, and had it not been for a Word that had gone forth before from your Lord, the case would have been judged between them, and indeed they are in grave doubt concerning it (this Qur'ân).

﴿ وَإِنَّ كُلًّا لَّمَّا لَيُوَفِّيَنَّهُمْ رَبُّكَ أَعْمَـٰلَهُمْ ۚ إِنَّهُ بِمَا يَعْمَلُونَ خَبِيرٌ ﴾

146. And verily, to each of them your Lord will repay their works in full. Surely, He is All-Aware of what they do.

### Transliteration

109. Fala taku fee miryatin mimma yaAAbudu haola-i ma yaAAbudoona illa kama yaAAbudu abaohum min qablu wa-inna lamuwaffoohum naseebahum ghayra manqoosin 110. Walaqad atayna moosa alkitaba faikhtulifa feehi walawla kalimatun sabaqat min rabbika laqudiya baynahum wa-innahum lafee shakkin minhu mureebun 111. Wa-inna kullan lamma layuwaffiyannahum rabbuka aAAmalahum innahu bima yaAAmaloona khabeerun

### Tafsir Ibn Kathir

### Associating Partners with Allah is no doubt Misguidance

Allah, the Exalted, says,

(So be not in doubt as to what these people worship.) This refers to the polytheists. Verily, what they are doing is falsehood, ignorance and misguidance. Verily, they are only worshipping what their fathers worshipped before. This means that they have no support for their Shirk. They are only mimicking their fathers in ignorance. Therefore, Allah will give them due recompense for that and He will punish them with a punishment the likes of which none can give besides Him. If they did any good deeds, then Allah will reward them for those good works in this life, before the life of the Hereafter. Concerning Allah's statement,

(And verily, We shall repay them in full their portion without diminution.) `Abdur-Rahman bin Zayd bin Aslam said, "We will pay them in full their portion of punishment without diminution." Then, Allah mentions that He gave Musa the Book, but the people differed concerning it. Some believed in it and some disbelieved in it. Therefore, you, Muhammad, have an example in the Prophets who came before you. So do not grieve or be upset by their denial of you.

(and had it not been for a Word (Kalimah) that had gone forth before from your Lord, the case would have been judged between them,) Ibn Jarir said, "If it were not that the punishment had already been delayed until an appointed time, then Allah would have decided the matter between you now. The word Kalimah carries the meaning that Allah will not punish anyone until the proof has been established against him and a Messenger has been sent to him." This is similar to Allah's statement,

(And We never punish until We have sent a Messenger (to give warning).) (17:15) For verily, Allah says in another verse,

G(And had it not been for a Word that went forth before from your Lord, and a term determined, (their punishment) must necessarily have come (in this world). So bear patiently what they say.)(20:129-130) Then, Allah informs that He will gather the early generations and the later generations from all of the nations. He will then reward them based upon their deeds. If they did good deeds, their reward will be good, and if they did evil deeds, their reward will be bad. Allah says,

(And verily, to each of them your Lord will repay their works in full. Surely, He is All-Aware of what they do.) This means that He is All-Knower of all of their deeds. This includes their honorable deeds and their despicable deeds, their small deeds and their great deeds. There are many different modes of recitation for this verse, yet all of their meanings agree with what we have mentioned. This is similar to Allah's statement,

(And surely, all - everyone of them will be brought before Us.)(36:32)

### Surah: 11 Ayah: 112 & Ayah: 113

﴿ فَٱسْتَقِمْ كَمَآ أُمِرْتَ وَمَن تَابَ مَعَكَ وَلَا تَطْغَوْاْ إِنَّهُ بِمَا تَعْمَلُونَ بَصِيرٌ ﴾

147. So stand (ask Allâh to make) you (Muhammad (peace be upon him)) firm and straight (on the religion of Islâmic Monotheism) as you are commanded and those (your companions) who turn in repentance (unto Allâh) with you, and transgress not (Allâh's Legal Limits). Verily, He is All-Seer of what you do.

﴿ وَلَا تَرْكَنُوٓاْ إِلَى ٱلَّذِينَ ظَلَمُواْ فَتَمَسَّكُمُ ٱلنَّارُ وَمَا لَكُم مِّن دُونِ ٱللَّهِ مِنْ أَوْلِيَآءَ ثُمَّ لَا تُنصَرُونَ ﴾

148. And incline not toward those who do wrong, lest the Fire should touch you, and you have no protectors other than Allâh, nor you would then be helped.

### Transliteration

112. Faistaqim kama omirta waman taba maAAaka wala tatghaw innahu bima taAAmaloona baseerun 113. Wala tarkanoo ila allatheena thalamoo fatamassakumu alnnaru wama lakum min dooni Allahi min awliyaa thumma la tunsaroona

### Tafsir Ibn Kathir

**The Command to Stand Firm and Straight**

Allah, the Exalted, commands His Messenger and His believing servants to be firm and to always be upright. This is of the greatest aid for gaining victory over the enemy and confronting the opposition. Allah also forbids transgression, which is to exceed the bounds (of what is allowed). Verily, transgression causes destruction to its practitioner, even if the transgression was directed against a polytheist. Then, Allah informs that He is All-Seer of the actions of His servants. He is not unaware of anything and nothing is hidden from Him. Concerning Allah's statement,

(And incline not toward those who do wrong,) `Ali bin Abi Talhah said that Ibn `Abbas said, "Do not compromise with them." Ibn Jarir said that Ibn `Abbas said, "Do not side with those who do wrong." This is a good statement. This means, "Do not seek assistance from wrongdoers, because it will be as if you are condoning their actions (of evil)."

Chapter 11: Hud (Hud), Verses 006-123

(lest the Fire should touch you, and you have no protectors other than Allah, nor you would then be helped.) This means that you will not have besides Allah any friend who can save you, nor any helper who can remove you from His torment.

### Surah: 11 Ayah: 114 & Ayah: 115

﴿ وَأَقِمِ ٱلصَّلَوٰةَ طَرَفَيِ ٱلنَّهَارِ وَزُلَفًا مِّنَ ٱلَّيْلِ ۚ إِنَّ ٱلْحَسَنَـٰتِ يُذْهِبْنَ ٱلسَّيِّـَٔاتِ ۚ ذَٰلِكَ ذِكْرَىٰ لِلذَّـٰكِرِينَ ﴾

149. And perform As-Salât (Iqâmat-as-Salât), at the two ends of the day and in some hours of the night (i.e. the five compulsory Salât (prayers)) Verily, the good deeds remove the evil deeds (i.e. small sins). That is a reminder (an advice) for the mindful (those who accept advice).

﴿ وَٱصْبِرْ فَإِنَّ ٱللَّهَ لَا يُضِيعُ أَجْرَ ٱلْمُحْسِنِينَ ﴾

150. And be patient; verily, Allâh wastes not the reward of the good-doers.

### Transliteration

114. Waaqimi alssalata tarafayi alnnahari wazulafan mina allayli inna alhasanati yuthhibna alssayyiati thalika thikra lilththakireena   115. Waisbir fa-inna Allaha la yudeeAAu ajra almuhsineena

### Tafsir Ibn Kathir

**The Command to establish the Prayer**

`Ali bin Abi Talhah reported that Ibn `Abbas said,

(And perform the Salah, at the two ends of the day) "This is referring to the morning prayer (Subh) and the evening prayer (Maghrib)." The same was said by Al-Hasan and `Abdur-Rahman bin Zayd bin Aslam. In one narration reported by Qatadah, Ad-Dahhak and others, Al-Hasan said, "It means the morning prayer (Subh) and the late afternoon prayer (`Asr)." Mujahid said, "It is the morning prayer at the beginning of the day and the noon prayer (Zuhr) and late afternoon prayer (`Asr) at the end of the day." This was also said by Muhammad bin Ka`b Al-Qurazi and Ad-Dahhak in one narration from him.

(and in some hours of the night.) Ibn `Abbas, Mujahid, Al-Hasan and others said, "This means the night prayer (`Isha')." Ibn Al-Mubarak reported from Mubarak bin Fadalah that Al-Hasan said,

(and in some hours of the night.) "This means the evening (Maghrib) and late night (`Isha') prayers. The Messenger of Allah said,

«هُمَا زُلَفَا اللَّيْلِ: الْمَغْرِبُ وَالْعِشَاءُ»

(They are the approach of the night: Maghrib and `Isha'.) The same was said by Mujahid, Muhammad bin Ka`b, Qatadah and Ad-Dahhak (that this means the Maghrib and `Isha' prayers). It should be noted that this verse was revealed before the five daily prayers were made obligatory during the night of Isra' (the Prophet's night journey to Jerusalem). At that time there were only two obligatory prayers: a prayer before sunrise and a prayer before sunset. During the late night another prayer (Tahajjud) was also made obligatory upon the Prophet and his nation. Later, this obligation was abrogated for his nation and remained obligatory upon him. Finally, this obligation was abrogated for the Prophet as well, according to one opinion. Allah knows best.

## The Good Deeds wipe away the Evil Deeds

Concerning Allah's statement,

(Verily, the good deeds remove the evil deeds.) This is saying that the performance of good deeds is an expiation of previous sins. This has been mentioned in a Hadith recorded by Imam Ahmad and the Sunan Compilers, that the Commander of the faithful, `Ali bin Abi Talib, said, "Whenever I used to hear a narration from the Messenger of Allah (), Allah would cause me to benefit by it however He willed. If anyone informed me of any statement that he said, I would make him swear (by Allah) that the Prophet said it. If he swore by Allah, then I would believe him. Abu Bakr once told me -- and Abu Bakr was truthful -- that he heard the Messenger of Allah say,

«مَا مِنْ مُسْلِمٍ يُذْنِبُ ذَنْبًا فَيَتَوَضَّأُ وَيُصَلِّي رَكْعَتَيْنِ إِلَّا غُفِرَ لَهُ»

(There is not any Muslim who commits a sin, then he makes Wudu' and prays two units of prayer, except that he will be forgiven (that sin).) In the Two Sahihs it is recorded that the Commander of the faithful, `Uthman bin `Affan made Wudu' for the people (to see), just like the Wudu' of the Messenger of Allah. Then he said, "I saw the Messenger of Allah make Wudu' like this, and he said,

«مَنْ تَوَضَّأَ وُضُوئِي هَذَا ثُمَّ صَلَّى رَكْعَتَيْنِ لَا يُحَدِّثُ فِيهِمَا نَفْسَهُ غُفِرَ لَهُ مَا تَقَدَّمَ مِنْ ذَنْبِهِ»

(Whoever makes Wudu' like this Wudu' of mine, then he prays two units of prayer in which he does not speak to himself, he will be forgiven for his previous sins.) In the Sahih it is recorded that Abu Hurayrah said that the Messenger of Allah said,

«أَرَأَيْتُمْ لَوْ أَنَّ بِبَابِ أَحَدِكُمْ نَهْرًا غَمْرًا، يَغْتَسِلُ فِيهِ كُلَّ يَوْمٍ خَمْسَ مَرَّاتٍ، هَلْ يُبْقِي مِنْ دَرَنِهِ شَيْئًا؟»

# Chapter 11: Hud (Hud), Verses 006-123

(Do you think that if there was a flowing river at the door of anyone of you and he bathed in it five times every day, would there be any dirt left on him) They said, "No, O Messenger of Allah!" He (peace and blessings of Allah be upon him) said,

»كَذَلِكَ الصَّلَوَاتُ الْخَمْسُ يَمْحُو اللهُ بِهِنَّ الذُّنُوبَ وَالْخَطَايَا«

(This is like the five daily prayers, for Allah uses them to wipe away the sins and wrongdoings.) Muslim recorded in his Sahih that Abu Hurayrah said that the Messenger of Allah used to say,

»الصَّلَوَاتُ الْخَمْسُ، وَالْجُمُعَةُ إِلَى الْجُمُعَةِ، وَرَمَضَانُ إِلَى رَمَضَانَ، مُكَفِّرَاتٌ لِمَا بَيْنَهُنَّ مَا اجْتُنِبَتِ الْكَبَائِرُ«

(The five daily prayers, Jumu`ah (Friday prayer) to Jumu`ah and (the fast of) Ramadan to Ramadan are expiations for whatever sins were committed between them, as long as you stay away from the major sins.) Al-Bukhari recorded Ibn Mas`ud saying that a man kissed a woman (who was not his relative or wife). He then came to the Prophet and informed him about the incident. Thus, Allah revealed,

(And perform Salah, at the two ends of the day and in some hours of the night. Verily, the good deeds remove the evil deeds.)(11:114) The man then said, "O Messenger of Allah, is this only for me" The Prophet replied,

»لِجَمِيعِ أُمَّتِي كُلِّهِم«

(This is for all of my (Ummah) followers.) Al-Bukhari recorded this narration in the Book of Prayer as well and the Book of Tafsir. Imam Ahmad recorded that Ibn `Abbas said that a man came to `Umar and said that a woman came to do business with him. During the course of their business, he took her into his place and did everything with her except the actual act of sexual intercourse. `Umar said, "Woe unto you! She probably was a woman whose husband is away (fighting) in the path of Allah." The man said, "Of course she was." `Umar then said, "Go to Abu Bakr and ask him about this." The man went to Abu Bakr and asked him about the matter. Abu Bakr said, "She probably was a woman whose husband is away (fighting) in the path of Allah," just as `Umar had said. Then he went to the Prophet and told him the same story. The Prophet said,

»فَلَعَلَّهَا مُغِيبَةٌ فِي سَبِيلِ الله«

(She probably was a woman whose husband is away (fighting) in the path of Allah.) Then a verse of Qur'an was revealed,

(And perform the Salah, at the two ends of the day and in some hours of the night. Verily, the good deeds remove the evil deeds.) The man then said, "O Messenger of Allah! Is this verse only for me, or does it apply to all of the people in general" `Umar then struck the man on his chest with his hand and said, "No, rather it is for all of the people in general." Then the Messenger of Allah said,

«صَدَقَ عُمَر»

(`Umar has spoken the truth.)

### Surah: 11 Ayah: 116 & Ayah: 117

﴿ فَلَوْلَا كَانَ مِنَ ٱلْقُرُونِ مِن قَبْلِكُمْ أُوْلُواْ بَقِيَّةٍ يَنْهَوْنَ عَنِ ٱلْفَسَادِ فِى ٱلْأَرْضِ إِلَّا قَلِيلًا مِّمَّنْ أَنجَيْنَا مِنْهُمْ ۗ وَٱتَّبَعَ ٱلَّذِينَ ظَلَمُواْ مَآ أُتْرِفُواْ فِيهِ وَكَانُواْ مُجْرِمِينَ ۝ ﴾

151. If only there had been among the generations before you persons having wisdom, prohibiting (others) from Al-Fasâd (disbelief, polytheism, and all kinds of crimes and sins) in the earth, (but there were none) - except a few of those whom We saved from among them. Those who did wrong pursued the enjoyment of good things of (this worldly) life, and were Mujrimûn (criminals, disbelievers in Allâh, polytheists, sinners).

﴿ وَمَا كَانَ رَبُّكَ لِيُهْلِكَ ٱلْقُرَىٰ بِظُلْمٍ وَأَهْلُهَا مُصْلِحُونَ ۝ ﴾

152. And your Lord would never destroy the towns wrongfully, while their people were right-doers.

### Transliteration

116. Falawla kana mina alqurooni min qablikum oloo baqiyyatin yanhawna AAani alfasadi fee al-ardi illa qaleelan mimman anjayna minhum waittabaAAa allatheena thalamoo ma otrifoo feehi wakanoo mujrimeena 117. Wama kana rabbuka liyuhlika alqura bithulmin waahluha muslihoona

### Tafsir Ibn Kathir

#### There must be a Group of People Who forbid Lewdness

Allah, the Exalted, says that there should have been a group of wise people present among the past generations who called to good and forbade the evil and corruption that took place among them in the land. His statement,

(except a few) This means that there were only a small number of people present among them who were of this caliber. They were those whom Allah saved at the sudden striking of His vengeance, when His anger was let lose. For this reason Allah commanded this noble Ummah (followers of Muhammad ) to always have among them those who command the good and forbid the evil. This is as Allah says,

(Let there arise out of you a group of people inviting to all that is good, enjoining righteousness and forbidding evil. And it is they who are the successful.)(3:104) It is related in a Hadith that the Prophet said,

»إِنَّ النَّاسَ إِذَا رَأَوُا الْمُنْكَرَ فَلَمْ يُغَيِّرُوهُ أَوْشَكَ أَنْ يَعُمَّهُمُ اللَّهُ بِعِقَابٍ«

(Verily, whenever a group of people see an evil and they do not change it, it is likely that Allah will cover them with (His) punishment.) Thus, Allah says,

(If only there had been among the generations before you persons having wisdom, There must be a Group of People Who forbid Lewdness Allah, the Exalted, says that there should have been a group of wise people present among the past generations who called to good and forbade the evil and corruption that took place among them in the land. His statement,

(except a few) This means that there were only a small number of people present among them who were of this caliber. They were those whom Allah saved at the sudden striking of His vengeance, when His anger was let lose. For this reason Allah commanded this noble Ummah (followers of Muhammad ) to always have among them those who command the good and forbid the evil. This is as Allah says,

(Let there arise out of you a group of people inviting to all that is good, enjoining righteousness and forbidding evil. And it is they who are the successful.)(3:104) It is related in a Hadith that the Prophet said,

»إِنَّ النَّاسَ إِذَا رَأَوُا الْمُنْكَرَ فَلَمْ يُغَيِّرُوهُ أَوْشَكَ أَنْ يَعُمَّهُمُ اللَّهُ بِعِقَابٍ«

(Verily, whenever a group of people see an evil and they do not change it, it is likely that Allah will cover them with (His) punishment.) Thus, Allah says,

(If only there had been among the generations before you persons having wisdom, prohibiting (others) from the Fasad in the earth,- except a few of those whom We saved from among them!) Concerning the statement,

(Those who did wrong pursued the enjoyment of good things of (this worldly) life,) This means that they continued in their ways of disobedience and evils and they did not heed the protesting of those righteous people, until the torment suddenly seized them.

(and were criminals.) Then, Allah informs that he does not destroy any town, except that it has wronged itself. No correctional punishment or torment comes to any town, except that its people were wrongdoers. This is as Allah says, s

(We wronged them not, but they wronged themselves.) (11:101) Allah also says,

(And your Lord is not at all unjust to (His) servants.) (41:46)

### Surah: 11 Ayah: 118 & Ayah: 119

﴿ وَلَوْ شَاءَ رَبُّكَ لَجَعَلَ ٱلنَّاسَ أُمَّةً وَٰحِدَةً وَلَا يَزَالُونَ مُخْتَلِفِينَ ۝ ﴾

153. And if your Lord had so willed, He could surely have made mankind one Ummah (nation or community (following one religion i.e. Islâm)) but they will not cease to disagree.

﴿ إِلَّا مَن رَّحِمَ رَبُّكَ ۚ وَلِذَٰلِكَ خَلَقَهُمْ ۗ وَتَمَّتْ كَلِمَةُ رَبِّكَ لَأَمْلَأَنَّ جَهَنَّمَ مِنَ ٱلْجِنَّةِ وَٱلنَّاسِ أَجْمَعِينَ ۝ ﴾

154. Except him on whom your Lord has bestowed His Mercy (the follower of truth - Islâmic Monotheism) and for that did He create them. And the Word of your Lord has been fulfilled (i.e. His Saying): "Surely, I shall fill Hell with jinn and men all together."

### Transliteration

118. Walaw shaa rabbuka lajaAAala alnnasa ommatan wahidatan wala yazaloona mukhtalifeena    119. Illa man rahima rabbuka walithalika khalaqahum watammat kalimatu rabbika laamlaanna jahannama mina aljinnati waalnnasi ajmaAAeena

### Tafsir Ibn Kathir

**Allah has not made Faith universally accepted**

Allah, the Exalted, informs that He is able to make all of mankind one nation upon belief, or disbelief. This is just as He said,

(And had your Lord willed, those on earth would have believed, all of them together.) (10:99) Allah goes on to say,

(but they will not cease to disagree. Except him on whom your Lord has bestowed His mercy,) This means that people will always differ in religions, creeds, beliefs, opinions and sects. Concerning Allah's statement,

(Except him on whom your Lord has bestowed His mercy,) This means that those who have received the mercy of Allah by following the Messengers are excluded from this. They are those who adhere to what they are commanded in the religion by the Messengers of Allah. That has always been their characteristic until the coming of the finality of the Prophets and Messengers (Muhammad). Those who received Allah's mercy are those who followed him, believed in him and supported him. Therefore, they succeeded by achieving happiness in this life and the Hereafter. They are the Saved Sect mentioned in the Hadith recorded in the Musnad and Sunan collections of Hadith. The routes of transmission of this Hadith all strengthen each other (in authenticity). In these narrations the Prophet said,

# Chapter 11: Hud (Hud), Verses 006-123

»إِنَّ الْيَهُودَ افْتَرَقَتْ عَلَى إِحْدَى وَسَبْعِينَ فِرْقَةً، وَإِنَّ النَّصَارَى افْتَرَقَتْ عَلَى اثْنَتَيْنِ وَسَبْعِينَ فِرْقَةً، وَسَتَفْتَرِقُ هَذِهِ الْأُمَّةُ عَلَى ثَلَاثٍ وَسَبْعِينَ فِرْقَةً، كُلُّهَا فِي النَّارِ إِلَّا فِرْقَةً وَاحِدَةً«

(Verily, the Jews split into seventy-one sects, and the Christians split into seventy-two sects, and this nation (of Muslims) will split into seventy-three sects. All of them will be in the Fire except one sect.) They (the Companions) said, "Who are they (the Saved Sect) O Messenger of Allah" He said,

»مَا أَنَا عَلَيْهِ وَأَصْحَابِي«

(The sect that is upon what my Companions and I are upon.) Al-Hakim recorded this narration in his Mustadrak with this additional wording. Concerning Allah's statement, (And the Word of your Lord has been fulfilled (His saying): "Surely, I shall fill Hell with Jinn and men all together.") Allah, the Exalted, informs that He precedes everything in His preordainment and decree, by His perfect knowledge and penetrating wisdom. The result of this decree is that from those whom He has created, some deserve the Paradise and some deserve the Hell Fire. From this decree is that He will fill the Hellfire with both mankind and Jinns. His is the profound evidence and the perfect wisdom. In the Two Sahihs it is recorded that Abu Hurayrah said that the Messenger of Allah said,

»اخْتَصَمَتِ الْجَنَّةُ وَالنَّارُ فَقَالَتِ الْجَنَّةُ: مَا لِي لَا يَدْخُلُنِي إِلَّا ضُعَفَاءُ النَّاسِ وَسَقَطُهُمْ وَقَالَتِ النَّارُ: أُوثِرْتُ بِالْمُتَكَبِّرِينَ وَالْمُتَجَبِّرِينَ. فَقَالَ اللَّهُ عَزَّ وَجَلَّ لِلْجَنَّةِ: أَنْتِ رَحْمَتِي أَرْحَمُ بِكِ مَنْ أَشَاءُ، وَقَالَ لِلنَّارِ: أَنْتِ عَذَابِي أَنْتَقِمُ بِكِ مِمَّنْ أَشَاءُ، وَلِكُلٍّ وَاحِدَةٍ مِنْكُمَا مِلْؤُهَا، فَأَمَّا الْجَنَّةُ فَلَا يَزَالُ فِيهَا فَضْلٌ، حَتَّى يُنْشِئَ اللَّهُ لَهَا خَلْقًا يُسْكِنُ فَضْلَ الْجَنَّةِ، وَأَمَّا النَّارُ فَلَا تَزَالُ تَقُولُ: هَلْ مِنْ مَزِيدٍ حَتَّى يَضَعَ عَلَيْهَا رَبُّ الْعِزَّةِ قَدَمَهُ فَتَقُولُ: قَطْ قَطْ وَعِزَّتِكَ«

(Paradise and the Hellfire debated. Paradise said, `None will enter me except the weak and despised of the people.' The Hellfire said, `I have inherited the haughty and the arrogant people.' Then Allah said to the Paradise, `You are My mercy and I grant mercy with you to whoever I wish.' Then He said to the Hellfire, `You are My torment and I take vengeance with you upon whoever I wish. I will fill each one of you.'

However, the Paradise will always have more bounties, to such an extent that Allah will create more creatures to dwell in it and enjoy its extra bounties. The Hellfire will continue saying, `Are there anymore (to enter me),' until the Lord of might places His Foot over it. Then it (Hell) will say, "Enough, enough, by Your might!")

### Surah: 11 Ayah: 120

﴿ وَكُلاًّ نَّقُصُّ عَلَيْكَ مِنْ أَنبَآءِ ٱلرُّسُلِ مَا نُثَبِّتُ بِهِۦ فُؤَادَكَ ۚ وَجَآءَكَ فِى هَـٰذِهِ ٱلْحَقُّ وَمَوْعِظَةٌ وَذِكْرَىٰ لِلْمُؤْمِنِينَ ﴿١٢٠﴾ ﴾

155. And all that We relate to you (O Muhammad (peace be upon him)) of the news of the Messengers is in order that We may make strong and firm your heart thereby. And in this (chapter of the Qur'an) has come to you the truth, as well as an admonition and a reminder for the believers.

### Transliteration

120. Wakullan naqussu AAalayka min anba-i alrrusuli ma nuthabbitu bihi fu-adaka wajaaka fee hathihi alhaqqu wamawAAithatun wathikra lilmu/mineena

### Tafsir Ibn Kathir

**The Conclusion**

Allah, the Exalted, is saying, `We relate all of these stories to you (Muhammad) concerning what happened with the Messengers who came before you with their nations. This is an explanation of what transpired in their arguments and disputes and how the Prophets were all rejected and harmed. These stories also explain how Allah helped His party of believers and disgraced His enemies, the disbelievers. We relate all of this to you (Muhammad) in order to make your heart firm and so that you may take an example from your brothers who passed before you of the Messengers.' Concerning Allah's statement,

(And in this has come to you the truth,) This is referring to this Surah itself. This was said by Ibn `Abbas, Mujahid and a group of the Salaf and it is the correct view. This means, `This comprehensive Surah contains the stories of the Prophets and how Allah saved them, and the believers along with them and how He destroyed the disbelievers. There has come to you (Muhammad) stories of truth and true events in this Surah. In this Surah is an admonition that prevents the disbelievers, and a reminder that causes the believers to reflect.'

### Surah: 11 Ayah: 121 & Ayah: 122

﴿ وَقُل لِّلَّذِينَ لَا يُؤْمِنُونَ ٱعْمَلُوا۟ عَلَىٰ مَكَانَتِكُمْ إِنَّا عَـٰمِلُونَ ﴿١٢١﴾ ﴾

156. And say to those who do not believe: "Act according to your ability and way, We are acting (in our way).

Chapter 11: Hud (Hud), Verses 006-123  91

$$\{ \text{وَٱنتَظِرُوٓاْ إِنَّا مُنتَظِرُونَ} ﴿١٢٢﴾ \}$$

157. And you wait ! We (too) are waiting."

### Transliteration

121. Waqul lillatheena la yu/minoona iAAmaloo AAala makanatikum inna AAamiloona
122. Waintathiroo inna muntathiroona

### Tafsir Ibn Kathir

**Allah, the Exalted, commands His Messenger to say to those who disbelieve in what he has come with from his Lord, by way of warning,**

(Act according to your ability) This means upon your path and your way.

(We are acting (in our way). This means that we are upon our path and our way (Islam).

(And you wait ! We (too) are waiting.) This means,

(And you will come to know for which of us will be the (happy) end in the Hereafter. Certainly the wrongdoers will not be successful.)(6:135) Verily, Allah fulfilled His promise to His Messenger , helped him and aided him. He made His Word uppermost (victorious), and the word of those who disbelieved lowly and disgraced. Allah is truly the Most Mighty, Most Wise.

### Surah: 11 Ayah: 123

$$\{ \text{وَلِلَّهِ غَيْبُ ٱلسَّمَٰوَٰتِ وَٱلْأَرْضِ وَإِلَيْهِ يُرْجَعُ ٱلْأَمْرُ كُلُّهُۥ فَٱعْبُدْهُ وَتَوَكَّلْ عَلَيْهِ ۚ وَمَا رَبُّكَ بِغَٰفِلٍ عَمَّا تَعْمَلُونَ} ﴿١٢٣﴾ \}$$

158. And to Allâh belongs the Ghaib (Unseen) of the heavens and the earth, and to Him return all affairs (for decision). So worship Him (O Muhammad (peace be upon him)) and put your trust in Him. And your Lord is not unaware of what you (people) do.

### Transliteration

123. Walillahi ghaybu alssamawati waal-ardi wa-ilayhi yurjaAAu al-amru kulluhu faoAAbudhu watawakkal AAalayhi wama rabbuka bighafilin AAamma taAAmaloona

### Tafsir Ibn Kathir

**Allah, the Exalted, informs that He is the All-Knower of the unseen of the heavens and the earth and that unto Him is the final return.**

He explains that everyone who does a deed, He will give them their deed (reward for it) on the Day of Reckoning. Unto Him belongs the creation and the command. Then

He, the Exalted, commands that He should be worshipped and relied upon, for verily, He is sufficient for whoever trusts and turns to Him. Concerning His statement,

(And your Lord is not unaware of what you do.) This means, `The lies (of the disbelievers) against you O Muhammad are not hidden from Him. He is the All-Knower of the conditions of His creatures and He will give them the perfect recompense for their deeds in this life and the Hereafter. He will aid you (Muhammad) and His party over the disbelievers in this life and in the Hereafter.' This is the end of the Tafsir of Surah Hud, and all praises and thanks are due to Allah.

## CHAPTER (SURAH) 12: YUSUF (JOSEPH), VERSES 001-052

﴿ بِسْمِ ٱللَّهِ ٱلرَّحْمَٰنِ ٱلرَّحِيمِ ﴾

In the Name of Allâh, the Most Gracious, the Most Merciful..

### Surah: 12 Ayah: 1, Ayah: 2 & Ayah: 3

﴿ الٓر تِلْكَ ءَايَٰتُ ٱلْكِتَٰبِ ٱلْمُبِينِ ﴾

1. Alif-Lâm-Râ. (These letters are one of the miracles of the Qur'an, and none but Allâh (Alone) knows their meanings). These are the Verses of the Clear Book (the Qur'ân that makes clear the legal and illegal things, legal laws, a guidance and a blessing).

﴿ إِنَّآ أَنزَلْنَٰهُ قُرْءَٰنًا عَرَبِيًّا لَّعَلَّكُمْ تَعْقِلُونَ ﴾

2. Verily, We have sent it down as an Arabic Qur'ân in order that you may understand.

﴿ نَحْنُ نَقُصُّ عَلَيْكَ أَحْسَنَ ٱلْقَصَصِ بِمَآ أَوْحَيْنَآ إِلَيْكَ هَٰذَا ٱلْقُرْءَانَ وَإِن كُنتَ مِن قَبْلِهِۦ لَمِنَ ٱلْغَٰفِلِينَ ﴾

3. We relate unto you (Muhammad (peace be upon him)) the best of stories through Our Revelations unto you, of this Qur'ân. And before this (i.e. before the coming of Divine Revelation to you), you were among those who knew nothing about it (the Qur'an).

### Transliteration

1. Alif-lam-ra tilka ayatu alkitabi almubeenu   2. Inna anzalnahu qur-anan AAarabiyyan laAAallakum taAAqiloona   3. Nahnu naqussu AAalayka ahsana alqasasi bima awhayna ilayka hatha alqur-ana wa-in kunta min qablihi lamina alghafileena

# Chapter 12: Yusuf (Joseph), Verses 001-052

## Tafsir Ibn Kathir

### Qualities of the Qur'an

In the beginning of Surat Al-Baqarah we talked about the separate letters, Allah said,

(These are the verses of the Book) in reference to the Clear Qur'an that is plain and apparent, and explains, clarifies and makes known the unclear matters. Allah said next,

(Verily, We have sent it down as an Arabic Qur'an in order that you may understand.) The Arabic language is the most eloquent, plain, deep and expressive of the meanings that might arise in one's mind. Therefore, the most honorable Book, was revealed in the most honorable language, to the most honorable Prophet and Messenger , delivered by the most honorable angel, in the most honorable land on earth, and its revelation started during the most honorable month of the year, Ramadan. Therefore, the Qur'an is perfect in every respect. So Allah said,

(We relate unto you the best of stories through Our revelations unto you, of this Qur'an.)

### Reason behind revealing Ayah (12:3)

On the reason behind revealing Ayah (12:3), Ibn Jarir At-Tabari recorded that `Abdullah bin `Abbas said, "They said, `O, Allah's Messenger! Why not narrate to us stories' Later on, this Ayah was revealed,

(We relate unto you the best of stories...)" There is a Hadith that is relevant upon mentioning this honorable Ayah, which praises the Qur'an and demonstrates that it is sufficient from needing all books besides it. Imam Ahmad recorded a narration from Jabir bin `Abdullah that `Umar bin Al-Khattab came to the Prophet with a book that he took from some of the People of the Book. `Umar began reading it to the Prophet who became angry. He said,

«أَمُتَهَوِّكُونَ فِيهَا يَا ابْنَ الْخَطَّابِ؟ وَالَّذِي نَفْسِي بِيَدِهِ، لَقَدْ جِئْتُكُمْ بِهَا بَيْضَاءَ نَقِيَّةً، لَا تَسْأَلُوهُمْ عَنْ شَيْءٍ فَيُخْبِرُوكُمْ بِحَقٍّ فَتُكَذِّبُونَهُ، أَوْ بِبَاطِلٍ فَتُصَدِّقُونَهُ، وَالَّذِي نَفْسِي بِيَدِهِ، لَوْ أَنَّ مُوسَى كَانَ حَيًّا مَا وَسِعَهُ إِلَّا أَنْ يَتَّبِعَنِي»

(Are you uncertain about it Ibn Al-Khattab By the One in Whose Hand is my soul! I have come to you with it white and pure. Do not ask them about anything, for they might tell you something true and you reject it, or they might tell you something false and you believe it. By the One in Whose Hand is my soul! If Musa were living, he would have no choice but to follow me.) Imam Ahmad also recorded a narration from `Abdullah bin Thabit who said, "`Umar came to Allah's Messenger and said; `O Messenger of Allah! I passed by a brother of mine from (the tribe of) Qurayzah, so he wrote some comprehensive statements from the Tawrah for me, should I read them to you' The face of Allah's Messenger changed (with anger). So I said to him, `Don't you see the face of Allah's Messenger" `Umar said, `We are pleased with Allah as our Lord, Islam as our religion, and Muhammad as our Messenger.' So the anger of the Prophet subsided, and he said,

»وَالَّذِي نَفْسُ مُحَمَّدٍ بِيَدِهِ، لَوْ أَصْبَحَ فِيكُمْ مُوسَى ثُمَّ اتَّبَعْتُمُوهُ وَتَرَكْتُمُونِي لَضَلَلْتُمْ، إِنَّكُمْ حَظِّي مِنَ الْأُمَمِ، وَأَنَا حَظُّكُمْ مِنَ النَّبِيِّينَ«

(By the One in Whose Hand is Muhammad's soul, if Musa appeared among you and you were to follow him, abandoning me, then you would have strayed. Indeed you are my share of the nations, and I am your share of the Prophets.)"

### Surah: 12 Ayah: 4

﴿ إِذْ قَالَ يُوسُفُ لِأَبِيهِ يَٰٓأَبَتِ إِنِّى رَأَيْتُ أَحَدَ عَشَرَ كَوْكَبًا وَٱلشَّمْسَ وَٱلْقَمَرَ رَأَيْتُهُمْ لِى سَٰجِدِينَ ﴾

4. (Remember) when Yûsuf (Joseph) said to his father: "O my father! Verily, I saw (in a dream) eleven stars and the sun and the moon - I saw them prostrating themselves to me."

### Transliteration

4. Ith qala yoosufu li-abeehi ya abati innee raaytu ahada AAashara kawkaban waalshshamsa waalqamara raaytuhum lee sajideena

### Tafsir Ibn Kathir

**Yusuf's Dream**

Allah says, `Mention to your people, O Muhammad, among the stories that you narrate to them, the story of Yusuf.' Prophet Yusuf (Joseph) mentioned his dream to his father, Prophet Ya`qub (Jacob), son of Prophet Ishaq (Isaac), son of Prophet Ibrahim (Abraham), peace be upon them all. `Abdullah bin `Abbas stated that the dreams of Prophets are revelations from Allah. Scholars of Tafsir explained that in Yusuf's dream the eleven stars represent his brothers, who were eleven, and the sun and the moon represent his father and mother. This explanation was collected from Ibn `Abbas, Ad-Dahhak, Qatadah, Sufyan Ath-Thawri and `Abdur-Rahman bin Zayd bin Aslam. Yusuf's vision became a reality forty years later, or as some say, eighty years, when Yusuf raised his parents to the throne while his brothers were before him,

(and they fell down before him prostrate. And he said: "O my father! This is the interpretation of my dream aforetime! My Lord has made it come true!")

# Chapter 12: Yusuf (Joseph), Verses 001-052

### Surah: 12 Ayah: 5

﴿ قَالَ يَـٰبُنَىَّ لَا تَقْصُصْ رُءْيَاكَ عَلَىٰٓ إِخْوَتِكَ فَيَكِيدُوا۟ لَكَ كَيْدًا ۖ إِنَّ ٱلشَّيْطَـٰنَ لِلْإِنسَـٰنِ عَدُوٌّ مُّبِينٌ ۝ ﴾

5. He (the father) said: "O my son! Relate not your vision to your brothers, lest they should arrange a plot against you. Verily! Shaitân (Satan) is to man an open enemy!

### Transliteration

5. Qala ya bunayya la taqsus ru/yaka AAala ikhwatika fayakeedoo laka kaydan inna alshshaytana lilinsani AAaduwwun mubeenun

### Tafsir Ibn Kathir

#### Ya`qub orders Yusuf to hide His Vision to avoid Shaytan's Plots

Allah narrates the reply Ya`qub gave his son Yusuf when he narrated to him the vision that he saw, which indicated that his brothers would be under his authority. They would be subjugated to Yusuf's authority to such an extent that they would prostrate before him in respect, honor and appreciation. Ya`qub feared that if Yusuf narrated his vision to any of his brothers, they would envy him and conspire evil plots against him. This is why Ya`qub said to Yusuf,

(Relate not your vision to your brothers, lest they should arrange a plot against you.) This Ayah means, "They might arrange a plot against you that causes your demise." In the Sunnah, there is a confirmed Hadith that states,

«إِذَا رَأَى أَحَدُكُمْ مَا يُحِبُّ فَلْيُحَدِّثْ بِهِ، وَإِذَا رَأَى مَا يَكْرَهُ فَلْيَتَحَوَّلْ إِلَى جَنْبِهِ الْآخَرِ، وَلْيَتْفُلْ عَنْ يَسَارِهِ ثَلَاثًا، وَلْيَسْتَعِذْ بِاللهِ مِنْ شَرِّهَا، وَلَا يُحَدِّثْ بِهَا أَحَدًا فَإِنَّهَا لَنْ تَضُرَّه»

(If any of you saw a vision that he likes, let him narrate it. If he saw a dream that he dislikes, let him turn on his other side, blow to his left thrice, seek refuge with Allah from its evil and not tell it to anyone. Verily, it will not harm him in this case.) In another Hadith that Imam Ahmad and collectors of the Sunan collected, Mu`awiyah bin Haydah Al-Qushayri said that the Messenger of Allah said,

«الرُّؤْيَا عَلَى رِجْلِ طَائِرٍ مَا لَمْ تُعْبَرْ، فَإِذَا عُبِرَتْ وَقَعَت»

(The dream is tied to a bird's leg, as long as it is not interpreted. If it is interpreted, it comes true.) Therefore, one should hide the prospects or the coming of a bounty until it comes into existence and becomes known. The Prophet said,

«اسْتَعِينُوا عَلَى قَضَاءِ الْحَوَائِجِ بِكِتْمَانِهَا، فَإِنَّ كُلَّ ذِي نِعْمَةٍ مَحْسُود»

(Earn help for fulfilling needs by being discrete, for every owner of a blessing is envied.)

### Surah: 12 Ayah: 6

﴿ وَكَذَلِكَ يَجْتَبِيكَ رَبُّكَ وَيُعَلِّمُكَ مِن تَأْوِيلِ ٱلْأَحَادِيثِ وَيُتِمُّ نِعْمَتَهُۥ عَلَيْكَ وَعَلَىٰٓ ءَالِ يَعْقُوبَ كَمَآ أَتَمَّهَا عَلَىٰٓ أَبَوَيْكَ مِن قَبْلُ إِبْرَٰهِيمَ وَإِسْحَٰقَ إِنَّ رَبَّكَ عَلِيمٌ حَكِيمٌ ۝ ﴾

6. "Thus will your Lord choose you and teach you the interpretation of dreams (and other things) and perfect His Favor on you and on the offspring of Ya'qûb (Jacob), as He perfected it on your fathers, Ibrâhîm (Abraham) and Ishâq (Isaac) aforetime! Verily, your Lord is All-Knowing, All-Wise."

### Transliteration

6. Wakathalika yajtabeeka rabbuka wayuAAallimuka min ta/weeli al-ahadeethi wayutimmu niAAmatahu AAalayka waAAala ali yaAAqooba kama atammaha AAala abawayka min qablu ibraheema wa-ishaqa inna rabbaka AAaleemun hakeemun

### Tafsir Ibn Kathir

#### Interpretation of Yusuf's Vision

Allah says that Ya`qub said to his son Yusuf, `Just as Allah chose you to see the eleven stars, the sun and the moon prostrate before you in a vision,

(Thus will your Lord choose you) designate and assign you to be a Prophet from Him,

(and teach you the interpretation of Ahadith).' Mujahid and several other scholars said that this part of the Ayah is in reference to the interpreting of dreams. He said next,

(and perfect His favor on you), `by His Message and revelation to you.' This is why Ya`qub said afterwards,

(as He perfected it aforetime on your fathers, Ibrahim...), Allah's intimate friend,

(and Ishaq), Ibrahim's son,

(Verily, your Lord is All-Knowing, All-Wise.) Allah knows best whom to chose for His Messages.

# Chapter 12: Yusuf (Joseph), Verses 001-052

## Surah: 12 Ayah: 7, Ayah: 8, Ayah: 9 & Ayah: 10

﴿ ۞ لَّقَدْ كَانَ فِى يُوسُفَ وَإِخْوَتِهِۦٓ ءَايَـٰتٌ لِّلسَّآئِلِينَ ﴾

7. Verily, in Yûsuf (Joseph) and his brethren, there were Ayât (proofs, evidences, verses, lessons, signs, revelations, etc.) for those who ask.

﴿ إِذْ قَالُوا۟ لَيُوسُفُ وَأَخُوهُ أَحَبُّ إِلَىٰٓ أَبِينَا مِنَّا وَنَحْنُ عُصْبَةٌ إِنَّ أَبَانَا لَفِى ضَلَـٰلٍ مُّبِينٍ ﴾

8. When they said: "Truly, Yûsuf (Joseph) and his brother (Benjamin) are dearer to our father than we, while we are a strong group. Really, our father is in a plain error.

﴿ ٱقْتُلُوا۟ يُوسُفَ أَوِ ٱطْرَحُوهُ أَرْضًا يَخْلُ لَكُمْ وَجْهُ أَبِيكُمْ وَتَكُونُوا۟ مِنْ بَعْدِهِۦ قَوْمًا صَـٰلِحِينَ ﴾

9. "Kill Yûsuf (Joseph) or cast him out to some (other) land, so that the favor of your father may be given to you alone, and after that you will be righteous folk (by intending repentance before committing the sin)."

﴿ قَالَ قَآئِلٌ مِّنْهُمْ لَا تَقْتُلُوا۟ يُوسُفَ وَأَلْقُوهُ فِى غَيَـٰبَتِ ٱلْجُبِّ يَلْتَقِطْهُ بَعْضُ ٱلسَّيَّارَةِ إِن كُنتُمْ فَـٰعِلِينَ ﴾

10. One from among them said: "Kill not Yûsuf (Joseph), but if you must do something, throw him down to the bottom of a well, he will be picked up by some caravan of travelers."

### Transliteration

7. Laqad kana fee yoosufa wa-ikhwatihi ayatun lilssa-ileena 8. Ith qaloo layoosufu waakhoohu ahabbu ila abeena minna wanahnu AAusbatun inna abana lafee dalalin mubeenin 9. Oqtuloo yoosufa awi itrahoohu ardan yakhlu lakum wajhu abeekum watakoonoo min baAAdihi qawman saliheena 10. Qala qa-ilun minhum la taqtuloo yoosufa waalqoohu fee ghayabati aljubbi yaltaqithu baAAdu alssayyarati in kuntum faAAileena

### Tafsir Ibn Kathir

#### There are Lessons to draw from the Story of Yusuf

Allah says that there are Ayat, lessons and wisdom to learn from the story of Yusuf and his brothers, for those who ask about their story and seek its knowledge. Surely, their story is unique and is worthy of being narrated.

(When they said: "Truly, Yusuf and his brother are dearer to our father than we...") They swore, according to their false thoughts, that Yusuf and his brother Binyamin (Benjamin), Yusuf's full brother,

(dearer to our father than we, while we are `Usbah.) meaning, a group. Therefore, they thought, how can he love these two more than the group,

(Really, our father is in a plain error.) because he preferred them and loved them more than us.

(Kill Yusuf or cast him out to some (other) land, so that the favor of your father may be given to you alone,) They said, `Remove Yusuf, who competes with you for your father's love, from in front of your father's face so that his favor is yours alone. Either kill Yusuf or banish him to a distant land so that you are rid of his trouble and you alone enjoy the love of your father. '

(and after that you will be righteous folk.), thus intending repentance before committing the sin,

(One from among them said...) Qatadah and Muhammad bin Ishaq said that he was the oldest among them and his name was Rubil (Reuben). As-Suddi said that his name was Yahudha (Judah). Mujahid said that it was Sham`un (Simeon) who said,

(Kill not Yusuf,), do not let your enmity and hatred towards him reach this level, of murder. However, their plot to kill Yusuf would not have succeeded, because Allah the Exalted willed that Yusuf fulfill a mission that must be fulfilled and complete; he would receive Allah's revelation and become His Prophet. Allah willed Yusuf to be a powerful man in Egypt and govern it. Consequently, Allah did not allow them to persist in their intent against Yusuf, through Rubil's words and his advice to them that if they must do something, they should throw him down to the bottom of a well,

(he will be picked up by some caravan) of travelers passing by. This way, he said, you will rid yourselves of this bother without having to kill him,

(if you must do something,) meaning, if you still insist on getting rid of him. Muhammad bin Ishaq bin Yasar said, "They agreed to a particularly vicious crime that involved cutting the relation of the womb, undutiful treatment of parents, and harshness towards the young, helpless and sinless. It was also harsh towards the old and weak who have the rights of being respected, honored and appreciated, as well as, being honored with Allah and having parental rights on their offspring. They sought to separate the beloved father, who had reached old age and his bones became weak, yet had a high status with Allah, from his beloved young son, in spite of his weakness, tender age and his need of his father's compassion and kindness. May Allah forgive them, and indeed, He is the Most Merciful among those who have mercy, for they intended to carry out a "grave error." Ibn Abi Hatim collected this state-ment, from the route of Salamah bin Al-Fadl from Muhammad bin Ishaq.

# Chapter 12: Yusuf (Joseph), Verses 001-052

### Surah: 12 Ayah: 11 & Ayah: 12

﴿ قَالُواْ يَٰٓأَبَانَا مَا لَكَ لَا تَأْمَنَّا عَلَىٰ يُوسُفَ وَإِنَّا لَهُۥ لَنَٰصِحُونَ ۝ ﴾

11. They said: "O our father! Why do you not trust us with Yûsuf (Joseph) though we are indeed his well-wishers?"

﴿ أَرْسِلْهُ مَعَنَا غَدًا يَرْتَعْ وَيَلْعَبْ وَإِنَّا لَهُۥ لَحَٰفِظُونَ ۝ ﴾

12. "Send him with us tomorrow to enjoy himself and play, and verily, we will take care of him."

### Transliteration

11. Qaloo ya abana ma laka la ta/manna AAala yoosufa wa-inna lahu lanasihoona
12. Arsilhu maAAana ghadan yartaAA wayalAAab wa-inna lahu lahafithoona

### Tafsir Ibn Kathir

**Yusuf's Brothers ask for Their Father's Permission to take Yusuf with Them**

When Yusuf's brothers agreed to take him and throw him down the well, taking the advice of their elder brother Rubil, they went to their father Ya`qub, peace be upon him. They said to him, "Why is it that you,

(do not trust us with Yusuf though we are indeed his well-wishers)." They started executing their plan by this introductory statement, even though they really intended its opposite, out of envy towards Yusuf for being loved by his father. They said,

"(Send him with us) tomorrow so that we all enjoy ourselves and play." Qatadah, Ad-Dahhak and As-Suddi said similarly. Yusuf's brothers said next,

(and verily, we will take care of him.), we will protect him and ensure his safety for you

### Surah: 12 Ayah: 13 & Ayah: 14

﴿ قَالَ إِنِّي لَيَحْزُنُنِي أَن تَذْهَبُواْ بِهِۦ وَأَخَافُ أَن يَأْكُلَهُ ٱلذِّئْبُ وَأَنتُمْ عَنْهُ غَٰفِلُونَ ۝ ﴾

13. He (Ya'qûb (Jacob)) said: "Truly, it saddens me that you should take him away. I fear lest a wolf should devour him, while you are careless of him."

﴿ قَالُواْ لَئِنْ أَكَلَهُ ٱلذِّئْبُ وَنَحْنُ عُصْبَةٌ إِنَّآ إِذًا لَّخَٰسِرُونَ ۝ ﴾

14. They said: "If a wolf devours him, while we are a strong group (to guard him), then surely, we are the losers."

### Transliteration

13. Qala innee layahzununee an thathhaboo bihi waakhafu an ya/kulahu aththi/bu waantum AAanhu ghafiloona   14. Qaloo la-in akalahu aththi/bu wanahnu AAusbatun inna ithan lakhasiroona

### Tafsir Ibn Kathir

#### Ya`qub's Answer to Their Request

Allah narrates to us that His Prophet Ya`qub said to his children, in response to their request that he send Yusuf with them to the desert to tend their cattle,

(Truly, it saddens me that you should take him away.) He said that it was hard on him that he be separated from Yusuf for the duration of their trip, until they came back. This demonstrates the deep love that Ya`qub had for his son, because he saw in Yusuf great goodness and exalted qualities with regards to conduct and physical attractiveness associated with the rank of prophethood. May Allah's peace and blessings be on him. Prophet Ya`qub's statement next,

(I fear lest a wolf should devour him, while you are careless of him.) He said to them, `I fear that you might be careless with him while you are tending the cattle and shooting, then a wolf might come and eat him while you are unaware.' They heard these words from his mouth and used them in their response for what they did afterwards. They also gave a spontaneous reply for their father's statement, saying,

(If a wolf devours him, while we are an `Usbah, then surely, we are the losers.) They said, `If a wolf should attack and devour him while we are all around him in a strong group, then indeed we are the losers and weak.'

### Surah: 12 Ayah: 15

﴿ فَلَمَّا ذَهَبُواْ بِهِ وَأَجْمَعُواْ أَن يَجْعَلُوهُ فِى غَيَبَتِ ٱلْجُبِّ وَأَوْحَيْنَآ إِلَيْهِ لَتُنَبِّئَنَّهُم بِأَمْرِهِمْ هَـٰذَا وَهُمْ لَا يَشْعُرُونَ ﴿١٥﴾

15. So, when they took him away and they all agreed to throw him down to the bottom of the well, (they did so) and We revealed to him: "Indeed, you shall (one day) inform them of this their affair, when they know (you) not."

### Transliteration

15. Falamma thahaboo bihi waajmaAAoo an yajAAaloohu fee ghayabati aljubbi waawhayna ilayhi latunabi-annahum bi-amrihim hatha wahum la yashAAuroona

### Tafsir Ibn Kathir

#### Yusuf is thrown in a Well

Allah says that when Yusuf's brothers took him from his father, after they requested him to permit that, (they all agreed to throw him down to the bottom of the well,) This part of the Ayah magnifies their crime, in that it mentions that they all agreed to throw him to the bottom of the well. This was their intent, yet when they took him from his father, they pretended otherwise, so that his father sends him with a good heart and feeling at ease and comfortable with his decision. It was reported that Ya`qub, peace be upon him, embraced Yusuf, kissed him and supplicated to Allah for him when he sent him with his brothers. As-Suddi said that the time spent between pretending to be well-wishers and harming Yusuf was no longer than their straying far from their father's eyes. They then started abusing Yusuf verbally, by cursing, and harming him by beating. When they reached the well that they agreed to throw him in, they tied him with rope and lowered him down. When Yusuf would beg one of them, he would smack and curse him. When he tried to hold to the sides of the well, they struck his hand and then cut the rope when he was only half the distance from the bottom of the well. He fell into the water and was submerged. However, he was able to ascend a stone that was in the well and stood on it. Allah said next,

(and We revealed to him: "Indeed, you shall (one day) inform them of this their affair, when they know (you) not. ") In this Ayah, Allah mentions His mercy and compassion and His compensation and relief that He sends in times of distress. Allah revealed to Yusuf, during that distressful time, in order to comfort his heart and strengthen his resolve, `Do not be saddened by what you have suffered. Surely, you will have a way out of this distress and a good end, for Allah will aid you against them, elevate your rank and raise your grade. Later on, you will remind them of what they did to you,' i

(when they know not.) "Ibn `Abbas commented on this Ayah, "You will remind them of this evil action against you, while they are unaware of your identity and unable to recognize you."

## Surah: 12 Ayah: 16, Ayah: 17 & Ayah: 18

﴿ وَجَآءُو أَبَاهُمْ عِشَآءً يَبْكُونَ ۞ ﴾

16. And they came to their father in the early part of the night weeping.

﴿ قَالُوا۟ يَٰٓأَبَانَآ إِنَّا ذَهَبْنَا نَسْتَبِقُ وَتَرَكْنَا يُوسُفَ عِندَ مَتَٰعِنَا فَأَكَلَهُ ٱلذِّئْبُ وَمَآ أَنتَ بِمُؤْمِنٍ لَّنَا وَلَوْ كُنَّا صَٰدِقِينَ ۞ ﴾

17. They said: "O our father! We went racing with one another, and left Yûsuf (Joseph) by our belongings and a wolf devoured him; but you will never believe us even when we speak the truth."

﴿ وَجَآءُو عَلَىٰ قَمِيصِهِۦ بِدَمٍ كَذِبٍ قَالَ بَلْ سَوَّلَتْ لَكُمْ أَنفُسُكُمْ أَمْرًا فَصَبْرٌ جَمِيلٌ وَٱللَّهُ ٱلْمُسْتَعَانُ عَلَىٰ مَا تَصِفُونَ ۞ ﴾

18. And they brought his shirt stained with false blood. He said: "Nay, but your own selves have made up a tale. So (for me) patience is most fitting. And it is Allâh (Alone) Whose help can be sought against that (lie) which you describe."

### Transliteration

16. Wajaoo abahum AAishaan yabkoona  17. Qaloo ya abana inna thahabna nastabiqu watarakna yoosufa AAinda mataAAina faakalahu alththi/bu wama anta bimu/minin lana walaw kunna sadiqeena  18. Wajaoo AAala qameesihi bidamin kathibin qala bal sawwalat lakum anfusukum amran fasabrun jameelun waAllahu almustaAAanu AAala ma tasifoona

### Tafsir Ibn Kathir

**Yusuf's Brothers try to deceive Their Father**

Allah narrates to us the deceit that Yusuf's brothers resorted to, after they threw him to the bottom of the well. They went back to their father, during the darkness of the night, crying and showing sorrow and grief for losing Yusuf. They started giving excuses to their father for what happened to Yusuf, falsely claiming that,

(We went racing with one another), or had a shooting competition,

(and left Yusuf by our belongings), guarding our clothes and luggage,

(and a wolf devoured him), which is exactly what their father told them he feared for Yusuf and warned against. They said next,

(but you will never believe us even when we speak the truth.) They tried to lessen the impact of the grave news they were delivering. They said, `We know that you will not believe this news, even if you consider us truthful. So what about when you suspect that we are not truthful, especially since you feared that the wolf might devour Yusuf and that is what happened' Therefore, they said, `You have reason not to believe us because of the strange coincidence and the amazing occurrence that happened to us.'

(And they brought his shirt stained with false blood.) on it, to help prove plot that they all agreed on. They slaughtered a sheep, according to Mujahid, As-Suddi and several other scholars, and stained Yusuf's shirt with its blood. They claimed that this was the shirt Yusuf was wearing when the wolf devoured him, being stained with his blood. But, they forgot to tear the shirt, and this is why Allah's Prophet Ya`qub did not believe them. Rather, he told them what he felt about what they said to him, thus refusing their false claim,

(Nay, but your ownselves have made up a tale. So (for me) patience is most fitting.) Ya`qub said, `I will firmly observe patience for this plot on which you agreed, until Allah relieves the distress with His aid and compassion,

(And it is Allah (alone) Whose help can be sought against that which you describe.), against the lies and unbelievable incident that you said had occurred.'

# Chapter 12: Yusuf (Joseph), Verses 001-052

### Surah: 12 Ayah: 19 & Ayah: 20

﴿ وَجَاءَتْ سَيَّارَةٌ فَأَرْسَلُوا وَارِدَهُمْ فَأَدْلَىٰ دَلْوَهُ ۖ قَالَ يَا بُشْرَىٰ هَـٰذَا غُلَامٌ ۚ وَأَسَرُّوهُ بِضَاعَةً ۚ وَاللَّهُ عَلِيمٌ بِمَا يَعْمَلُونَ ۝ ﴾

19. And there came a caravan of travelers and they sent their water-drawer, and he let down his bucket (into the well). He said: "What good news! Here is a boy." So they hid him as merchandise (a slave). And Allâh was the All-Knower of what they did.

﴿ وَشَرَوْهُ بِثَمَنٍ بَخْسٍ دَرَاهِمَ مَعْدُودَةٍ وَكَانُوا فِيهِ مِنَ الزَّاهِدِينَ ۝ ﴾

20. And they sold him for a low price - for a few Dirhams (i.e. for a few silver coins). And they were of those who regarded him insignificant.

### Transliteration

19. Wajaat sayyaratun faarsaloo waridahum faadla dalwahu qala ya bushra hatha ghulamun waasarroohu bidaAAatan waAllahu AAaleemun bima yaAAmaloona 20. Washarawhu bithamanin bakhsin darahima maAAdoodatin wakanoo feehi mina alzzahideena

### Tafsir Ibn Kathir

#### Yusuf is Rescued from the Well and sold as a Slave

Allah narrates what happened to Yusuf, peace be upon him, after his brothers threw him down the well and left him in it, alone, where he remained for three days, according to Abu Bakr bin `Ayyash. Muhammad bin Ishaq said, "After Yusuf's brothers threw him down the well, they remained around the well for the rest of the day to see what he might do and what would happen to him. Allah sent a caravan of travelers that camped near that well, and they sent to it the man responsible for drawing water for them. When he approached the well, he lowered his bucket down into it, Yusuf held on to it and the man rescued him and felt happy,

("What good news! Here is a boy.") Al-`Awfi reported that Ibn `Abbas commented, "Allah's statement,

(So they hid him as merchandise), is in reference to Yusuf's brothers, who hid the news that he was their brother. Yusuf hid this news for fear that his brothers might kill him and preferred to be sold instead. Consequently, Yusuf's brothers told the water drawer about him and that man said to his companions,

("What good news! Here is a boy."), a slave whom we can sell. Therefore, Yusuf's own brothers sold him." Allah's statement,

(And Allah was the All-Knower of what they did. ) states that Allah knew what Yusuf's brothers, and those who bought him, did. He was able to stop them and prevent them from committing their actions, but out of His perfect wisdom He decreed otherwise.

He let them do what they did, so that His decision prevails and His appointed destiny rules,

(Surely, His is the creation and commandment. Blessed is Allah, the Lord of the all that exists!) (7:54) This reminds Allah's Messenger Muhammad , that Allah has perfect knowledge in the persecution that his people committed against him and that He is able to stop them. However, He decided to give them respite, then give Muhammad the victory and make him prevail over them, just as He gave Yusuf victory and made him prevail over his brothers. Allah said next,

(And they sold him for a Bakhs price, - for a few Dirhams) in reference to Yusuf's brothers selling him for a little price, according to Mujahid and `Ikrimah. `Bakhs' means decreased, just as Allah the Exalted said in another Ayah,

(shall have no fear, either of a Bakhs (a decrease in the reward of his good deeds) or a Rahaq (an increase in the punishment for his sins).) (72:13) meaning that Yusuf's brothers exchanged him for a miserably low price. Yet, he was so insignificant to them that had the caravan people wanted him for free, they would have given him for free to them! Ibn `Abbas, Mujahid and Ad-Dahhak said that,

(And they sold him), is in reference to Yusuf's brothers. They sold Yusuf for the lowest price, as indicated by Allah's statement next,

(for a few Dirhams), twenty Dirhams, according to `Abdullah bin Mas`ud. Similar was said by Ibn `Abbas, Nawf Al-Bikali, As-Suddi, Qatadah and `Atiyah Al-`Awfi, who added that they divided the Dirhams among themselves, each getting two Dirhams. Ad-Dahhak commented on Allah's statement,

(And they were of those who regarded him insignificant.) "Because they had no knowledge of his prophethood and glorious rank with Allah, the Exalted and Most Honored."

### Surah: 12 Ayah: 21 & Ayah: 22

﴿ وَقَالَ ٱلَّذِى ٱشْتَرَىٰهُ مِن مِّصْرَ لِٱمْرَأَتِهِۦٓ أَكْرِمِى مَثْوَىٰهُ عَسَىٰٓ أَن يَنفَعَنَآ أَوْ نَتَّخِذَهُۥ وَلَدًا ۚ وَكَذَٰلِكَ مَكَّنَّا لِيُوسُفَ فِى ٱلْأَرْضِ وَلِنُعَلِّمَهُۥ مِن تَأْوِيلِ ٱلْأَحَادِيثِ ۚ وَٱللَّهُ غَالِبٌ عَلَىٰٓ أَمْرِهِۦ وَلَٰكِنَّ أَكْثَرَ ٱلنَّاسِ لَا يَعْلَمُونَ ﴾

21. And he (the man) from Egypt who bought him, said to his wife: "Make his stay comfortable, may be he will profit us or we shall adopt him as a son." Thus did We establish Yûsuf (Joseph) in the land, that We might teach him the interpretation of events. And Allâh has full power and control over His Affairs, but most of men know not.

﴿ وَلَمَّا بَلَغَ أَشُدَّهُۥٓ ءَاتَيْنَٰهُ حُكْمًا وَعِلْمًا ۚ وَكَذَٰلِكَ نَجْزِى ٱلْمُحْسِنِينَ ﴾

22. And when he (Yûsuf (Joseph)) attained his full manhood, We gave him wisdom and knowledge (the Prophethood); thus We reward the Muhsinûn (doers of good).

### Transliteration

21. Waqala allathee ishtarahu min misra liimraatihi akrimee mathwahu AAasa an yanfaAAana aw nattakhithahu waladan wakathalika makkanna liyoosufa fee al-ardi walinuAAallimahu min ta/weeli alahadeethi waAllahu ghalibun AAala amrihi walakinna akthara alnnasi la yaAAlamoona 22. Walamma balagha ashuddahu ataynahu hukman waAAilman wakathalika najzee almuhsineena

### Tafsir Ibn Kathir

#### Yusuf in Egypt

Allah mentions the favors that He granted Yusuf, peace be on him, by which He made the man from Egypt who bought him, take care of him and provide him with a comfortable life. He also ordered his wife to be kind to Yusuf and had good hopes for his future, because of his firm righteous behavior. He said to his wife,

(Make his stay comfortable, maybe he will profit us or we shall adopt him as a son.) The man who bought Yusuf was the minister of Egypt at the time, and his title was `Aziz'. Abu Ishaq narrated that Abu `Ubaydah said that `Abdullah bin Mas`ud said, "Three had the most insight: the `Aziz of Egypt, who said to his wife,

(Make his stay comfortable...), the woman who said to her father,

(O my father! Hire him...), (28:26) and Abu Bakr As-Siddiq when he appointed `Umar bin Al-Khattab to be the Khalifah after him, may Allah be pleased with them both." Allah said next that just as He saved Yusuf from his brothers,

(Thus did We establish Yusuf in the land), in reference to Egypt,

(that We might teach him the interpretation of events.) the interpretation of dreams, according to Mujahid and As-Suddi. Allah said next,

(And Allah has full power and control over His affairs,) if He wills something, then there is no averting His decision, nor can it ever be stopped or contradicted. Rather, Allah has full power over everything and everyone else. Sa`id bin Jubayr said while commenting on Allah's statement,

(And Allah has full power and control over His affairs,) "He does what ever He wills." Allah said,

(but most of men know not.) meaning, have no knowledge of Allah's wisdom with regards to His creation, compassion and doing what He wills. Allah said next,

(And when he attained), in reference to Prophet Yusuf, peace be upon him,

(his full manhood), sound in mind and perfect in body,

(We gave him wisdom and knowledge), which is the prophethood that Allah sent him with for the people he lived among,

(thus We reward the doers of good.) because Yusuf used to do good in the obedience of Allah the Exalted.

### Surah: 12 Ayah: 23

﴿ وَرَاوَدَتْهُ ٱلَّتِي هُوَ فِى بَيْتِهَا عَن نَّفْسِهِۦ وَغَلَّقَتِ ٱلْأَبْوَٰبَ وَقَالَتْ هَيْتَ لَكَ قَالَ مَعَاذَ ٱللَّهِ إِنَّهُۥ رَبِّىٓ أَحْسَنَ مَثْوَاىَ إِنَّهُۥ لَا يُفْلِحُ ٱلظَّٰلِمُونَ ۝ ﴾

23. And she, in whose house he was, sought to seduce him (to do an evil act), and she closed the doors and said: "Come on, O you." He said: "I seek refuge in Allâh (or Allâh forbid)! Truly, he (your husband) is my master! He made my living in a great comfort! (So I will never betray him). Verily, the Zâlimûn (wrong and evil-doers) will never be successful."

### Transliteration

23. Warawadat-hu allatee huwa fee baytiha AAan nafsihi waghallaqati al-abwaba waqalat hayta laka qala maAAatha Allahi innahu rabbee ahsana mathwaya innahu la yuflihu alththalimoona

### Tafsir Ibn Kathir

#### Wife of the `Aziz loves Yusuf and plots against Him

Allah states that the wife of the `Aziz of Egypt, in whose house Yusuf resided and whose husband recommended that she takes care of him and be generous to him, tried to seduce Yusuf! She called him to do an evil act with her, because she loved him very much. Yusuf was very handsome, filled with manhood and beauty. She beautified herself for him, closed the doors and called him,

(and (she) said: "Come on, O you.") But he categorically refused her call,

(He said: "I seek refuge in Allah! Truly, he is my Rabb! He made my living in a great comfort!") as they used to call the chief and master a `Rabb', Yusuf said to her, `your husband is my master who provided me with comfortable living and was kind to me, so I will never betray him by committing immoral sins with his wife,'

(Verily, the wrongdoers will never be successful.) This was said by Mujahid, As-Suddi, Muhammad bin Ishaq and several others. The scholars differ in their recitation of,

(Hayta Laka), whereby Ibn `Abbas, Mujahid and several other scholars said that it means that she was calling him to herself. Al-Bukhari said; "Ikrimah said that,

(Hayta Laka') means, `come on, O you', in the Aramaic language." Al-Bukhari collected this statement from `Ikrimah without a chain of narration. Other scholars read it with the meaning, `I am ready for you'. Ibn `Abbas, Abu `Abdur-Rahman As-

Sulami, Abu Wa'il, `Ikrimah and Qatadah were reported to have read this part of the Ayah this way and explained it in the manner we mentioned, as `I am ready for you'.

### Surah: 12 Ayah: 24

﴿ وَلَقَدْ هَمَّتْ بِهِ ۖ وَهَمَّ بِهَا لَوْلَآ أَن رَّءَا بُرْهَٰنَ رَبِّهِۦ ۚ كَذَٰلِكَ لِنَصْرِفَ عَنْهُ ٱلسُّوٓءَ وَٱلْفَحْشَآءَ ۚ إِنَّهُۥ مِنْ عِبَادِنَا ٱلْمُخْلَصِينَ ﴾ ۝

24. And indeed she did desire him, and he would have inclined to her desire, had he not seen the evidence of his Lord. Thus it was, that We might turn away from him evil and illegal sexual intercourse. Surely, he was one of Our chosen (guided) slaves.

### Transliteration

24. Walaqad hammat bihi wahamma biha lawla an raa burhana rabbihi kathalika linasrifa AAanhu alssoo-a waalfahshaa innahu min AAibadina almukhlaseena

### Tafsir Ibn Kathir

This is about the thoughts that cross the mind, according to Al-Baghawi who mentioned this opinion from some of the analysts. Al-Baghawi next mentioned here a Hadith that he narrated from `Abdur Razzaq, from Ma`mar, from Hammam, from Abu Hurayrah, from the Messenger of Allah,

»يَقُولُ اللهُ تَعَالَى: إِذَا هَمَّ عَبْدِي بِحَسَنَةٍ فَاكْتُبُوهَا لَهُ حَسَنَةً، فَإِنْ عَمِلَهَا فَاكْتُبُوهَا لَهُ بِعَشْرِ أَمْثَالِهَا، وَإِنْ هَمَّ بِسَيِّئَةٍ فَلَمْ يَعْمَلْهَا فَاكْتُبُوهَا حَسَنَةً، فَإِنَّمَا تَرَكَهَا مِنْ جَرَّائِي، فَإِنْ عَمِلَهَا فَاكْتُبُوهَا بِمِثْلِهَا«

(Allah the Exalted said, `If my slave intends to perform a good deed, then record it for him as one good deed; if he performs it, then record it for him multiplied ten folds. If he intends to commit an evil act but did not commit it, then record it for him as one good deed, if he left it for My sake. But if he commits it, then write it as one evil deed.') This Hadith was also collected in the Two Sahihs using various wording, this is one of them. It was also reported that the Ayah means that Yusuf was about to beat her. As for the evidence that Yusuf saw at that moment, there are conflicting opinions to what it was. Ibn Jarir At-Tabari said, "The correct opinion is that we should say that he saw an Ayah from among Allah's Ayat that repelled the thought that crossed his mind. This evidence might have been the image of Ya`qub, or the image of an angel, or a divine statement that forbade him from doing that evil sin, etc. There are no clear proofs to support any of these statements in specific, so it should be left vague, as Allah left it. Allah's statement next,

(Thus it was, that We might turn away from him evil and immoral sins.) means, `Just as We showed him the evidence that turned him away from that sin, We save him from all types of evil and illegal sexual activity in all his affairs,' because,

(Surely, he was one of Our Mukhlasin servants.) meaning, chosen, purified, designated, appointed and righte- ous. May Allah's peace and blessings be on him."

### Surah: 12 Ayah: 25, Ayah: 26, Ayah: 27, Ayah: 28 & Ayah: 29

﴿ وَٱسْتَبَقَا ٱلْبَابَ وَقَدَّتْ قَمِيصَهُۥ مِن دُبُرٍ وَأَلْفَيَا سَيِّدَهَا لَدَا ٱلْبَابِ ۚ قَالَتْ مَا جَزَآءُ مَنْ أَرَادَ بِأَهْلِكَ سُوٓءًا إِلَّآ أَن يُسْجَنَ أَوْ عَذَابٌ أَلِيمٌ ﴾

25. So they raced with one another to the door, and she tore his shirt from the back. They both found her lord (i.e. her husband) at the door. She said: "What is the recompense (punishment) for him who intended an evil design against your wife, except that he be put in prison or a painful torment?"

﴿ قَالَ هِىَ رَٰوَدَتْنِى عَن نَّفْسِى ۚ وَشَهِدَ شَاهِدٌ مِّنْ أَهْلِهَآ إِن كَانَ قَمِيصُهُۥ قُدَّ مِن قُبُلٍ فَصَدَقَتْ وَهُوَ مِنَ ٱلْكَٰذِبِينَ ﴾

26. He (Yûsuf (Joseph)) said: "It was she that sought to seduce me;" and a witness of her household bore witness (saying): "If it be that his shirt is torn from the front, then her tale is true and he is a liar!

﴿ وَإِن كَانَ قَمِيصُهُۥ قُدَّ مِن دُبُرٍ فَكَذَبَتْ وَهُوَ مِنَ ٱلصَّٰدِقِينَ ﴾

27. "But if it be that his shirt is torn from the back, then she has told a lie and he is speaking the truth!"

﴿ فَلَمَّا رَءَا قَمِيصَهُۥ قُدَّ مِن دُبُرٍ قَالَ إِنَّهُۥ مِن كَيْدِكُنَّ ۖ إِنَّ كَيْدَكُنَّ عَظِيمٌ ﴾

28. So when he (her husband) saw his ((Yûsuf's (Joseph)) shirt torn at the back, (her husband) said: "Surely, it is a plot of you women! Certainly mighty is your plot!

﴿ يُوسُفُ أَعْرِضْ عَنْ هَٰذَا ۚ وَٱسْتَغْفِرِى لِذَنۢبِكِ ۖ إِنَّكِ كُنتِ مِنَ ٱلْخَاطِـِٔينَ ﴾

29. "O Yûsuf (Joseph)! Turn away from this! (O woman!) Ask forgiveness for your sin. Verily, you were of the sinful."

### Transliteration

25. Waistabaqa albaba waqaddat qameesahu min duburin waalfaya sayyidaha lada albabi qalat ma jazao man arada bi-ahlika soo-an illa an yusjana aw AAathabun aleemun  26. Qala hiya rawadatnee AAan nafsee washahida shahidun min ahliha in

## Chapter 12: Yusuf (Joseph), Verses 001-052

kana qameesuhu qudda min qubulin fasadaqat wahuwa mina alkathibeena 27. Wa-in kana qameesuhu qudda min duburin fakathabat wahuwa mina alssadiqeena 28. Falamma raa qameesahu qudda min duburin qala innahu min kaydikunna inna kaydakunna AAatheemun 29. Yoosufu aAArid AAan hatha waistaghfiree lithanbiki innaki kunti mina alkhati-eena

### Tafsir Ibn Kathir

Allah says that Yusuf and the wife of the `Aziz raced to the door, Yusuf running away from her and her running after him to bring him back to the room. She caught up with him and held on to his shirt from the back, tearing it so terribly that it fell off Yusuf's back. Yusuf continued running from her, with her in pursuit. However, they found her master, her husband, at the front door. This is when she responded by deceit and evil plots, trying to exonerate herself and implicate him, saying,

(What is the recompense (punishment) for him who intended an evil design against your wife...), in reference to illegal sexual intercourse,

(except that he be put in prison)

(or a painful torment) tormented severely with painful beating. Yusuf did not stand idle, but he declared the truth and exonerated himself from the betrayal she accused him of,

(He (Yusuf) said), in truth and honesty,

(It was she that sought to seduce me), and mentioned that she pursued him and pulled him towards her until she tore his shirt.

(And a witness of her household bore witness (saying): "If it be that his shirt is torn from the front..."), not from the back,

(then her tale is true) that he tried to commit an illegal sexual act with her. Had he called her to have sex with him and she refused, she would have pushed him away from her and tore his shirt from the front,

(But if it be that his shirt is torn from the back, then she has told a lie and he is speaking the truth!) Had Yusuf run away from her, and this is what truly happened, and she set in his pursuit, she would have held to his shirt from the back to bring him back to her, thus tearing his shirt from the back. There is a difference of opinion over the age and gender of the witness mentioned here. `Abdur-Razzaq recorded that Ibn `Abbas said that,

(and a witness of her household bore witness) "was a bearded man," meaning an adult male. Ath-Thawri reported that Jabir said that Ibn Abi Mulaykah said that Ibn `Abbas said, "He was from the king's entourage." Mujahid, `Ikrimah, Al-Hasan, Qatadah, As-Suddi, Muhammad bin Ishaq and others also said that the witness was an adult male. Al-`Awfi reported that Ibn `Abbas said about Allah's statement, (and a witness of her household bore witness) "He was a babe in the cradle." Similar was reported from Abu Hurayrah, Hilal bin Yasaf, Al-Hasan, Sa`id bin Jubayr and Ad-Dahhak bin Muzahim, that the witness was a young boy who lived in the `Aziz's house. Ibn Jarir At-Tabari preferred this view. Allah's statement,

(So when he saw his (Yusuf's) shirt torn at the back,) indicates that when her husband became certain that Yusuf was telling the truth and that his wife was lying when she heralded the accusation of betrayal at Yusuf,

(he said: "Surely, it is a plot of you women!...") He said, `This false accusation and staining the young man's reputation is but a plot of many that you, women, have,'

(Certainly mighty is your plot!) The `Aziz ordered Yusuf, peace be upon him, to be discrete about what happened,

(O Yusuf ! Turn away from this!), do not mention to anyone what has happened,

(And ask forgiveness for your sin, ) addressing his wife. The `Aziz was an easy man, or gave excuse to his wife because she saw in Yusuf an appeal she could not resist. He said to her, `Ask forgiveness for your sin, the evil desire that you wanted to satisfy with this young man, and then inventing false accusations about him,'

(verily, you were of the sinful.)

## Surah: 12 Ayah: 30, Ayah: 31, Ayah: 32, Ayah: 33 & Ayah: 34

﴿ ۞ وَقَالَ نِسْوَةٌ فِى ٱلْمَدِينَةِ ٱمْرَأَتُ ٱلْعَزِيزِ تُرَٰوِدُ فَتَىٰهَا عَن نَّفْسِهِۦ ۖ قَدْ شَغَفَهَا حُبًّا ۖ إِنَّا لَنَرَىٰهَا فِى ضَلَـٰلٍ مُّبِينٍ ﴾

30. And women in the city said: "The wife of Al-'Azîz is seeking to seduce her (slave) young man, indeed she loves him violently; verily we see her in plain error."

﴿ فَلَمَّا سَمِعَتْ بِمَكْرِهِنَّ أَرْسَلَتْ إِلَيْهِنَّ وَأَعْتَدَتْ لَهُنَّ مُتَّكَـًٔا وَءَاتَتْ كُلَّ وَٰحِدَةٍ مِّنْهُنَّ سِكِّينًا وَقَالَتِ ٱخْرُجْ عَلَيْهِنَّ ۖ فَلَمَّا رَأَيْنَهُۥٓ أَكْبَرْنَهُۥ وَقَطَّعْنَ أَيْدِيَهُنَّ وَقُلْنَ حَـٰشَ لِلَّهِ مَا هَـٰذَا بَشَرًا إِنْ هَـٰذَآ إِلَّا مَلَكٌ كَرِيمٌ ﴾

31. So when she heard of their accusation, she sent for them and prepared a banquet for them; she gave each one of them a knife (to cut the foodstuff with), and she said ((to Yûsuf (Joseph)) "Come out before them." Then, when they saw him, they exalted him (at his beauty) and (in their astonishment) cut their hands. They said: "How perfect is Allâh (or Allâh forbid)! No man is this! This is none other than a noble angel!"

﴿ قَالَتْ فَذَٰلِكُنَّ ٱلَّذِى لُمْتُنَّنِى فِيهِ ۖ وَلَقَدْ رَٰوَدتُّهُۥ عَن نَّفْسِهِۦ فَٱسْتَعْصَمَ ۖ وَلَئِن لَّمْ يَفْعَلْ مَآ ءَامُرُهُۥ لَيُسْجَنَنَّ وَلَيَكُونًا مِّنَ ٱلصَّٰغِرِينَ ۝ ﴾

32. She said: "This is he (the young man) about whom you did blame me, and I did seek to seduce him, but he refused. And now if he refuses to obey my order, he shall certainly be cast into prison, and will be one of those who are disgraced."

﴿ قَالَ رَبِّ ٱلسِّجْنُ أَحَبُّ إِلَىَّ مِمَّا يَدْعُونَنِى إِلَيْهِ ۖ وَإِلَّا تَصْرِفْ عَنِّى كَيْدَهُنَّ أَصْبُ إِلَيْهِنَّ وَأَكُن مِّنَ ٱلْجَٰهِلِينَ ۝ ﴾

33. He said: "O my Lord! Prison is dearer to me than that to which they invite me. Unless You turn away their plot from me, I will feel inclined towards them and be one (of those who commit sin and deserve blame or those who do deeds) of the ignorant."

﴿ فَٱسْتَجَابَ لَهُۥ رَبُّهُۥ فَصَرَفَ عَنْهُ كَيْدَهُنَّ ۚ إِنَّهُۥ هُوَ ٱلسَّمِيعُ ٱلْعَلِيمُ ۝ ﴾

34. So his Lord answered his invocation and turned away from him their plot. Verily, He is the All-Hearer, the All-Knower.

### Transliteration

30. Waqala niswatun fee almadeenati imraatu alAAazeezi turawidu fataha AAan nafsihi qad shaghafaha hubban inna lanaraha fee dalalin mubeenin 31. Falamma samiAAat bimakrihinna arsalat ilayhinna waaAAtadat lahunna muttakaan waatat kulla wahidatin minhunna sikkeenan waqalati okhruj AAalayhinna falamma raaynahu akbarnahu waqattaAAna aydiyahunna waqulna hasha lillahi ma hatha basharan in hatha illa malakun kareemun 32. Qalat fathalikunna allathee lumtunnanee feehi walaqad rawadtuhu AAan nafsihi faistAAsama wala-in lam yafAAal ma amuruhu layusjananna walayakoonan mina alssaghireena 33. Qala rabbi alssijnu ahabbu ilayya mimma yadAAoonanee ilayhi wa-illa tasrif AAannee kaydahunna asbu ilayhinna waakun mina aljahileena 34. Faistajaba lahu rabbuhu fasarafa AAanhu kaydahunna innahu huwa alssameeAAu alAAaleemu

### Tafsir Ibn Kathir

### The News reaches Women in the City, Who also plot against Yusuf

Allah states that the news of what happened between the wife of the `Aziz and Yusuf spread in the city, that is, Egypt, and people talked about it,

(And women in the city said...), such as women of chiefs and princes said, while admonishing and criticizing the wife of the `Aziz,

(The wife of the `Aziz is seeking to seduce her (slave) young man,), she is luring her servant to have sex with her, (indeed she loves him violently;), her love for him filled her heart and engulfed it,

(verily, we see her in plain error.), by loving him and trying to seduce him.

(So when she heard of their accusation,) especially their statement, "indeed she loves him violently." Muhammad bin Ishaq commented, "They heard of Yusuf's beauty and wanted to see him, so they said these words in order to get a look at him. " This is when,

(she sent for them), invited them to her house,

(and prepared a banquet for them.) Ibn `Abbas, Sa'id bin Jubayr, Mujahid, Al-Hasan, As-Suddi and several others commented that she prepared a sitting room which had couches, pillows (to recline on) and food that requires knives to cut, such as citron. This is why Allah said next,

(and she gave each one of them a knife), as a part of her plan of revenge for their plot to see Yusuf,

(and she said (to Yusuf): "Come out before them."), for she had asked him to stay somewhere else in the house,

(Then, when) he went out and,

(they saw him, they exalted him) they thought highly of him and were astonished at what they saw. They started cutting their hands in amazement at his beauty, while thinking that they were cutting the citron with their knives. Therefore, they injured their hands with the knives they were holding, according to several reports of Tafsir. Others said that after they ate and felt comfortable, and after having placed citron in front of them, giving each one of them a knife, the wife of the `Aziz asked them, "Would you like to see Yusuf" They said, "Yes." So she sent for him to come in front of them and when they saw him, they started cutting their hands. She ordered him to keep coming and going, so that they saw him from all sides, and he went back in while they were still cutting their hands. When they felt the pain, they started screaming and she said to them, "You did all this from one look at him, so how can I be blamed

(They said: "How perfect is Allah! No man is this! This is none other than a noble angel!") They said to her, "We do not blame you anymore after the sight that we saw." They never saw anyone like Yusuf before, for he, peace be upon him, was given half of all beauty. An authentic Hadith stated that the Messenger of Allah passed by Prophet Yusuf, during the Night of Isra' in the third heaven and commented,

《فَإِذَا هُوَ قَدْ أُعْطِيَ شَطْرَ الْحُسْنِ》

(He was given a half of all beauty.) Mujahid and others said (they said): "We seek refuge from Allah,"

# Chapter 12: Yusuf (Joseph), Verses 001-052

(No man is this!) They said next,

("This is none other than a noble angel!" She said: "This is he (the young man) about whom you did blame me...") She said these words to them so that they excuse her behavior, for a man who looks this beautiful and perfect, is worthy of being loved, she thought. She said,

(and I did seek to seduce him, but he refused) to obey me. Some scholars said that when the women saw Yusuf's beauty, she told them about his inner beauty that they did not know of, being chaste and beautiful from the inside and outside. She then threatened him,

(And now if he refuses to obey my order, he shall certainly be cast into prison, and will be one of those who are disgraced.) This is when Prophet Yusuf sought refuge with Allah from their evil and wicked plots,

(He said: "O my Lord! Prison is dearer to me than that to which they invite me...") illegal sexual acts,

(Unless You turn away their plot from me, I will feel inclined towards them) Yusuf invoked Allah: If You abandon me and I am reliant on myself, then I have no power over myself, nor can I bring harm or benefit to myself, except with Your power and will. Verily, You are sought for each and everything, and our total reliance is on You Alone for each and everything. Please, do not abandon me and leave me to rely on myself, for then,

("I will feel inclined towards them and be one of the ignorant." So his Lord answered his invocation) Yusuf, peace be upon him, was immune from error by Allah's will, and He saved him from accepting the advances of the wife of the `Aziz'. He preferred prison, rather than accept her illicit call. This indicates the best and most perfect grade in this case, for Yusuf was youthful, beautiful and full of manhood. His master's wife was calling him to herself, and she was the wife of the `Aziz of Egypt. She was also very beautiful and wealthy, as well as having a great social rank. He refused all this and preferred prison, for he feared Allah and hoped to earn His reward. It is recorded in the Two Sahihs that the Messenger of Allah said,

«سَبْعَةٌ يُظِلُّهُمُ اللهُ فِي ظِلِّهِ يَوْمَ لَا ظِلَّ إِلَّا ظِلُّهُ: إِمَامٌ عَادِلٌ، وَشَابٌّ نَشَأَ فِي عِبَادَةِ اللهِ، وَرَجُلٌ قَلْبُهُ مُعَلَّقٌ بِالْمَسْجِدِ إِذَا خَرَجَ مِنْهُ حَتَّى يَعُودَ إِلَيْهِ، وَرَجُلَانِ تَحَابَّا فِي اللهِ، اجْتَمَعَا عَلَيْهِ وَتَفَرَّقَا عَلَيْهِ، وَرَجُلٌ تَصَدَّقَ بِصَدَقَةٍ فَأَخْفَاهَا حَتَّى لَا تَعْلَمَ شِمَالُهُ مَا أَنْفَقَتْ يَمِينُهُ، وَرَجُلٌ دَعَتْهُ امْرَأَةٌ ذَاتُ مَنْصِبٍ وَجَمَالٍ فَقَالَ: إِنِّي أَخَافُ اللهَ، وَرَجُلٌ ذَكَرَ اللهَ خَالِيًا فَفَاضَتْ عَيْنَاهُ»

(Allah will give shade to seven, on the Day when there will be no shade but His: A just ruler, a youth who has been brought up in the worship of Allah, a man whose heart is attached to the Masjid, from the time he goes out of the Masjid until he gets back to it, two persons who love each other only for Allah's sake and they meet and part in Allah's cause only, a man who gives charitable gifts so secretly that his left hand does not know what his right hand has given, a man who refuses the call of a charming woman of noble birth for illicit intercourse with her and says: "I am afraid of Allah, and a person who remembers Allah in seclusion and his eyes are then flooded with tears.")

### Surah: 12 Ayah: 35

﴿ ثُمَّ بَدَا لَهُم مِّنْ بَعْدِ مَا رَأَوُاْ ٱلْأَيَـٰتِ لَيَسْجُنُنَّهُۥ حَتَّىٰ حِينٍ ﴾

35. Then it occurred to them, after they had seen the proofs (of his innocence), to imprison him for a time.

### Transliteration

35. Thumma bada lahum min baAAdi ma raawoo al-ayati layasjununnahu hatta heenin

### Tafsir Ibn Kathir

#### Yusuf is imprisoned without Justification

Allah says, `Then it occurred to them that it would be in their interest to imprison Yusuf for a time, even after they were convinced of his innocence and saw the proofs of his truth, honesty and chastity.' It appears, and Allah knows best, that they imprisoned him after the news of what happened spread. They wanted to pretend that Yusuf was the one who tried to seduce the `Aziz's wife and that they punished him with imprisonment. This is why when the Pharaoh asked Yusuf to leave jail a long time afterwards, he refused to leave until his innocence was acertained and the allegation of his betrayal was refuted. When this was successfully achieved, Yusuf left the prison with his honor intact, peace be upon him.

### Surah: 12 Ayah: 36

﴿ وَدَخَلَ مَعَهُ ٱلسِّجْنَ فَتَيَانِ قَالَ أَحَدُهُمَآ إِنِّىٓ أَرَىٰنِىٓ أَعْصِرُ خَمْرًا وَقَالَ ٱلْأَخَرُ إِنِّىٓ أَرَىٰنِىٓ أَحْمِلُ فَوْقَ رَأْسِى خُبْزًا تَأْكُلُ ٱلطَّيْرُ مِنْهُ نَبِّئْنَا بِتَأْوِيلِهِۦٓ إِنَّا نَرَىٰكَ مِنَ ٱلْمُحْسِنِينَ ﴾

36. And there entered with him two young men in the prison. One of them said: "Verily, I saw myself (in a dream) pressing wine." The other said: "Verily, I saw myself (in a dream) carrying bread on my head and birds were eating thereof." (They said): "Inform us of the interpretation of this. Verily, we think you are one of the Muhsinûn (doers of good)."

## Transliteration

36. Wadakhala maAAahu alssijna fatayani qala ahaduhuma innee aranee aAAsiru khamran waqala alakharu innee aranee ahmilu fawqa ra/see khubzan ta/kulu alttayru minhu nabbi/na bita/weelihi inna naraka mina almuhsineena

## Tafsir Ibn Kathir

### Two Jail Mates ask Yusuf to interpret their Dreams

Qatadah said, "One of them was the king's distiller and the other was his baker." Each of these two men had a dream and asked Yusuf to interpret it for them.

### Surah: 12 Ayah: 37 & Ayah: 38

﴿ قَالَ لَا يَأْتِيكُمَا طَعَامٌ تُرْزَقَانِهِ إِلَّا نَبَّأْتُكُمَا بِتَأْوِيلِهِ قَبْلَ أَن يَأْتِيَكُمَا ذَٰلِكُمَا مِمَّا عَلَّمَنِى رَبِّى إِنِّى تَرَكْتُ مِلَّةَ قَوْمٍ لَّا يُؤْمِنُونَ بِٱللَّهِ وَهُم بِٱلْأَخِرَةِ هُمْ كَٰفِرُونَ ﴾

37. He said: "No food will come to you (in wakefulness or in dream) as your provision, but I will inform (in wakefulness) its interpretation before it (the food) comes. This is of that which my Lord has taught me. Verily, I have abandoned the religion of a people that believe not in Allâh and are disbelievers in the Hereafter (i.e. the Kan'anyyûn of Egypt who were polytheists and used to worship sun and other false deities).

﴿ وَٱتَّبَعْتُ مِلَّةَ ءَابَآءِى إِبْرَٰهِيمَ وَإِسْحَٰقَ وَيَعْقُوبَ مَا كَانَ لَنَآ أَن نُّشْرِكَ بِٱللَّهِ مِن شَىْءٍ ذَٰلِكَ مِن فَضْلِ ٱللَّهِ عَلَيْنَا وَعَلَى ٱلنَّاسِ وَلَٰكِنَّ أَكْثَرَ ٱلنَّاسِ لَا يَشْكُرُونَ ﴾

38. "And I have followed the religion of my fathers - Ibrâhîm (Abraham), Ishâq (Isaac) and Ya'qûb (Jacob) (peace be upon them), and never could we attribute any partners whatsoever to Allâh. This is from the Grace of Allâh to us and to mankind, but most men thank not (i.e. they neither believe in Allâh, nor worship Him).

## Transliteration

37. Qala la ya/teekuma taAAamun turzaqanihi illa nabba/tukuma bita/weelihi qabla an ya/tiyakuma thalikuma mimma AAallamanee rabbee innee taraktu millata qawmin la yu/minoona biAllahi wahum bial-akhirati hum kafiroona 38. WaittabaAAtu millata aba-ee ibraheema wa-ishaqa wayaAAqooba ma kana lana an nushrika biAllahi min shay-in thalika min fadli Allahi AAalayna waAAala alnnasi walakinna akthara alnnasi la yashkuroona

## Tafsir Ibn Kathir

### Yusuf calls His Jail Mates to Tawhid even before He interprets Their Dreams

Yusuf, peace be upon him, told the two men that he has knowledge in the interpretation of whatever they saw in their dream, and that he will tell them about the interpretation of the dreams before they become a reality. This is why he said,

(No food will come to you as your provision, but I will inform you of its interpretation) Mujahid commented,

(No food will come to you as your provision,) this day,

(but I will inform you of its interpretation before it comes.) As-Suddi said similarly. Yusuf said that, this knowledge is from Allah Who taught it to me, because I shunned the religion of those who disbelieve in Him and the Last Day, who neither hope for Allah's reward nor fear His punishment on the Day of Return,

(And I have followed the religion of my fathers, - Ibrahim, Ishaq and Ya`qub) Yusuf said, `I have avoided the way of disbelief and polytheism, and followed the way of these honorable Messengers,' may Allah's peace and blessings be on them. This, indeed, is the way of he who seeks the path of guidance and follows the way of the Messengers, all the while shunning the path of deviation. It is he whose heart Allah will guide, teaching him what he did not know beforehand. It is he whom Allah will make an Imam who is imitated in the way of righteousness, and a caller to the path of goodness. Yusuf said next,

(and never could we attribute any partners whatsoever to Allah. This is from the grace of Allah to us and to mankind,) this Tawhid -Monotheism-, affirming that there is no deity worthy of worship except Allah alone without partners,

(is from the grace of Allah to us), He has revealed it to us and ordained it on us,

(and to mankind,), to whom He has sent us as callers to Tawhid,

(but most men thank not.) they do not admit Allah's favor and blessing of sending the Messengers to them, but rather,

(Have changed the blessings of Allah into disbelief, and caused their people to dwell in the house of destruction.) (14:28)

### Surah: 12 Ayah: 39 & Ayah: 40

﴿يَـٰصَىحِبَىِ ٱلسِّجْنِ ءَأَرْبَابٌ مُّتَفَرِّقُونَ خَيْرٌ أَمِ ٱللَّهُ ٱلْوَٰحِدُ ٱلْقَهَّارُ ۝﴾

39. "O two companions of the prison! Are many different lords (gods) better or Allâh, the One, the Irresistible?

﴿ مَا تَعْبُدُونَ مِن دُونِهِ إِلَّا أَسْمَاءً سَمَّيْتُمُوهَا أَنتُمْ وَءَابَاؤُكُم مَّا أَنزَلَ ٱللَّهُ بِهَا مِن سُلْطَانٍ إِنِ ٱلْحُكْمُ إِلَّا لِلَّهِ أَمَرَ أَلَّا تَعْبُدُوٓا۟ إِلَّآ إِيَّاهُ ذَٰلِكَ ٱلدِّينُ ٱلْقَيِّمُ وَلَٰكِنَّ أَكْثَرَ ٱلنَّاسِ لَا يَعْلَمُونَ ۝ ﴾

40. "You do not worship besides Him but only names which you have named (forged) - you and your fathers - for which Allâh has sent down no authority. The command (or the judgement) is for none but Allâh. He has commanded that you worship none but Him (i.e. His Monotheism); that is the (true) straight religion, but most men know not.

### Transliteration

39. Ya sahibayi alssijni aarbabun mutafarriqoona khayrun ami Allahu alwahidu alqahharu   40. Ma taAAbudoona min doonihi illa asmaan sammaytumooha antum waabaokum ma anzala Allahu biha min sultanin ini alhukmu illa lillahi amara alla taAAbudoo illa iyyahu thalika alddeenu alqayyimu walakinna akthara alnnasi la yaAAlamoona

### Tafsir Ibn Kathir

Prophet Yusuf went on calling his two prison companions to worship Allah alone, without partners, and to reject whatever is being worshipped instead of Him like the idols, which were worshipped by the people of the two men, Yusuf said,

(Are many different lords (gods) better or Allah, the One, the Irresistible) to Whose grace and infinite kingdom everything and everyone has submitted in humiliation. Prophet Yusuf explained to them next that it is because of their ignorance that they worship false deities and give them names, for these names were forged and are being transferred from one generation to the next generation. They have no proof or authority that supports this practice, hence his statement to them,

(for which Allah has sent down no authority) or proof and evidence. He then affirmed that the judgement, decision, will and kingdom are all for Allah alone, and He has commanded all of His servants to worship none but Him. He said,

(that is the straight religion,) `this, Tawhid of Allah and directing all acts of worship at Him alone in sincerity, that I am calling you to is the right, straight religion that Allah has ordained and for which He has revealed what He wills of proofs and evidences,'

(but most men know not.), and this is why most of them are idolators,

(And most of mankind will not believe even if you eagerly desire it.) (12:103) When Yusuf finished calling them, he started interpreting their dreams for them,

### Surah: 12 Ayah: 41

﴿يَـٰصَىحِبَىِ ٱلسِّجْنِ أَمَّآ أَحَدُكُمَا فَيَسْقِى رَبَّهُۥ خَمْرًا ۖ وَأَمَّا ٱلْءَاخَرُ فَيُصْلَبُ فَتَأْكُلُ ٱلطَّيْرُ مِن رَّأْسِهِۦ ۚ قُضِىَ ٱلْأَمْرُ ٱلَّذِى فِيهِ تَسْتَفْتِيَانِ ۝﴾

41. "O two companions of the prison! As for one of you, he (as a servant) will pour out wine for his lord (king or master) to drink; and as for the other, he will be crucified and birds will eat from his head. Thus is the case judged concerning which you both did inquire."

### Transliteration

41. Ya sahibayi alssijni amma ahadukuma fayasqee rabbahu khamran waamma al-akharu fayuslabu fata/kulu alttayru min ra/sihi qudiya al-amru allathee feehi tastaftiyani

### Tafsir Ibn Kathir

#### The Interpretation of the Dreams

Yusuf said,

(O two companions of the prison! As for one of you, he will pour out wine for his master to drink;) to the man who saw in a dream that he was pressing wine. He did not direct this speech at him, however, so that to lessen the grief of the other person. This is why he made his statement indirect,

(and as for the other, he will be crucified and birds will eat from his head.) which is the interpretation of the other man's dream in which he saw himself carrying bread above his head. Yusuf told them that the decision about their matter has already been taken and it shall come to pass. This is because the dream is tied to a bird's leg, as long as it is not truthfully interpreted. If it is interpreted, then it becomes a reality. Ath-Thawri said that `Imarah bin Al-Qa`qa` narrated that Ibrahim said that `Abdullah bin Mas`ud said, "When they said what they said to him, and he explained their dreams to them, they replied, `We did not see anything at all.' This is when he said,

(Thus is the case judged concerning which you both did inquire.)" The understanding in this is that he who claims that he saw a dream and was given its interpretation, then he will be tied to its interpretation, and Allah has the best knowledge. There is an honorable Hadith that Imam Ahmad collected from Mu`awiyah bin Haydah that the Prophet said,

«الرُّؤْيَا عَلَى رِجْلِ طَائِرٍ مَا لَمْ تُعْبَرْ، فَإِذَا عُبِرَتْ وَقَعَت»

(The dream is tied to a bird's leg, as long as it is not interpreted. If it is interpreted, it becomes a reality.)

## Surah: 12 Ayah: 42

﴿ وَقَالَ لِلَّذِى ظَنَّ أَنَّهُ نَاجٍ مِّنْهُمَا ٱذْكُرْنِى عِندَ رَبِّكَ فَأَنسَىٰهُ ٱلشَّيْطَٰنُ ذِكْرَ رَبِّهِۦ فَلَبِثَ فِى ٱلسِّجْنِ بِضْعَ سِنِينَ ۞ ﴾

42. And he said to the one whom he knew to be saved: "Mention me to your lord (i.e. your king, so as to get me out of the prison)." But Shaitân (Satan) made him forget to mention it to his Lord (or Satan made Yûsuf (Joseph) to forget the remembrance of his Lord (Allâh) as to ask for His Help, instead of others). So (Yûsuf (Joseph)) stayed in prison a few (more) years.

### Transliteration

42. Waqala lillathee thanna annahu najin minhuma othkurnee AAinda rabbika faansahu alshshaytanu thikra rabbihi falabitha fee alssijni bidAAa sineena

### Tafsir Ibn Kathir

#### Yusuf asks the King's Distiller to mention Him to the King

Yusuf knew that the distiller would be saved. So discretely, so that the other man's suspicion that he would be crucified would not intensify, he said,

(Mention me to your King.) asking him to mention his story to the king. That man forgot Yusuf's request and did not mention his story to the king, a plot from the devil, so that Allah's Prophet would not leave the prison. This is the correct meaning of,

(But Shaytan made him forget to mention it to his master.) that it refers to the man who was saved. As was said by Mujahid, Muhammad bin Ishaq and several others. As for, `a few years', or, Bida` in Arabic, it means between three and nine, according to Mujahid and Qatadah. Wahb bin Munabbih said, "Ayyub suffered from the illness for seven years, Yusuf remained in prison for seven years and Bukhtanassar (Nebuchadnezzar - Chaldean king of Babylon) was tormented for seven years."

## Surah: 12 Ayah: 43, Ayah: 44, Ayah: 45, Ayah: 46, Ayah: 47, Ayah: 48 & Ayah: 49

﴿ وَقَالَ ٱلْمَلِكُ إِنِّى أَرَىٰ سَبْعَ بَقَرَٰتٍ سِمَانٍ يَأْكُلُهُنَّ سَبْعٌ عِجَافٌ وَسَبْعَ سُنۢبُلَٰتٍ خُضْرٍ وَأُخَرَ يَابِسَٰتٍ يَٰٓأَيُّهَا ٱلْمَلَأُ أَفْتُونِى فِى رُءْيَٰىَ إِن كُنتُمْ لِلرُّءْيَا تَعْبُرُونَ ۞ ﴾

43. And the king (of Egypt) said: "Verily, I saw (in a dream) seven fat cows, whom seven lean ones were devouring, and seven green ears of corn, and (seven) others dry. O notables! Explain to me my dream, if it be that you can interpret dreams."

﴿ قَالُوٓاْ أَضْغَٰثُ أَحْلَٰمٖۖ وَمَا نَحْنُ بِتَأْوِيلِ ٱلْأَحْلَٰمِ بِعَٰلِمِينَ ۝ ﴾

44. They said: "Mixed up false dreams and we are not skilled in the interpretation of dreams."

﴿ وَقَالَ ٱلَّذِى نَجَا مِنْهُمَا وَٱدَّكَرَ بَعْدَ أُمَّةٍ أَنَا۠ أُنَبِّئُكُم بِتَأْوِيلِهِۦ فَأَرْسِلُونِ ۝ ﴾

45. Then the man who was released (one of the two who were in prison), now at length remembered and said: "I will tell you its interpretation, so send me forth."

﴿ يُوسُفُ أَيُّهَا ٱلصِّدِّيقُ أَفْتِنَا فِى سَبْعِ بَقَرَٰتٖ سِمَانٍ يَأْكُلُهُنَّ سَبْعٌ عِجَافٌ وَسَبْعِ سُنۢبُلَٰتٍ خُضْرٍ وَأُخَرَ يَابِسَٰتٖ لَّعَلِّىٓ أَرْجِعُ إِلَى ٱلنَّاسِ لَعَلَّهُمْ يَعْلَمُونَ ۝ ﴾

46. (He said): "O Yûsuf (Joseph), the man of truth! Explain to us (the dream) of seven fat cows whom seven lean ones were devouring, and of seven green ears of corn, and (seven) others dry, that I may return to the people, and that they may know."

﴿ قَالَ تَزْرَعُونَ سَبْعَ سِنِينَ دَأَبٗا فَمَا حَصَدتُّمْ فَذَرُوهُ فِى سُنۢبُلِهِۦٓ إِلَّا قَلِيلٗا مِّمَّا تَأْكُلُونَ ۝ ﴾

47. (Yûsuf (Joseph)) said: "For seven consecutive years, you shall sow as usual and that (the harvest) which you reap you shall leave in ears, (all) except a little of it which you may eat.

﴿ ثُمَّ يَأْتِى مِنۢ بَعْدِ ذَٰلِكَ سَبْعٌ شِدَادٞ يَأْكُلْنَ مَا قَدَّمْتُمْ لَهُنَّ إِلَّا قَلِيلٗا مِّمَّا تُحْصِنُونَ ۝ ﴾

48. "Then will come after that, seven hard (years), which will devour what you have laid by in advance for them, (all) except a little of that which you have guarded (stored).

﴿ ثُمَّ يَأْتِى مِنۢ بَعْدِ ذَٰلِكَ عَامٞ فِيهِ يُغَاثُ ٱلنَّاسُ وَفِيهِ يَعْصِرُونَ ۝ ﴾

49. "Then thereafter will come a year in which people will have abundant rain and in which they will press (wine and oil)."

**Transliteration**

43. Waqala almaliku innee ara sabAAa baqaratin simanin ya/kuluhunna sabAAun AAijafun wasabAAa sunbulatin khudrin waokhara yabisatin ya ayyuha almalao aftoonee fee ru/yaya in kuntum lilrru/ya taAAburoona 44. Qaloo adghathu ahlamin wama nahnu bita/weeli al-ahlami biAAalimeena 45. Waqala allathee naja minhuma waiddakara baAAda ommatin ana onabbi-okum bita/weelihi faarsilooni 46. Yoosufu

Chapter 12: Yusuf (Joseph), Verses 001-052                                                                 121

ayyuha alssiddeequ aftina fee sabAAi baqaratin simanin ya/kuluhunna sabAAun AAijafun wasabAAi sunbulatin khudrin waokhara yabisatin laAAallee arjiAAu ila alnnasi laAAallahum yaAAlamoona  47. Qala tazraAAoona sabAAa sineena daaban fama hasadtum fatharoohu fee sunbulihi illa qaleelan mimma ta/kuloona  48. Thumma ya/tee min baAAdi thalika sabAAun shidadun ya/kulna ma qaddamtum lahunna illa qaleelan mimma tuhsinoona  49. Thumma ya/tee min baAAdi thalika AAamun feehi yughathu alnnasu wafeehi yaAAsiroona

### Tafsir Ibn Kathir

### The Dream of the King of Egypt

The King of Egypt had a dream that Allah the Exalted made a reason for Yusuf's release from prison, with his honor and reputation preserved. When the king had this dream, he was astonished and fearful and sought its interpretation. He gathered the priests, the chiefs of his state and the princes and told them what he had seen in a dream, asking them to interpret it for him. They did not know its interpretation and as an excuse, they said,

(Mixed up false dreams), which you saw,

(and we are not skilled in the interpretation of dreams.) They said, had your dream been a vision rather than a mixed up false dream, we would not have known its interpretation. The man who was saved from the two, who were Yusuf's companions in prison, remembered. Shaytan plotted to make him forget the request of Yusuf, to mention his story to the king. Now, years later, he remembered after forgetfulness and said to the king and his entourage,

(I will tell you its interpretation,) he interpretation of this dream,

(so send me forth.) to the prison, to Yusuf, the man of truth. So they sent him, and he said to Yusuf,

(O Yusuf, the man of truth! Explain to us..) and mentioned the king's dream to him.

### Yusuf's Interpretation of the King's Dream

This is when Yusuf, peace be upon him, told the interpretation of the dream, without criticizing the man for forgetting his request that he had made to him. Neither did he make a precondition that he be released before explaining the meaning. Rather, he said,

(For seven consecutive years, you shall sow as usual) `you will receive the usual amount of rain and fertility for seven consecutive years.' He interpreted the cows to be years, because cows till the land that produce fruits and vegetables, which represent the green ears of corn in the dream. He next recommended what they should do during these fertile years,

(and that (the harvest) which you reap you shall leave it in the ears, (all) except a little of it which you may eat.) He said, `Whatever you harvest during those seven fertile years, leave it in the ears so as to preserve it better. This will help the harvest stay healthy longer, except the amount that you need to eat, which should not be substantial. Stay away from extravagance, so that you use what remains of the harvest during the seven years of drought that will follow the seven fertile years.' This was represented by the seven lean cows that eat the seven fat cows. During the seven years of drought, they will eat from the harvest they collected during the seven fertile years, as represented by the dry ears of corn in the dream. Yusuf told them that during these years, the remaining ears will not produce anything and whatever they try to plant, will not produce any harvest, so he said,

(which will devour what you have laid by in advance for them, (all) except a little of that which you have guarded (stored).) He delivered the good news to them that after the consecutive years of drought, there will come a fertile year, during which people will receive rain and the land will produce in abundance. The people will then press wine and oil as usual.

### Surah: 12 Ayah: 50, Ayah: 51 & Ayah: 52

﴿ وَقَالَ ٱلْمَلِكُ ٱئْتُونِى بِهِۦ ۖ فَلَمَّا جَآءَهُ ٱلرَّسُولُ قَالَ ٱرْجِعْ إِلَىٰ رَبِّكَ فَسْـَٔلْهُ مَا بَالُ ٱلنِّسْوَةِ ٱلَّـٰتِى قَطَّعْنَ أَيْدِيَهُنَّ ۚ إِنَّ رَبِّى بِكَيْدِهِنَّ عَلِيمٌ ﴾

50. And the king said: "Bring him to me." But when the messenger came to him, (Yûsuf (Joseph)) said: "Return to your lord and ask him, 'What happened to the women who cut their hands? Surely, my Lord (Allâh) is Well-Aware of their plot.'"

﴿ قَالَ مَا خَطْبُكُنَّ إِذْ رَٰوَدتُّنَّ يُوسُفَ عَن نَّفْسِهِۦ ۚ قُلْنَ حَـٰشَ لِلَّهِ مَا عَلِمْنَا عَلَيْهِ مِن سُوٓءٍ ۚ قَالَتِ ٱمْرَأَتُ ٱلْعَزِيزِ ٱلْـَٔـٰنَ حَصْحَصَ ٱلْحَقُّ أَنَا۠ رَٰوَدتُّهُۥ عَن نَّفْسِهِۦ وَإِنَّهُۥ لَمِنَ ٱلصَّـٰدِقِينَ ﴾

51. (The King) said (to the women): "What was your affair when you did seek to seduce Yûsuf (Joseph)?" The women said: "Allâh forbid! No evil know we against him!" The wife of Al-'Azîz said: "Now the truth is manifest (to all), it was I who sought to seduce him, and he is surely of the truthful."

﴿ ذَٰلِكَ لِيَعْلَمَ أَنِّى لَمْ أَخُنْهُ بِٱلْغَيْبِ وَأَنَّ ٱللَّهَ لَا يَهْدِى كَيْدَ ٱلْخَآئِنِينَ ﴾

52. (Then Yûsuf (Joseph) said: "I asked for this inquiry) in order that he (Al-'Azîz) may know that I betrayed him not in (his) absence. And, verily! Allâh guides not the plot of the betrayers."

### Transliteration

50. Waqala almaliku i/toonee bihi falamma jaahu alrrasoolu qala irjiAA ila rabbika fais-alhu ma balu alnniswati allatee qattaAAna aydiyahunna inna rabbee bikaydihinna AAaleemun 51. Qala ma khatbukunna ith rawadtunna yoosufa AAan nafsihi qulna hasha lillahi ma AAalimna AAalayhi min soo-in qalati imraatu alAAazeezi al-ana

hashasa alhaqqu ana rawadtuhu AAan nafsihi wa-innahu lamina alssadiqeena 52. Thalika liyaAAlama annee lam akhunhu bialghaybi waanna Allaha la yahdee kayda alkha-ineena

### Tafsir Ibn Kathir

## The King investigates what happened between the Wife of the `Aziz, the Women in the City, and Yusuf

Allah narrates to us that when the king was conveyed the interpretation of his dream, he liked Yusuf's interpretation and felt sure that it was true. He realized the virtue of Prophet Yusuf, recognized his knowledge in the interpretation of dreams and valued his good conduct with his subjects in his country. The king said,

(Bring him to me.) `Release him from prison and bring him to me.' When the king's emissary came to Yusuf and conveyed the news of his imminent release, Yusuf refused to leave the prison until the king and his subjects declare his innocence and the integrity of his honor, denouncing the false accusation that the wife of the `Aziz made against him. He wanted them to know that sending him to prison was an act of injustice and aggression, not that he committed an offense that warranted it. He said,

(Return to your lord (i.e. king...) The Sunnah of our Prophet praised Prophet Yusuf and asserted his virtues, honor, elevated rank and patience, may Allah's peace and blessings be on him. The Musnad and the Two Sahihs recorded that Abu Hurayrah said that the Messenger of Allah said,

«نَحْنُ أَحَقُّ بِالشَّكِّ مِنْ إِبْرَاهِيمَ إِذْ قَالَ»

(We are more liable to be in doubt than Ibrahim when he said,)

(رَبِّ أَرِنِي كَيْفَ تُحْيِي الْمَوْتَى)

(My Lord! Show me how You give life to the dead. ..)

«وَيَرْحَمُ اللهُ لُوطًا لَقَدْ كَانَ يَأْوِي إِلَى رُكْنٍ شَدِيدٍ، وَلَوْ لَبِثْتُ فِي السِّجْنِ مَا لَبِثَ يُوسُفُ لَأَجَبْتُ الدَّاعِي»

(And may Allah send His mercy on Lut! He wished to have powerful support! If I were to stay in prison for such a long time as Yusuf did, I would have accepted the offer.) In another narration collected by Ahmad from Abu Hurayrah, the Prophet said about Yusuf's statement,

("...and ask him, `What happened to the women who cut their hands Surely, my Lord (Allah) is Well-Aware of their plot.'")

»لَوْ كُنْتُ أَنَا، لَأَسْرَعْتُ الْإِجَابَةَ وَمَا ابْتَغَيْتُ الْعُذْرِ«

(If it was me, I would have accepted the offer rather than await my exoneration first.) Allah said (that the king asked),

(He said, "What was your affair when you did seek to seduce Yusuf") The king gathered those women who cut their hands, while being hosted at the house of the wife of the `Aziz. He asked them all, even though he was directing his speech at the wife of his minister, the `Aziz in particular. He asked the women who cut their hands,

(What was your affair...), what was your story with regards to,

(when you did seek to seduce Yusuf) on the day of the banquet

(The women said: "Allah forbid! No evil know we against him!") The women answered the king, `Allah forbid that Yusuf be guilty of this, for by Allah, we never knew him to do evil.' This is when,

(The wife of the `Aziz said: "Now the truth has Hashasa...") or the truth is manifest to all, according to Ibn `Abbas, Mujahid and others. Hashasa also means, `became clear and plain',

(it was I who sought to seduce him, and he is surely of the truthful.) when he said,

(It was she that sought to seduce me.)

(in order that he may know that I betrayed him not in (his) absence. ) She said, `I admit this against myself so that my husband knows that I did not betray him in his absence and that adultery did not occur. I tried to seduce this young man and he refused, and I am admitting this so that he knows I am innocent,'

(And, verily, Allah guides not the plot of the betrayers. And I free not myself (from the blame).) She said, `I do not exonerate myself from blame, because the soul wishes and lusts, and this is what made me seduce him,' for,

(Verily, the (human) self is inclined to evil, except when my Lord bestows His mercy (upon whom He wills).) whom Allah the Exalted wills to grant them immunity,

(Verily, my Lord is Oft-Forgiving, Most Merciful.) This is the most viable and suitable understanding for the continuity of the story and the meanings of Arabic speech. Al-Mawardi mentioned this in his Tafsir, in support of it, it was also preferred by Imam Abu Al-`Abbas Ibn Taymiyyah who wrote about it in detail in a separate work.

www.ingramcontent.com/pod-product-compliance
Lightning Source LLC
Chambersburg PA
CBHW081114080526
44587CB00021B/3586